Democracy and Imperialism

After costly US engagement in two major wars in the Middle East, foreign policy debates are dominated by questions about the appropriateness of American military interventions. A central issue is whether an interventionist foreign policy is compatible with the American constitutional tradition and the temperament this tradition requires.

The book examines the unique contribution made by Irving Babbitt (1865–1933) to understanding the quality of foreign policy leadership in a democracy. Babbitt explored how a democratic nation's foreign policy is a product of the moral and cultural tendencies of its leaders and how the substitution of expansive, sentimental Romanticism for the religious and ethical traditions of the West would lead to imperialism.

Democracies that lack political restraint and tend toward plebiscitary practices and outcomes are more likely to be warlike and imperialistic. The United States has been moving away from the restraining order of sound constitutionalism and increasingly trying to impose its will on other nations, a trend that will inevitably cause the United States to clash with the "civilizational" regions that have emerged in recent decades. How to address the problem of tension between civilizations is a subject to which Babbitt, showing characteristic foresight, devoted much attention. This book brings the question of soul types to issues of foreign policy leadership and discusses the qualities in leaders that are necessary for sound foreign policy.

William S. Smith is Research Fellow and Managing Director of the Center for the Study of Statesmanship at the Catholic University of America.

Democracy and Imperialism

IRVING BABBITT AND
WARLIKE DEMOCRACIES

William S. Smith

UNIVERSITY OF MICHIGAN PRESS
ANN ARBOR

Copyright © 2019 by William S. Smith
All rights reserved

This book may not be reproduced, in whole or in part, including illustrations, in any form (beyond that copying permitted by Sections 107 and 108 of the U.S. Copyright Law and except by reviewers for the public press), without written permission from the publisher.

Published in the United States of America by the
University of Michigan Press
Manufactured in the United States of America
Printed on acid-free paper
First published August 2019

A CIP catalog record for this book is available from the British Library.

Library of Congress Cataloging-in-Publication data has been applied for.

ISBN 978-0-472-13153-2 (hardcover : alk. paper)
ISBN 978-0-472-12593-7 (e-book)

Cover credit: US Air Force photo/Tech. Sgt. Mark R. W. Orders-Woempner.

To Laura
Amor Vinci Omnia

Acknowledgments

T.S. Eliot wrote of Irving Babbitt, "To have been once a pupil of Babbitt's was to always remain in that position . . . His ideas are permanently with one, as a measurement and test of one's own." Such sentiments reflect mine regarding my mentor, Professor Claes Ryn of The Catholic University of America. Professor Ryn's personal support for my academic work, extending now over many decades, has only been surpassed by the influence of his ideas on my own and their relevance to the contemporary challenges of the United States.

This book would not have been possible without my wife, Laura. When I left a business career and pursued a path in academia, she offered the same unwavering support and encouragement that she has always provided to all of our family. My thanks also to my dear children, Therese, Burke, and Margaret, for their interest in their father's new endeavors, and their understanding about how important this subject is to me.

I would like to offer additional words of gratitude to our friends and family whose constant enthusiasm provided needed ballast to my work, especially Page and Katie Wilson, Patrick and Jennifer Donovan, Dana Nickel, Celeste Wilson, and Nadia Schadlow.

I am grateful to the superb team at the Harvard University Archives where Irving Babbitt's papers are held. I also cannot neglect to note my admiration for my colleagues at Catholic University who courageously pursue a constant stream of ideas that will not ingratiate them to the foreign policy establishment, a mark of distinction.

My editors at the University of Michigan Press, Elizabeth Demers and Kevin Rennells, are consummate professionals and they made the load of such a challenging project so much lighter.

Finally, to the men and women of the American military and their families, who have borne the terrible burden of America's recent wars of choice, may you be blessed with temperate leaders like George Washington, who understood that America's true calling is to be a virtuous republic, not an empire.

Contents

Introduction   1

CHAPTER 1   Babbitt and Human Nature   17

CHAPTER 2   Modernity as Naturalism   29

CHAPTER 3   Two Types of Democracy   53

CHAPTER 4   Democracy as Revolution   77

CHAPTER 5   Democracy as Imperialism   99

CHAPTER 6   True and False Cosmopolitanism   139

CHAPTER 7   Babbitt and Contemporary Theories of World Order   155

Conclusion   177

Notes   183

Bibliography   203

Index   209

Digital materials related to this title can be found on the Fulcrum platform via the following citable URL: https://doi.org/10.3998/mpub.11301249

Introduction

> The fortune of princes changes with their character.
> —Sallust, *The War with Catiline*

Imperialism, as a national motivation, generally has pejorative connotations across the political spectrum. Imperialism implies the forced imposition of the will of one people upon another people who oppose the political, cultural, or economic changes being imposed. Imperialism is widely viewed as an unjustified violation of national sovereignty.

While imperialism, as an abstract concept, meets with near universal opprobrium, in concrete historical circumstances actions that constitute genuine imperialism are sometimes in the eye of the beholder. Historians of ancient Rome, for example, have regularly debated whether the growth of Roman power derived from a culture with imperial ambitions or whether pervasive outside threats to the Roman republic caused Rome to conquer other peoples.

Recent US foreign policy actions have generated similar debates. During the Cold War, left-leaning foreign policy observers viewed American interventions in nations such as Vietnam as imperialistic adventurism, while right-leaning observers viewed such interventions as strategic responses to existential threats to US security. In the post–Cold War environment, similar disagreements have emerged. President George W. Bush, for example, argued that the spread of freedom and democracy through military interventions was a humanitarian cause and represented a defensive strategy by the United States to prevent future terrorist attacks, while critics argued that such military interventionism embodied military, political, and cultural imperialism.

Arriving at precise agreement about the nature of imperialism seems to take on added complexity in democratic regimes. Imperialism is readily recognized in tyrannical regimes that brutally suppress internal dissent and invade their neighbors for obvious economic, strategic, or political advantage. Democratic nations, however, with their implicit popular legitimacy, seem to enjoy a certain inoculation against having their foreign wars characterized as imperialistic. To secure popular support for foreign policy initiatives, leaders of democracies tend to assert altruistic or humanitarian motivations. For this reason, the citizens of democratic nations may have difficulty in recognizing imperialism on the part of their own countries because of the assumption that the nations' actions have pure motives and popular sanction.

While democracies seem weaker at self-diagnosing imperialism, the historical record reflects some ambiguity about whether democracies are indeed less disposed to imperialism than other regime types. Numerous historical examples point to democratic or quasi-democratic regimes that did in fact develop unjust and tyrannical characteristics and tended toward imperialism. Ancient Greece and Rome as well as Jacobin France are but three important examples.[1] The Framers of the American Constitution were acutely aware of the decline of democracy in the classical world and, when constructing the Constitution, attempted to install bulwarks against the tendency of democracies to degenerate into class conflict, to suffer a loss of liberty at home, and to engage in foreign adventurism abroad. One could make the argument that the spirit of the original Constitution was anti-imperialistic.

Because of the ambiguity of imperialism in democracies, it would seem a worthy task of scholarship to refine and enlarge the nation's understanding of imperialism and examine how democratic leaders might avoid a drift into imperialism as a matter of national policy. Such a project would involve a form of national self-examination to consider whether there are certain qualities in a democracy that pull it toward peace and other traits that pull it toward conquest.

Developing a deeper understanding of the nature of imperialism seems an especially necessary task for contemporary Americans. The United States has, in recent decades, launched lengthy wars in far-flung corners of the world. Supporters of these wars claimed that they were essential for both humanitarian and security reasons, and there is indeed evidence of terroristic threats and humanitarian crises in the regions where the United States has intervened. But given the weakness democracies tend to exhibit in diagnosing their own imperialism, it also seems incumbent on scholars to ask if America's wars may be symptomatic of the kind of moral and cultural developments that coincided with the decline and wars of ancient Athens, the Roman republic, and revolutionary France.

Irving Babbitt, who lived through the Great War and spent much of his life studying the intellectual origins of the French Revolution, wrote extensively about what he believed to be the virtues or vices within democracy that might hold the balance between war and peace. Because Babbitt's analysis of imperialism was philosophically penetrating, Babbitt, I argue, developed a useful guide to diagnosing genuine imperialism, a guide that transcends the typical back-and-forth arguments regarding whether certain historical and concrete cases entail imperialism.

In approaching the problem of imperialism in a democracy, Babbitt adopted an important part of the framework of classical political philosophy by asserting that the most important question is *Who will rule?* Babbitt believed that democracies were little different from other forms of government in that the quality most required for a successful political order is high moral character in leaders. Modern democracies, Babbitt argued, had a tendency to evade this problem of ethical leadership by hiding behind appeals to popular will and democratic legitimacy. A numerical majority, he pointed out, might or might not embrace sound and just policies but are far more likely to go morally astray if they are poorly led.

Babbitt's theory of imperialism makes a unique contribution to political theory because he systematically applied the classical question of who should rule to international problems of war and peace. Irrespective of the form of government, Babbitt asserted that leaders of poor moral character who would easily cast aside conscience would be far more likely to embody a spirit of imperialism and exhibit a stronger inclination to impose their wills on others. Unjust military adventurism, Babbitt believed, was inevitably rooted in intemperate leaders with a will to power, and democracies with decadent leadership therefore enjoyed no special immunity against engaging in imperialism. On the other hand, leaders who had mastered themselves in an ethical sense would be far less likely to aspire to dominion over others.

As Babbitt might have predicted, throughout the last century and particularly since the conclusion of the Cold War, Western elites have tended to evade the central issue of ethical leadership and have expressed confidence that principles of peace and international order could be found either through robust military power or through the proper support for international institutions. Whether they were advocates of the use of soft power or hard power, most American leaders of both parties have been united in their belief that the purpose of American foreign policy is to promote humanitarian goals.

Some believers in humanitarianism have expressed confidence that peace would triumph if the world would only finally accept the fact of global diversity and the requirements of international law and international institutions. As the historian Samuel Huntington wrote, the globalists believed that peace would be the inevitable result of "an open society with open borders, encouraging subnational ethnic, racial, and cultural identities, dual citizenship, diasporas, and led by elites who increasingly identified with global institutions, norms, and rules rather than national ones."[2] This type of idealism and globalism might, if Babbitt is right, be charged with combining "the pretence to a vast illumination with the utmost degree of spiritual and intellectual emptiness and vagueness."[3]

Other American foreign policy elites have criticized this type of globalism and argued for a different humanitarian vision—the worldwide triumph of democracy through American military assertiveness. Unlike the vision of the sentimental globalists, this worldwide democratic aspiration would be advanced through great American military strength. Worldwide peace and humanitarian goals should be promoted by American hegemony. As Huntington said, "At the start of the new millennium conservatives accepted and endorsed the idea of an American empire and the use of American power to reshape the world according to American values."[4] In defending his use of hard power in Iraq, President George W. Bush expressed his humanitarian goals this way: "The best hope for peace in our world is the expansion of freedom in all the world."[5]

The idealistic and globalist aspirations of US elites for the past one hundred years, whether of the sentimental humanitarian or the more militaristic humanitarian, appear to have clashed with historical reality: the twentieth and twenty-first centuries have witnessed brutality and suffering on an unprecedented scale as well as never-ending wars. Rather than speak of an era of global peace and democracy, the cynic might agree with remarks attributed to the French philosopher Émile Boutroux, who in 1912, just before the outbreak of the Great War, told a reporter "that from the amount of peace talk abroad, he inferred that the future was likely to be 'supremely warlike and bloody.'"[6]

Irving Babbitt diagnosed what he saw as profound intellectual and moral errors underlying the dominant notions of international peace and democracy. He had seen similar arguments made both prior to and after the catastrophic

Great War, and he pleaded with Western intellectuals to reconsider their assumptions about what might promote peace among Western nations. Contemporary paradigms of world order were based, he argued, on a Romantic idealism that denied central facts of human existence. Restoring a sounder, more realistic view of human nature was essential: "It is pleasanter, after all, to be awakened by a douche of ice-water than by an explosion of dynamite under the bed; and that has been the frequent fate of the romantic idealist."[7]

The central issue, Babbitt argued, is not distinguishing between sound and unsound types of humanitarianism in foreign policy but recognizing the reality that humanitarianism is largely indistinguishable from imperialism. The hubris of the meddling humanitarian stands in stark contrast to the humility and sobriety of George Washington's Farewell Address, arguably the foreign policy expression of the spirit of the Constitution.

Babbitt understood that Western culture was so saturated with the erroneous understanding that humanitarianism represented the only moral reality that his task involved bringing to life the centuries-buried understanding of moral reality on which the West—and all great cultures—had once rested. To reconstruct this moral reality, he employed the perspective of classical moral and political philosophy and built his arguments about war and peace from the ground up, starting with a careful examination of human nature and its moral and spiritual characteristics. Babbitt argued that any realistic understanding of human nature placed the ultimate source of political disorders—local, national, and international—in the individual human soul.

Human beings were subject to a "human law" that required them to exhibit "ethical concentration" to control their own merely impulsive, selfish desires. All disorder among human beings derives, in some way, from the inability of individual human beings to rein in their own selfish desires. Without some form of ethical control, conflict is inevitable. As Babbitt concisely insisted, "temperament is what separates."[8] Babbitt based his theories of societal and international order on a simple Confucian premise that has parallel Western counterparts in classical Greek philosophy: "There may be something after all in the Confucian idea that if a man only sets himself right, the rightness will extend to his family first of all, and finally in widening circles to the whole community."[9]

Babbitt was well informed about contemporary events and did not ignore the complexity of foreign affairs, the requirements of military preparedness, and the fragility of any international order. But he sought to break down these problems to their most basic elements. He insisted that societies without leaders who shared a culture of character would be prone to war. Intemperate leaders beget an intemperate culture, which begets a decaying constitutional order, which begets a grasping, even warlike regime. The imperialistic personality writ large is the imperialistic state. The Athens of an Alcibiades will not be a peaceful Athens, democracy or not.

Both sentimental humanitarianism and hard-power humanitarianism evade the problem of what Babbitt called the human law, which is an ethical standard standing athwart humanity's lower nature. Sentimental globalism argues that a heartfelt and sincere desire for worldwide peace can breathe life, authority, and efficacy into international institutions, creating order and protecting human rights. To paraphrase Babbitt, the globalists believe that peace is not the fruit of a common discipline among the world's leaders and nations but rather results from a common emotion.

Likewise, those humanitarians who advocate the promotion of democracy around the world through military power, advancing a so-called Freedom Agenda, do not regard popular sovereignty as subject to the human law as understood by Babbitt.[10] The Freedom Agenda is based on something like Rousseau's democratic theory, which postulated that when popular sentiment is unleashed and the "people" become free of dictators and tyrants, the "will" of the people then rises to the fore, ensuring peace and freedom. Democracy is peace, and peace is democracy.

In this type of Rousseauistic democracy, the popular will becomes antinomian, a mysterious moral force that, in the collective, is exempted from any law above itself. In revolutionary France, the popular will expressed itself in the guillotining of many innocents. As Babbitt noted in a 1923 Sorbonne lecture, "Radical democracy can lead to imperialism and tyranny since the sovereign people wants no obstacle to its will."[11]

Babbitt argued that idealistic imperialism was always a danger lurking in American popular culture: "An unchecked expansiveness on the national scale is always imperialistic. Among the ingredients of a possible American imperialism M. Siegfried enumerates the American's 'great self-satisfaction, his rather brutal sense of his own interests, and *the consciousness, still more dangerous, of his "duties" towards humanity.'* M. Siegfried admits however that our imperialism is likely to be of a new and subtle essence, not primarily concerned with territorial aggrandizement."[12]

The very first sentence in Babbitt's 1923 Sorbonne lecture, titled "Democracy and Imperialism," told the audience that "the connection between the two phenomena is not always acknowledged."[13] History would warn that democracies provide no insulation against imperialism and, under the wrong leadership, can be quite warlike. "Democracy in the sense of direct and unlimited democracy is, as was pointed out by Aristotle, the death of liberty; in virtue of its tyrannical temper, it is likewise, in the broad sense in which I have been using the term, closely akin to imperialism."[14]

After years of costly US wars, a consideration of Babbitt's ideas may be indispensable to the crafting of an American foreign policy that is based not on sentimental hopes or utopian ideologies but on a genuine moral realism. Through Babbitt's ideas, an American foreign policy might be constructed that jettisons the imperial and utopian projects that have emerged from humanitarianism but also refuses to concede important principles to the amoral darkness of a nihilistic realism.

At this point, a note regarding the chief emphasis of this book is required. This examination of Babbitt and international relations and foreign policy is not one of international relations theory as ordinarily understood but is primarily one of political philosophy, though especially as related to international relations and foreign policy. It is freely granted that scholars of international relations and foreign policy in the more narrow sense make important contributions to understanding the nature of the international order and trends in military and diplomatic affairs that will impact that order. Policymakers do well to pay heed to those who think and write about the practice of foreign policy, but foreign policy scholars likewise need to learn from the practitioners of foreign policy, which is a form of prudential statecraft. As Edmund Burke remarked, in any prudential endeavor, be it politics or farming or medicine, "I shall always advise to call in the aid of the farmer and the physician rather than the professor of metaphysics."[15]

While recognizing the importance of other approaches to international relations and foreign policy, this study stresses certain philosophical considerations as a means of offering building blocks essential to any sound theory of international affairs. None of what is discussed or argued here is intended to deny or discount the great complexity of this field of scholarly research. As it explores central philosophical questions, this book may suggest new ways of thinking about or approaching international relations but does not provide specific answers for many of the large and bewildering challenges of US foreign policy.

On the other hand, any theory of international relations that fancies a future utopian or millenarian paradise on earth or postulates the possibility of a fundamental transformation of human nature through political action can, ipso facto, be considered a work of intellectual malpractice. This book conveys that according to Irving Babbitt, certain ideas about international affairs are in fact rooted in fantasy, in a Romantic idealism that exhibits a false understanding of reality and will likely disturb rather than improve world order. To the extent that this study finds Babbitt's views plausible, it challenges some widely held views of international relations and foreign policy.

From the time of the ancient Greeks, political philosophy has analyzed politics from the perspective of what can be expected from human nature. Political philosophers have examined political regimes or theories about potential regimes by tracing political forms back to characteristics found in the individual human soul or to misunderstandings about its nature. The regime with leaders and citizens inclined toward material possessions will, for example, desire commerce and trade above other goals. Eric Voegelin has described classical political philosophy in particular as applying "the anthropological principle that society is man written in larger letters."[16]

Babbitt's unique contribution to international relations theory, I argue, is that his concept of imperialism and of restraint in foreign policy systematically and in distinctive ways applies the anthropological principle to a level above regime types and demonstrates that the international order is also the sum total of "man written in larger letters." In his lectures at the Sorbonne, Babbitt described his project this way: "At the end, I will leave behind the political aspects of the relationship between democracy and imperialism and try to study the root of this problem in the psychology of the individual."[17] Babbitt's central thesis, so counterintuitive in today's Western outlook, is that morality is found not in humanitarian projects, no matter how noble sounding, but in the human heart. It is this moral confusion, more than any other, that has set American foreign policy on the wrong path.

The international order is undoubtedly affected by balances of military power, economic interdependencies and rivalries, ethnic tensions, and a host of complex factors studied by international relations theorists, just as relations among individuals may be shaped by dependencies and conflicts as well as characteristics of the individual person such as willpower, health, intelligence, physical strength, and other factors that influence success or failure. Yet Babbitt insisted that theories of international affairs that ignore or distort the immutable tendencies within the human soul are superficial at best and pernicious at worst. The anthropological principle applies to the analysis of world affairs in the same way that it applies to the analysis of regime types.

The challenges of international relations in the twenty-first century differ significantly from those faced at the turn of the twentieth century. In Babbitt's time, two centuries of Romanticism of a certain type had bred an aggressive form of nationalism in Europe. Babbitt applied his ideas to the contemporary interactions among European nation-states and especially to the misunderstandings about human nature that he felt had helped to usher in the Great War.

In our time, the likelihood of nationalistic wars between Western European nation-states is more remote, but Babbitt's insights can be applied to a different set of events and circumstances within the international order. At the close of this book, I examine two contrasting theories of world order that attempt to explain contemporary events: the amoral realism of Henry Kissinger and the Hegelian idealism of Francis Fukuyama. Both frameworks, I argue, fundamentally misunderstand the nature of morality in relation to world affairs. I contrast these two theories with the arguments of Samuel Huntington, which, I believe, come closest to Irving Babbitt's understanding of how morality might shape a sound foreign policy.

Huntington is a realist, and his theory lays out the hard realities of the current world order: the great challenges of current world affairs are found less in clashes between individual nation-states than in "clashes of civilizations." The clash between Islamic and Western societies is one obvious example. However, other significant international challenges fit the Huntington paradigm. The current tension between the United States and Russia, for example, may seem a clash of individual nation-states, but this tension is probably more deeply rooted in the US conviction that it represents a universal civilizational order of "democracy and freedom," while Russia feels it is the primary defender of a far-reaching Orthodox civilization and a culture also found in numerous neighboring nations.

Huntington's conclusions about how the character of leaders can manage this situation are very similar to Babbitt's. World leaders must be realistic but also magnanimous and must celebrate what is best in their own civilizations while recognizing the richness and nobility of other great civilizations. Both Babbitt and Huntington advised Western leaders to seek what is at once common and highest in human nature; only a cosmopolitanism rooted in a common understanding about what is most noble in the human soul might unite centrifugal forces among leaders and nations. In our time, Huntington points out that the challenge is even more daunting and complex: to develop a rich cosmopolitanism that unites across culturally diverse civilizations—a project for which Babbitt's moral-religious and humanistic philosophy and his extensive discussion of East and West laid a philosophical foundation.

Babbitt's study of the great humanistic and religious sages of Asian civilization and their commonalities with Western Christianity points to the possibility that with proper leadership, bridges between civilizations might be built. If, as Babbitt insisted, human experience, despite its infinite variety, is at its core always and everywhere the same, and "the best books of the world seem to have been written, as Emerson puts it, by one all-wise, all-seeing gentleman,"[18] then our task is to find the higher values that can unite the world's leaders across the world's civilizations and to recognize that these higher things are a unifying, peace-inducing force. Nations and civilizations may have trade and military alliances, but the only source of true peace is found in the souls of cultural and political leaders who share a higher nobility.

War will persist in human history because human nature always has the potential for moral indolence or evil. Despite his realism about the strenuous challenge of uniting human beings through ethical work, Babbitt believed that this common ground among diverse peoples and cultures was both real and possible for properly educated people to discern. Leaders across civilizations who share the proper temperament and character may "go beyond the convention of a particular time and country, and lay hold in varying degrees on 'the unwritten laws of heaven.'"[19] Babbitt's quest was to locate and elucidate the part of the human soul that is either divine or most deeply human, because it is the wisdom of the ages that what is divine or most deeply human is what unites human beings, whereas what is merely temperamental or impulsive, untouched by a higher discipline, is what divides them.

This book examines Babbitt's central ideas with special reference to their relevance for foreign policy and international relations and with emphasis on what he has to say explicitly about those subjects. The first chapter discusses Babbitt's view of human nature, a view that, with respect to the higher potential of every human's "worldly" or "temporal" existence, he labeled *humanism*. That view, he argued, is shared by numerous philosophical thinkers across civilizations who have expressed the same idea in a diversity of ways. Humanism, Babbitt said, is compatible with but not identical to the great religious traditions of East and West. The second chapter explains Babbitt's view that a modern movement, naturalism, has gained wide currency in the West and that this movement provides a distorted and erroneous understanding of human nature, repudiating the West's cultural and religious heritage. The errors concerning human nature found in naturalism, Babbitt argued, spawned two superficially very different but closely aligned and often cooperating currents: first, a reliance on natural science as the way to progress, and second, a sentimental humanitarianism that wholly rejects the old Western view of human nature and society. Sentimental humanitarianism has become most influential as the source of radical democracy theory as developed by Jean-Jacques Rousseau. That theory is discussed in the third chapter. In practice, radical democracy engenders two prominent characteristics, revolutionary disorder in domestic politics (discussed in chapter 4) and imperialistic aggression in foreign policy (chapter 5). The only effective antidote to the imperialistic aggression of radical democracy, Babbitt argued, is a return to a sounder understanding of human nature and recognition that political disorder is rooted in disorders of the soul. As discussed in the sixth chapter, Babbitt argued that human beings can become genuinely "cosmopolitan" and move toward peace with other nations and civilizations only when their leaders share an ethical center, which is possible only when they have achieved a certain moral character. Temperamental, morally undisciplined leaders who cannot control their passions will never find peace with one another. The final chapter compares Babbitt's theory of peace and good relations among nations and civilizations with three representative contemporary theories of world order. The book concludes by applying Babbitt's ideas to current world affairs and discussing their significance for supplementing and enriching theories of foreign policy and international relations.

Biographical and Bibliographical Information

Because of the death of his mother at an early age, Irving Babbitt grew up under a diversity of circumstances, working as a paperboy in New York City, as a farmhand in Ohio, and as a cowhand in Wyoming. Babbitt's love of languages and their corresponding cultures eventually brought him to Harvard, where he worried that his professors were concentrating on superficial issues of philology rather than a more important philosophical subject matter. He graduated with high honors in Classics and eventually found his way to the Sorbonne, where he studied Eastern languages such as Sanskrit and Pali and where he developed a profound respect for Eastern religions, especially Buddhism. After earning a master's degree at Harvard, he was offered a faculty position as an instructor of French. Babbitt was well qualified to teach Classics, but the Classics requirement had been eased for Harvard students, probably leading to Babbitt's intellectual sparring with Harvard president Charles W. Eliot, a prominent education reformer and proponent of the modern system of electives for undergraduates. Babbitt, particularly in his first book, *Literature and the American College*, adamantly opposed the democratization of the curriculum under the elective system. Babbitt enjoyed a long career at Harvard, where he was a popular professor and influenced a number of figures, such as T. S. Eliot, who would become famous in their own right. Babbitt remained on the Harvard faculty until his death on July 15, 1933.[20]

Babbitt achieved national fame during his lifetime for his advocacy of a "New Humanism" rooted in ethical discipline that stood in opposition to the cult of science and Romanticism. For example, an event at Carnegie Hall to discuss the New Humanism with Babbitt as the featured speaker reportedly drew three thousand people. The debate and controversy surrounding Babbitt involved some of the most prominent intellectual and literary figures of his age, including Edmund Wilson, Ernest Hemingway, T. S. Eliot, Arthur Lovejoy, Sinclair Lewis, H. L. Mencken, and Allen Tate. In Babbitt's last decades, he wrote extensively about politics and war and peace.

The first body of scholarly literature around Babbitt's thought came in his lifetime with the intellectual ferment caused by his advocacy of a New Humanism. Two important books published in 1930 discussed Babbitt's ideas. A defense of the New Humanism was made in *Humanism in America*, edited by Norman Foerster, while *The Critique of Humanism*, edited by C. Hartley Grattan, took the opposite tack.

Babbitt's contemporary intellectual critics ranged from Mencken, who was largely out of his depth in critiquing Babbitt's interpretation of Rousseau, to intellectually more formidable interlocutors who were sympathetic but not in full agreement with Babbitt. In this latter category was his student Eliot, who was more sympathetic to orthodox religion than was Babbitt, and Lovejoy, who engaged with Babbitt in a relatively public dispute concerning his interpretation of Romanticism and Rousseau. With Babbitt's death, debate over the New Humanism subsided, although in 1941 Oscar Cargill published *Intellectual America: Ideas on the March*, which contained a rather polemical attack on Babbitt's ideas on humanism and education.

Prominent intellectuals during and just after World War II who were deeply influenced by Babbitt included the historian and Pulitzer Prize–winning poet Peter Viereck and the historian and classicist Nathan Pusey, who became president of Harvard in 1953 and in 1960 inaugurated the Irving Babbitt Chair of Comparative Literature. Russell Kirk's treatment of Babbitt in *The Conservative Mind* (1953) helped attract interest in Babbitt. Scholarship on his work expanded markedly in the 1970s with the contributions of such scholars as Thomas Nevin, George Panichas, and Claes G. Ryn. Kirk assisted this new era of Babbitt scholarship by founding the conservative intellectual journal *Modern Age* in 1957. In time, *Modern Age* became a vehicle for a considerable body of Babbitt scholarship. Ryn and Panichas in particular have done a great deal to correct older and misleading interpretations of Babbitt's ideas. In 1983 a two-day conference on Babbitt at The Catholic University of America in Washington, DC, commemorated the fiftieth anniversary of Babbitt's death. In 1984 the National Humanities Institute was founded, in part to carry forward Babbitt's intellectual legacy. For a quarter of a century, writings on Babbitt or related to his work have appeared in the interdisciplinary and international journal *Humanitas*, which continues to publish articles about Babbitt's thought. A growing number of scholars have applied, extended, revised, or developed Babbitt's central ideas, integrating them into work of their own.

Overall, the considerable body of scholarship about Babbitt falls into several distinct categories. In addition to the scholarship regarding the New Humanism, there is considerable scholarship on Babbitt's religious thought and his comparisons between religions of the East and West as found in his *Dhammapada* and *Democracy and Leadership*: Babbitt's ideas, for example, have scholarly followers in China. Related to Babbitt's religious thought, there also is some formidable philosophical scholarship surrounding his contributions to epistemology and to his general ideas, such as Ryn's *Will, Imagination, and Reason* and Folke Leander's *Humanism and Naturalism: A Comparative Study of Ernest Seillière, Irving Babbitt, and Paul Elmer More*. Over the years, scholars have also examined Babbitt's theories on education and his disagreements with Charles Eliot. One recent such article is Kipton D. Smilie's "Humanitarian and Humanistic ideals: Charles W. Eliot, Irving Babbitt, and the American Curriculum at the Turn of the 20th Century" in the *Journal of Thought*. Babbitt was a considerable force in comparative literature, and there is a body of work around his critique of romanticism, mostly famously in Lovejoy's review of *Rousseau and Romanticism* in *Modern Language Notes* (1920). Babbitt's views on Rousseauistic democracy also generated considerable controversy, and a number of scholars accused him of anti-democratic sentiments. A representative example is David Spitz's "The Undesirability of Democracy" in *Patterns of Anti-Democratic Thought* (1965). Finally, excellent and more sweeping considerations of Babbitt's ideas may be found in *Irving Babbitt in Our Time*, edited by Claes Ryn and George Panichas, as well as Thomas Nevin's *Irving Babbitt: An Intellectual Study*, both generally reliable surveys of Babbitt's ideas. A voluminous body of literature surrounds Babbitt's ideas, and these works are merely a representative sample drawn from a few key areas of scholarly interest.

For the purposes of the present study, what is lacking in the scholarly treatment of Babbitt is a thorough discussion of his ideas on war and peace and on democracy and imperialism. Given the presence of these themes throughout Babbitt's works and his considerable interest in the origins of both the French Revolution and the Great War, this represents a considerable intellectual gap that requires attention.

Only a single scholarly article gives exclusive attention to Babbitt's ideas on war and peace, Richard Gamble's "The 'Fatal Flaw' of Internationalism: Babbitt on Humanitarianism" in *Humanitas* (1996). Gamble's article is a very reliable and sound interpretation of Babbitt's ideas, but its focus is largely limited to a two-part essay written by Babbitt in *Nation* (1915). Babbitt's ideas on imperialism are spread through much of his writings, and Gamble's essay is therefore not a systematic consideration of the sweep of Babbitt's thought on the issue. Likewise, Nevin's book contains an important chapter on "Humanism in a Political Context" that mentions the connection Babbitt made between humanitarianism and "ideological imperialism" and how "Rousseau had produced Robespierre and Napoleon."[21] But Nevin's treatment of Babbitt's political thought is confined largely to a discussion of Babbitt's ideas on democratic theory generally and not include a discussion of the implications of democratic theory for foreign policy. Kirk's famous treatment of Babbitt in *The Conservative Mind* does mention the term *imperialism* once but does so in the context of human psychology, not foreign affairs. Likewise, Henry Kariel's essay "Democracy Limited: Irving Babbitt's Classicism" in the *Review of Politics* (1951) features substantial discussion of Babbitt's political ideas but only one small mention of the danger of nations "meddling" in the operations of other nations.

Claes Ryn is one scholar who has written prolifically about foreign policy and clearly has been heavily influenced by Babbitt. In *America the Virtuous*, for example, Ryn draws on and enlarges many of Babbitt's ideas about war and peace and, like Babbitt, examines how Rousseau's ideas seem to serve as an important intellectual basis for democratic imperialism in foreign policy and the fraying of the constitutional order in domestic affairs. However, Ryn's scholarship in this area is not a systematic treatment of Babbitt's ideas specifically. Drawing on Babbitt, Ryn instead builds his own theory of imperialism, offers a more systematic philosophical treatment of epistemology, and engages in a more contemporary discussion of current foreign policy events. For example, in *America the Virtuous*, which deals prominently with foreign affairs, Ryn mentions Babbitt's name on only seven pages.

Given the paucity of scholarship about Babbitt's theory of imperialism and the recent wars prosecuted by the American democracy, the time seems ripe for a systematic treatment of Babbitt's thoughts on the tendencies that may make democracies warlike and for creating a scholarly basis for applying those ideas to the contemporary challenges of world order.

CHAPTER 1

Babbitt and Human Nature

> There are two laws discrete,
> Not reconciled,—
> Law for man, and law for thing;
> The last builds the town and fleet,
> But it runs wild,
> And doth the man unking.
>
> —Ralph Waldo Emerson, ode inscribed to W. H. Channing

Much of international relations theory rests on analysis of "macro" trends in world affairs: studies of economic interdependence among nations, catalogs of military spending and weaponry, discussions of influential political ideologies and revolutions, detailed analyses of common interests among nations, or studies focused on international institutions. These analyses of the international system may yield significant insights about global trends and therefore may enlighten leaders about looming dangers to world order. Yet each of these analyses also operates under certain "micro" assumptions about the nature of human beings and the potentialities therein. The superstructures of these theories have a deeper, philosophical basis. To understand Irving Babbitt's theory of democratic imperialism, one needs to examine carefully Babbitt's theory of human nature: his larger theory of democracy is based on the constituent parts of his insights into the human psyche.

Babbitt developed his theory in a manner similar to that of the classical Greek philosophers—that is, on the anthropological principle that the political order is a larger reflection of individual souls, particularly those of its leaders. Babbitt noticed that both classical Greek and Asian philosophers, such as Aristotle and Confucius, shared a common understanding that peace in the polity was intimately related to a certain ethical harmony in the souls of individuals. Babbitt concluded that true peace, as opposed to a temporary balance of forces or an agreement on common interests, is rooted in spiritual agreement. Just as intemperate individuals are prone to conflict and insensitive to the interests of others, nations with intemperate leaders are likewise quick to assert a certain moral superiority and are prone to seek dominion over others. Babbitt, an admirer and scholar of Confucian ethics, saw that Confucius traced a very clear line from the virtuous individual to the peaceful nation:

> Wanting to govern well their states, they first harmonized their own clans.
> Wanting to harmonize their own clan, they first cultivated themselves.
> Wanting to cultivate themselves, they first corrected their minds.
> Wanting to correct their minds, they first made their wills sincere.
> Wanting to make their wills sincere, they first extended their knowledge.
> When things are investigated, knowledge is extended.
> When the will is sincere, the mind is correct.
> When the mind is correct, the self is cultivated.
> When the self is cultivated, the clan is harmonized.
> When the clan is harmonized, the country is well governed.
> When the country is well governed, there will be peace throughout the land.[1]

These philosophers believed that the ability of people and nations to get along in peace would ultimately be found in the ability of human beings to fulfill the requirements found in the moral and spiritual components of their nature. When one is searching for peace in the world, it is proper therefore to begin by searching for how human beings find peace within themselves. That is where we begin, with Irving Babbitt's understanding of the human soul. How is the soul called to virtue and orderliness? What is a proper understanding of virtue, and what steps that must be taken to form a superior moral character?

Emerson's lines represent one of Babbitt's most frequently quoted passages of poetry.[2] Emerson's poem provides a concise exposition of Babbitt's understanding of human nature and concept of humanism: human beings are unique in the universe because they are not simply subject to the laws of nature and science; they are also subject to a uniquely human law that is a guide for their behavior. In Christian terminology, the requirements of Babbitt's human law might be described as the callings of conscience. Like conscience, the human law is distinct from and above the laws of nature that apply to the animal kingdom and the material world. The human law is not an abstract dogma but a fact of everyday experience, as human beings are free to live to excess or to avoid excess, to give in to impulse or control impulse, to act with malice or act with kindness.

Because of the existence of the human law, counterpoised to the laws of physical nature, human beings sense a dualism within themselves: they are pulled between a higher self and a lower self. As Babbitt describes the experience, "Anyone who sets out to live temperately and proportionately will find that he will need to impose upon himself a difficult discipline. His attitude toward life will necessarily be dualistic. It will be dualistic in the sense that he recognizes in man a 'self' that is capable of exercising control and another 'self' that needs controlling."[3] The central feature of Babbitt's humanism is his affirmation of this dualism.

Babbitt pointed to classical Greece and Rome for the West's original understanding of this dualism. "Aristotle recognizes that man is the creature of two laws: he has an ordinary or natural self of impulse and desire and a human self that is known practically as a power of control over impulse and desire. If man is to become human he must not let impulse and desire run wild, but most oppose to everything excessive in his ordinary self, whether in thought or deed or emotion, the law of measure."[4]

Society, for Aristotle, did not exist as a vehicle for humanitarian "service." Instead, Babbitt's interpretation of Aristotle was that society existed to assist the individual in mediating the law of measure within one's own soul. "Aristotle, who would attach the individual by a thousand bonds to society, who even makes ethics only a branch of politics, does not, therefore, fall into the humanitarian error of making social service the goal of the individual. Society is chiefly important in the eyes of Aristotle for the aid it may give the individual in realizing his higher self."[5]

Babbitt also looked to Cicero as "one of the most influential of occidental humanists" who also asserted the dualism of human nature.[6] For Babbitt, the essence of Cicero was found in the belief that "one becomes humanistic in proportion as he grows aware of the law of order and measure and decorum that, according to Cicero, distinguishes man from other living creatures, and in proportion as he imposes the discipline of this law upon his ordinary or animal self."[7]

Despite the clear influence of classical Greek and Roman philosophers,

Babbitt's humanism was also heavily influenced by his study of Confucius and early Buddhism. We see this Asian influence in Babbitt's assertion that the uniquely human law is accessed through the power of a "higher will," an assertion of self-control and self mastery. The requirements of conscience are fulfilled not by contemplating virtue but through acts of will. For much of Eastern philosophy, the power of reason—so prominent in classical Greek philosophy—gives way to the primacy of will. Reflecting a sympathy with Eastern philosophy, Babbitt believed that individuals do not "think" their way to good behavior; they restrain their will and therefore avoid bad behavior.

While it is intellectually perilous to oversimplify the distinction between East and West on the importance of will versus intellect, it seems reasonable to assert that the Greek tradition of philosophy and even the Christian scholastic tradition tend to associate the divine quality in human beings with intellect. Babbitt countered that the true divine quality in human nature was will: "As against the expansionists of every kind, I do not hesitate to affirm that what is specifically human in man and ultimately divine is a certain quality of will, a will that is felt in its relation to his ordinary self as a will to refrain."[8]

While Babbitt argued that although Plato and Aristotle tended to give primacy to reason rather than will, both Aristotle and Christianity nonetheless possess a clear understanding of the power of will. "Though Aristotle, after the Greek fashion, gives primacy not to will but to mind, the power of which I am speaking is surely related to his 'energy of the soul,' the form of activity distinct from mere outer working, deemed by him appropriate for the life of leisure that he proposes as the goal of a liberal education."[9]

Because of this intellectual ambiguity in the epistemology of the ancient Greeks, Babbitt tended to see more clarity in Confucius and Buddha, who more unambiguously ranked will as superior to reason and who pointed to a higher will as the central locus of the divine in human beings: "Reason that has the support of a higher will, that is, in the Confucian phrase, submissive to 'the will of heaven' would seem better able to exercise control over natural man than a reason that is purely self-reliant."[10] Babbitt shared the Confucian belief that reason and knowledge would represent a superior moral compass only if rooted in the well-trained will. Without this higher will, reason alone would have little power to lead a human being toward a higher plane of existence: "One may well come to agree with certain Asiatics, in contrast at this point with the European intellectual, that the good life is not primarily something to be *known* but something to be *willed*. There is warrant for the belief that if a man *acts* on the light he already has the light will grow."[11]

Despite this emphasis, Babbitt was not antirational. The intellect, he believed, was not blindly directed by the higher will but could support the higher will in helping to formulate correct moral choices. Nonetheless, the obligation to *act* when facing moral choices required the intellect to be subordinated to the higher will. As he explained the role of intellect in supporting the higher will, "If anyone sets himself the humanistic task of achieving the intermediary term between extremes, he will find that it is not enough to exercise an inner check on temperament, he will need to exercise this check intelligently; and to exercise it intelligently he will need to look up to some norm."[12]

Therefore, Babbitt's position was that the intellect played a supporting role in the search for proper moral choices, but the true human law was accessed through acts of volition. When human beings took concrete steps to improve their character, they were fulfilling their truest nature. More specifically, Babbitt argued that a proper exercise of the higher will possessed a negative quality in the sense that the higher will served to override or check impulse and desire. To capture this quality of negation, Babbitt used the term *inner check*, a concept found in ancient Hindu texts. The inner check is the instrumental component of the will that prevents human beings from yielding to the ordinary desires of their selfish nature. "Instead of conceiving of the divine in terms of expansion the Oriental sage defines it experimentally as the 'inner check.' No more fundamental distinction perhaps can be made than that between those who associate the good with the yes-principle and those who associate it rather with the no-principle."[13] (Babbitt also described the negative quality of the higher will as a "veto power.")[14]

Properly understood, the inner check is not spontaneous, nor does it come naturally. Babbitt said that it must be cultivated—that is, it develops a stronger pull in the soul when it is regularly exercised. "'That wherein the superior man cannot be equaled,' says Confucius, 'is simply this—his work which other men cannot see.' It is this inner work and habits that result from it that above all humanize a man and make him exemplary to the multitude."[15]

For those human beings who fail to exercise the inner check, the result will be a lack of meaning, direction, and purpose. A lack of inner work and surrender to impulse dehumanizes human beings because it represents a failure to exercise the quality in their nature that is most uniquely human. "The man who drifts supinely with the current desire is guilty according to Buddha of the gravest of all vices—spiritual or moral indolence (*pamāda*). He on the contrary who curbs or reins in his expansive desires is displaying the chief of all virtues, spiritual vigilance or strenuousness (*appamāda*). The man who is spiritually strenuous has entered upon the 'path.'"[16]

Babbitt considered this Eastern ethical view, with its emphasis on will, to be among the most spiritually strenuous doctrines ever propagated. Of Buddha, he said, "No one ever put so squarely upon the individual what the individual is ever seeking to evade—the burden of moral responsibility." Babbitt quoted the *Dhammapada*: "Self is the lord of self. Who else can be the lord? . . . You yourself must make the effort. The Buddhas are only teachers."[17] In the ancient Hindu, Babbitt said, the divine is an "inner check."[18] In Buddha's terminology, "the permanent or ethical element in himself towards which he should strive to move is known to him practically as a power of inhibition or inner check upon expansive desire. Vital impulse (*élan vital*) may be subjected to vital control (*frein vital*)."[19]

Babbitt also seemed to imply that the tendency in Western thinkers to overstate the role of reason actually might be found less in the original classical and Christian thinkers themselves than in subsequent interpretations, such as scholastic philosophy. When read carefully, he argued, the great thinkers of East and West shared some agreement that the highest divine part of humanity might also be characterized as a certain quality of the will found in the veto power. "In the past, the spirit that says no has been associated rather with the divine. Socrates tells us that the counsels of his 'voice' were always negative, never positive."[20]

Babbitt did not view the higher will as an abstract mechanism of thought, such as Kant's categorical imperative. Babbitt said that the higher will is not an "ideal" but an immediate fact of experience. "Positively, one may define it as the higher immediacy that is known in its relation to the lower immediacy—the merely temperamental man with his impressions and emotions and expansive desires—as a power of vital control (*frein vital*). Failure to exercise this control is the spiritual indolence that is for both the Christian and the Buddhist a chief source, if not the chief source, of evil."[21]

A third important concept in Babbitt's thought is the imagination, which, like reason, is shaped by the quality of a person's will. For Babbitt, the imagination serves as a kind of cognitive filter, sorting reality based on the nature of the soul that deploys it. Therefore, if a person is materialistic, for example, his imagination will tend to focus attention on material possessions and the acquisition of money. If a person has cultivated and exercised the higher will, in contrast, her imagination will draw attention to nobler things. Babbitt did not display a systematic epistemology, but he did regularly describe a complex theory about the interplay among will, imagination, and reason. In these descriptions, he consistently viewed the mechanics of the soul as a process in which individuals listen to the voice of their inner check, which, in turn, tends to influence a person's imagination, which, in turn, influences the individual's ideas.

People who have exercised and cultivated their higher will develop an outlook that Babbitt calls the "ethical imagination."[22] When the higher will is exercised, will, imagination, and reason cooperate in leading the individual toward a higher reality. "The imagination that Joubert calls the 'eye of the soul' is fully conscious and also creative, though in a different sense: it creates values. It does so by coöperating with reason in service of the higher will. The unconscious activities must be controlled with reference to the values thus created with the help of the ethical imagination, as one may term it, if they are to have direction and purpose, in other words, human significance."[23] Babbitt contrasted this ethical or moral imagination with the "idyllic" imagination of modernity—an imagination that is not disciplined or pulled back to an ethical center by the higher will and an imagination that, because of its lack of control, may lose touch with reality.

Babbitt saw a corrective to the Western tendency to intellectualize virtue in Edmund Burke, who gave the imagination a new and important role. Babbitt wrote that Burke added a new insight to the Western tradition by emphasizing a quality in the soul that moves people to virtue that is neither rational nor subrational but suprarational and imaginative. For example, of Burke Babbitt said,

> And then he was familiar, as we are all familiar, with persons who give no reasons at all, or the wrong reasons, for doing the right thing, and with other persons who give the most logical and ingenious reasons for doing the wrong thing. The basis for right conduct is not reasoning but experience, and experience much wider than that of the individual, the secure possession of which can result only from the early acquisition of right habits.[24]

Claes G. Ryn has explored in depth the interplay among will, imagination, and reason, showing that the will is preeminent because it shapes the outlook of the individual. Ryn emphasizes that the ethical imagination does not arise spontaneously but is a result of the will's ethical work: "Babbitt finds the ultimate criterion of reality in the universal ordering power of the higher will. To know the essence of life, man must act to change his character. Without the sense of reality that comes with the exercise of the higher will no adequate perception of life is possible."[25]

The degree to which human beings are guided by their higher rather than their lower selves shapes or even determines their outlook on every human endeavor, including their aesthetical, moral, cultural, and political outlooks. In fact, much of Babbitt's early writing applied his views on human nature not to politics but to aesthetics. For example, Babbitt wrote extensively about the Romantic critique of classical form. In the eighteenth and nineteenth centuries, the Romantics argued that a hollow formalism had crept into classical art and that these standards should be jettisoned. The Romantics believed that classical art and literature could be replaced by a new form, that of impulsive spontaneity and novelty.

Babbitt in fact agreed with some of this critique of classical formalism, but he argued that in the attempt to replace classicism, new and sound standards of taste would only be found in the souls of individuals who were operating on a higher ethical level. Spontaneity and novelty were not a substitute for sound standards: "Taste is attained only when this sensibility is rectified with reference to standard inwardly apprehended, and in this sense may be defined as a man's literary conscience; it is, in short, only one aspect of the struggle between our lower and higher selves."[26] Art and literature would be of the highest order only when they emerged from the orderly soul. "The humanist maintains that man attains the truth of his nature only by imposing decorum upon his ordinary self."[27]

Babbitt not only noted the importance of the higher will over imagination and reason in humanistic philosophers such as Confucius and Socrates but also found it a common essence at the core of the world's great religions, including Christianity, which he asserted were rooted in Asia: "The mention of Christ and Buddha (of Confucius as a typical Asiatic I shall have more to say presently) is hardly necessary to remind us that it is the distinction of Asia as compared to Europe and other parts of the world to have been the mother of religions."[28] And, he argued that the core of Asian religions is an emphasis on will. Christianity, for example, encourages human beings to submit their own selfish will to the divine will. "Dante has caught the inmost spirit of Christianity in his reply to this question: 'In his will is our peace.' This idea that man needs to submit his ordinary self to a higher or divine will is essential not merely to Christianity, but to all genuine religion. Muhammad is at one here with Buddha and Christ. The word Islam means submission."[29]

Babbitt's most oft-quoted Christian saint is Paul, who emphasized "spiritual concentration." "Now Christ, for St. Paul, is evidently the living intuition of a law that is set above the ordinary self; by taking on the yoke of the law men are drawn together as to common centre."[30] In a review of Ernest Renan, for example, Babbitt argued that Renan had missed the core teaching of St. Paul: "He calls him the second founder of Christianity, but he has little sympathy for the distinctive feature of the Pauline religion, its haunting sense of sin and the stress it lays on the struggle between a lower and a higher self, between a law of the flesh and a law of the spirit."[31]

In Christian terms, the ultimate goal of human beings is to discover the divine will and conform one's own will to it. Babbitt therefore found true Christianity to be a religion of severe moral obligations and rejected the romanticizing of Christ as a Romantic aesthete.[32] In his chapter on Renan in *Masters of Modern French Criticism*, Babbitt criticized Renan's portrayal of Jesus as a Romantic sentimentalist: "Perhaps nothing so offends the serious reader of the 'Vie de Jésus' as Renan's assumption that the highest praise he can give Jesus is to say that he satisfies the aesthetic sense. He multiplies in speaking of him such adjectives as *doux, beau, exquis, charmant, ravissant, délicieux*."[33] Renan "reduces the mission of Jesus, so far as possible, to sentimental and humanitarian effusions . . . religion of the will is almost entirely sacrificed . . . to . . . religion of the heart."[34]

On the contrary, Babbitt viewed true Christianity as a religion that places great demands on the conscience of individuals. "For the man who imitates Christ in any traditional sense this world is not an Arcadian dream but a place of trial and probation. 'Take up your cross and follow me.' . . . Genuine religion must always have in some form the sense of a deep inner cleft between man's ordinary self and the divine."[35]

Babbitt argued that the Christian emphasis on will was sometimes obscured by classical influences. At its core, Christianity is an Asian religion, but it is an Asian religion that, he argued, had incorporated aspects of "Platonic, Aristotelian, Stoical, Neoplatonic; also a strong Roman element."[36]

At this point, we should be careful to avoid blurring the important distinction found in Babbitt's thought between religion and humanism. Babbitt developed his concept of humanism in part by distilling some of the common moral premises found in different religious traditions. However, he was careful to argue that humanism operates on a separate plane of existence and does not incorporate the otherworldly saintliness found in the great religious traditions. Humanism, he said, is a system of ethics for the worldly, not the otherworldly.

> The point on which Christ and Buddha are in accord is the need of renunciation. It should be abundantly plain from all I have said that the higher will is felt in its relation to the expansive desires as a will to refrain. The humanist does not carry the exercise of this will beyond a subduing of his desires to the law of measure; but it may be carried much further until it amounts to a turning away from the desires of the natural man altogether—the "dying to the world" of the Christian.[37]

Babbitt's humanism did not serve as an alternative religion; it was instead an acknowledgment that on an ethical and experiential level, human beings may come together on a moral and ethical level even if they do not share doctrinal or dogmatic beliefs. This was an essential point to be made in the context of a discussion of war and peace, as Babbitt pointed to the possibility that people across religious traditions could find common ground. As Ryn explains Babbitt's goal, "In formulating the idea of higher will Babbitt is not trying to talk Christians out of their beliefs. He is addressing all those in the modern world who are not willing to accept ethical or religious truth on the authority of inherited dogmas. To these skeptics he argues, not that traditional Western beliefs are wrong, but that ethics and religion do not stand or fall with Church authority. The have an experiential foundation."[38]

In his time, Babbitt failed to persuade a number of religiously inclined intellectuals that his version of humanism did not represent a critique or a substitute for Christianity. Tension developed between Babbitt and some of his followers such as T. S. Eliot as well as Babbitt's closest friend, Paul Elmer More.[39]

Babbitt's complaint about Christianity was not that its doctrines, properly understood, were erroneous and did not have a basis in human experience. Nor did he believe that humanism could serve as a substitute theology to provide understanding about eternal mysteries traditionally addressed by religion. Babbitt in fact insisted that Christian doctrine was fully in keeping with human experience and human nature and went further than humanism in addressing otherworldly questions. His complaint was that in historical practice, Christian dogma had sometimes pointed adherents to an overemphasis on the outwardly concept of divinely given "grace" that distracted human beings from their obligation to rein in their own selfish desires. In these cases, an overemphasis on "grace" or "providence" took away from the "works" brought about by individual effort and conduct. Babbitt pointed to historical examples in which the contemplation of the genuine mystery of grace had resulted in metaphysical concepts and theological dogmas that tended to drift away from actual human experience. In one example, Babbitt pointed to the church doctrine of "infant damnation" as the abdication of the "critical spirit" to "outer authority—that of revelation and the church."[40]

Babbitt's concern was that rigid dogmatism might take the concept of grace too far, weakening the sense of obligation that individuals require to be sensitive to the callings of the higher will. "It may be said of the ultramontane Catholic, as of the extreme partisan of grace, though in a very different sense, that he has simply repudiated self-reliance."[41] Babbitt recoiled from any religious doctrine that might lead an individual away from the obligation of self-mastery. He felt that theological doctrines should not distract from the experiential reality and obligation of ethical work. Even the greatest saints, he believed, had taken their first steps toward otherworldliness on the path of everyday ethical work.

For Babbitt, when an overemphasis on grace led to a neglect of ethical concentration, religion could become a bewildering mystery. "We can infer what Buddha would have thought of the Augustinian Christians who would have man turn away from works and brood everlastingly on the mystery of grace. He would have agreed with Holmes that the only decent thing for a consistent Calvinist to do is to go mad."[42]

Babbitt emphasized that his critique involved erroneous historical tendencies found in some theological dogma; he was not criticizing Christianity's core doctrines. During one of his discussions on grace, he remarked in a footnote, "I do not mean to say that St. Augustine did not put great emphasis on works, but merely that side of Christianity which shows most clearly his influence has put an even greater emphasis on grace."[43] Of Christian civilization, Babbitt remarked on the century of Dante, Aquinas, and Giotto, "The achievements of the thirteenth century which mark perhaps the culmination of Christian civilization were very splendid not only from a religious but also from a humanistic point of view."[44]

Many of Babbitt's critics either did not understand or did not accept his humanistic project. As Thomas Nevin pointed out, "Babbitt's humanism was more than an ethic but less than a religion, and so it was fit to satisfy neither the secular nor the spiritual temperaments."[45] With his promotion of New Humanism, Babbitt won neither a broad religious nor a secular following. Despite public criticism of his views on religion, Babbitt did not revise them.[46] Toward the end of his life, in 1932, Babbitt wrote to More some comments that reflected the consistent view that when religious dogmas diverted from actual human experience, religion could go astray: "There is a side of Christianity for which I do feel a real antipathy—namely the fanaticism and intolerance that it has so often displayed as a historical religion, so much so that you yourself would have been persecuted for certain statements in your last volume during the genuine ages of faith."[47]

Babbitt believed that very few individuals could genuinely ascend to the level of supernaturalism embodied in the life of an ascetic Christian saint, and the monastic life was losing favor because Christianity had been losing moral authority since the Enlightenment. The problems he saw in the West would not therefore be solved by an appeal for everyone to become a Christian saint. "Perhaps" he said, "the world would have been a better place if more people had made sure that they were human before setting out to be superhuman."[48]

The intellectual controversy between those with an orthodox religious leaning such as More and Eliot and Babbitt's non-orthodox humanism is not the subject of this book. Babbitt was generally an ally of traditional religion, seeing religious faith as encouraging ethical concentration on the part of the individual. Babbitt's intellectual sparring with some advocates of orthodox Christianity did, however, highlight Babbitt's foremost doctrine: ethical concentration of the individual is the key to ordering reality and to social peace.

Human nature's most prominent feature for Babbitt was the challenge of conforming one's behavior to the requirements of the human law, a law that is felt in the soul of every human being as an inner check on impulse, emotion, and passion. The modern world, he felt, had gone wrong by adopting philosophies of "naturalism" that deny this essential aspect of human nature.

CHAPTER 2

Modernity as Naturalism

A remarkable feature of the modern man indeed is that he does not propose to renounce anything and at the same time hopes to achieve the peace and brotherhood that are, according to Buddha and Christ, to be achieved only by renunciation. If these great religious teachers are right, it follows that what one finds when one penetrates beneath the surface of our contemporary life is a monstrous huddle of incompatible desires.

—Irving Babbitt, *On Being Creative*

During his time studying at the Sorbonne, when Irving Babbitt entered the library's great Reading Room, he was confronted by two large mural paintings. As Babbitt described it, "On either side of the entrance . . . are mural paintings of two female figures: one of strenuous aspect, and with a contracted brow, is entitled Science; the other in floating draperies, and with vague, far-away eye, is entitled Rêve."[1] To Babbitt, these murals represented the West's intellectual drift away from a true humanism, rooted in ethical self-control, and toward two forms of what he called naturalism. For Babbitt, the two greatest influences in modernity were a worship of science, rooted in the ideas of Francis Bacon and given wide currency during the Enlightenment, and a sentimental Romanticism, a philosophy that had a pedigree in the West going back to Aristophanes but that found its most powerful modern expression in Jean-Jacques Rousseau. Babbitt stated quite simply, "I define two main forms of naturalism—on the one hand, utilitarian and scientific and, on the other, emotional naturalism."[2]

While these two forms of naturalism had roots going back many centuries,

Babbitt contended that they found their fullest expression in the eighteenth and nineteenth centuries, when they undergirded the two dominant social movements in the West, scientific and sentimental humanitarianism. "The positive and utilitarian movements, we should add, have been inspired mainly by scientific humanitarianism, and sentimental naturalism again has been an important element, if not the most important element, in the so-called Romantic movement."[3]

For many intellectual historians, scientific naturalism and the sentimental naturalism of Romanticism seem to be opposing philosophies. Was not Romanticism a reaction against science? What does the scientist in the laboratory have in common with the pastoral poet? For Babbitt, however, the two naturalisms were close intellectual cousins because in their purest ideological forms, both denied the importance of the human law and the moral struggle found in the inner life of human beings. They both denied the "dualism" of human nature and the importance of cultivating a higher will that could check selfish and impulsive desires. These two strains of naturalism, he insisted, had corrupted ethics by placing the locus of ethics in the struggle for social justice, so-called humanitarianism, rather than rooting justice in the moral choices of individuals.

Babbitt believed that because these two forms of naturalism had corrupted modern ethics, they had also succeeded in creating a distorted picture of human nature and politics. His concept of democratic imperialism grew out of his belief that these two forms of naturalism had jettisoned the classical and Christian obligation of individuals to engage in introspection and self-reform, an error that would foster leaders who lacked self-control. Babbitt quoted Walter Lippmann as differentiating the "naturalists" of modernity from the "supernaturalists" of humanism and genuine religion: "According to Mr. Walter Lippmann, the conviction the modern man has lost is that 'there is an immortal essence presiding like a king over his appetites.'"[4]

At the same time, while denying individual's obligation to conform their own behavior to a higher law, these two philosophies existed side by side in modernity to unite a worship of scientific power with a worship of emotion and unchecked impulse. The modern marriage of technology and impulse was, Babbitt believed, a sure invitation to war.

Toward the end of his life, Babbitt penned a seminal essay in which he attempted to define humanism and contrast it with these two types of humanitarianism. Humanism is not primarily concerned with expanding scientific knowledge or with expressing sympathy or pity for the downtrodden; it is concerned with individual moral choices that will build character. "Humanism appears primarily, not in the enlargement of comprehension and sympathy, desirable though this enlargement may be, but in the act of selection, in the final imposition on mere multiplicity of a scale of values."[5] Humanists can be found in any age or civilization, reflecting a temperament, not a religious dogma. "Humanists . . . are those who, in any age, aim at proportionateness through a cultivation of the law of measure."[6] Proportion, spiritual effort, self-control, and decorum are the marks of the humanist. "'Nothing too much' is indeed the central maxim of all genuine humanists, ancient and modern."[7] As Babbitt explained, the focus of the humanitarian is not self-mastery but progress for society: "A person who has sympathy for mankind in the lump, faith in future progress, and desire to serve the great cause of this progress, should be called not a humanist, but a humanitarian."[8]

Humanism contrasts with modern humanitarianism, where ethical strenuousness plays little role. As Babbitt scholar Thomas Nevin summarized Babbitt's view of humanitarianism, "He ascribed to Bacon the modern impetus for *libido sciendi*, the passion for knowledge as gathered data, pursued on the premise that scientific investigation determines the progress of humanity. Complementary to this scientific naturalism was a sentimental naturalism, or *libido sentiendi*, a passion for feeling at the expense of self-discipline and restraint, for moral impressionism in lieu of conscience. The archetypal intellect of this aberration was Jean-Jacques Rousseau. . . . [T]he Renaissance and Enlightenment had furthered these two naturalistic or humanitarian tendencies while eroding the authority of institutional Christianity."[9] Rather than standing for the law of measure, Babbitt said that Rousseau's emotional humanitarianism "was above all for free temperamental expansion. He was himself emotionally expansive to a degree that was incompatible not only with artificial but with real decorum. He encouraged the humanitarian hope that brotherhood among men may be based on emotional overflow."[10]

Likewise, Babbitt pointed out that scientific humanitarianism shared Rousseau's repudiation of the human law as scientific inquiry came to replace the law of measure and the obligation to rein in one's own expansive desires. Babbitt argued that the scientific humanitarian displays a boundless desire simply to acquire knowledge and is quite agnostic about or even hostile to the great moral questions raised by religious and humanistic thinkers. "The humanitarian has favoured not only temperamental expansion; he has also, as a rule, favoured the utmost expansion of scientific knowledge with a view to realising the Baconian ideal. Perhaps indeed the chief driving power behind the humanitarian movement has been the confidence inspired in man by the progressive control physical science has enabled him to acquire over forces of nature."[11]

In its purest ideological form, scientific humanitarianism argues that scientific inquiry represents the only true knowledge and that the accumulation of information developed using the scientific method represents the key to humanity's progress. With a focus on the endless accumulation of data points, Babbitt said that the struggle within the soul of human beings disappears as the primary moral force shaping society.

> The humanitarians, as I have pointed out, from Bacon down, are extraordinarily superficial in their definition of work. Even when they do not fall into the cruder quantitative fallacies, they conceive of work in terms of the natural law and of the outer world and not in terms of the inner life. They do not take account of that form of work which consists in the superimposition of the ethical will upon the natural self and its expansive desires.[12]

While Babbitt was critical of scientific humanitarianism as a guide for human conduct, he was not a Luddite. He thought science to be perfectly healthy when it remained in its proper moral place. Scientific humanitarianism became problematic when it developed into an all-encompassing ideology and when it denied Emerson's law for man and the law for thing. On this point, Babbitt seemed to have been influenced by M. Edmond Scherer:

> Industrial and scientific progress he grants is possible, since each new invention or discovery becomes the point of departure for further conquests. The error begins when we transfer what is true of the practical and positive order to the world of moral values; when we suppose that society increases in uprightness, equity, moderation, modesty, delicacy of feeling by a necessary evolution and an automatic development.[13]

Babbitt maintained that there is a vain conceit in human nature that draws people to scientific humanitarianism. True ethical work, he said, involves exertion, self-scrutiny, and personal renunciation; scientific humanitarianism requires only "wonder and curiosity." Critiques of scientific humanitarianism, Babbitt therefore pointed out, tend to be unwelcome: "Tell the average person that someone is planning to get into wireless communication with Mars, or to shoot a rocket to the moon, and he is all respectful interest and attention at once. Tell him, on the contrary, that he needs, in the interest of his own happiness, to walk in the path of humility and self-control, and he will be indifferent, or even actively resentful."[14]

Babbitt insisted that he was not hostile to the acquisition of scientific knowledge or even to a fanciful, Romantic work of art, but he argued that these scientific and Romantic pursuits would become pernicious if they pretended to serve as a substitute for the obligations found in the moral life of individual human beings. "It goes without saying that the humanist is not hostile to science as such but only to a science that has overstepped its due bounds, and in general to every form of naturalism, whether rationalistic or emotional, that sets up as a substitute for humanism or religion. In the case of such encroachments there is not only a quarrel between the naturalist and the humanist, but a quarrel of first principles."[15]

These two forms of humanitarianism, Babbitt argued, found their penultimate expressions in two philosophers who, again, have been traditionally viewed as being in opposition: Rousseau and Bacon.

> Very diverse elements enter into the writings of Bacon as into those of Rousseau, but, like those of Rousseau, they have a central drive: they always have encouraged and, one may safely say, always will encourage the substitution of a kingdom of man for the traditional Kingdom of God—the exultation of material over spiritual "comfort," the glorification of man's increasing control over the forces of nature under the name of progress.[16]

The modern version of scientific humanitarianism came first and, Babbitt argued, was nearly fully formed in the ideas of Bacon, while elements of Romanticism did not coalesce into the modern form of sentimental humanitarianism until Rousseau: "We already have in the sixteenth century a perfect example of scientific naturalist and humanitarian, in Bacon. For sentimental naturalism, on the other hand, we have to wait until the eighteenth century, when it is embodied with extraordinary completeness in the personality and writings of Rousseau."[17]

Babbitt viewed Francis Bacon as the intellectual father of scientific naturalism and the author of the moral breakdown that it fostered. "He was led to neglect the human law through a too subservient pursuit of the natural law; in seeking to gain dominion over things he lost dominion over himself; he is a notable example of how a man may be 'unkinged' as Emerson phrases it, when overmastered by the naturalistic temper and unduly fascinated by power and success."[18]

Babbitt considered Bacon's and Rousseau's modern understanding of the human person to contrast strongly with a dualistic view of human nature offered by St. Paul or Buddha. By refusing to recognize the ethical and spiritual struggle within the soul, unique to human nature, the naturalists had rejected "the duality of human experience."[19] As has been discussed, for those of a religious or humanistic outlook, life is characterized by the dualistic challenge of self-mastery; one must overcome the pulls of the natural passions found in the lower parts of the human soul and exert a higher discipline. Babbitt believed that the denial of the duality of human nature embodied in naturalism was an overt repudiation of religious and humanistic ethics.

> The naturalist no longer looks on man as subject to a law of his own distinct from that of the material order—a law, the acceptance of which leads, on the religious level, to the miracles of other-worldliness that one finds in Christians and Buddhists at their best, and the acceptance of which, in this world, leads to the subduing of the ordinary self and its spontaneous impulses to the law of measure that one finds in Confucianists and Aristotelians.[20]

With naturalism's denial of a special law for man, Babbitt argued that the West had abandoned its core ethical principle: "What the naturalists have neglected is not something that is on the fringe or outer rim of human experience, but something, on the contrary, that is very central. . . . I have already said that the element in man that has been overlooked by the naturalistic psychology is felt in relation to his ordinary self negatively. If instead of taking the point of view of one's ordinary self, one heeds the admonitions of the inner monitor, the result is two of the most positive of all things: character and happiness."[21]

With naturalism, the West had thrown off both medieval religion and classical humanism as humanitarian ethics denied the centrality of the human law. Babbitt contrasted Sophocles's and Dante's view of human nature with that of a later Romantic poet, Keats: "Yet Sophocles and Dante are not only superior to Keats, but in virtue of the presence of the ethical imagination in their work, superior not merely in degree but in kind."[22] Keats's "Prometheus Unbound" was "flimsy" as a solution to the problem of evil because it wholly lacked an "imaginative concentration on the human law."[23]

In *Rousseau and Romanticism*, Babbitt presented a systematic intellectual (and roughly chronological) argument demonstrating Western civilization's devolution from its humanistic and medieval religious roots into the naturalistic philosophies of the seventeenth and eighteenth centuries. He pointed to two general trends in this devolution. First, Babbitt argued that medieval Christianity had checked humankind's expansive desires through its emphasis on humility and through the outer authority of the church. Overall, Babbitt emphasized that the dualistic view of human nature embraced by the church had helped with the "rescue of civilization from the wreck of pagan antiquity and the welter of the barbarian invasions."[24] But by its frequent emphasis on outer authority, orthodox Christianity also tended to make man "entirely distrustful of himself and entirely dependent upon God," which meant that "in practice," humans became "entirely dependent upon the Church." In the daily life of human beings, this dependence on the church put the administration of human nature "in receivership."[25]

Babbitt pointed to Pascal's writings on Catholicism as tending to assert fear rather than self-control. The control imposed by the church sometimes tended toward relying on an outer control of behavior rather than an inner control by the self-exertion of the individual. "For Pascal, religion was not only the 'mother of form and fear,' but he and the whole side of Christianity for which he stands pushed the form to a point where it became a strait-jacket for the human spirit, the fear to a point where it amounted to a theological reign of terror."[26] Babbitt argued that immediately prior to the Renaissance, the institutional church's sale of dispensations sent a signal to the faithful that outer authority mattered more than self-mastery.

As the West became more secure in the late medieval period, Babbitt argued, "the critical spirit began to awaken" and "human nature showed itself tired of being treated as bankrupt, of being governed from without and from above." The resultant self-confidence helped usher in the Renaissance, during which the West "aspired to become autonomous," with a "strong trend in many quarters toward individualism."[27]

The Renaissance, Babbitt said, contained a variety of intellectual threads in which "naturalistic, humanistic, and religious elements are mingled in almost every conceivable proportion in" a "vast and complex movement." One strong element that emerged in the Renaissance, however, was a naturalism that tended to obscure the dual nature of the human soul and the potentiality for evil. Babbitt saw this tendency in a sixteenth-century writer, Rabelais, who "in his extreme opposition to the monkish ideal, already proclaims, like Rousseau, the intrinsic excellence of man." From Rabelais, there was clear line to "Rousseau's educational naturalism—his exaltation of the spontaneity and genius of the child."[28] An overemphasis on the "intrinsic excellence of man" by some Renaissance thinkers would later progress to an affirmation of the "natural goodness" of humankind, as asserted by Rousseau, and a loss of the sense of duality in human nature.

In reaction to this element of naturalism in the Renaissance, religious leaders of the sixteenth and seventeenth centuries sensed a danger that naturalism might repudiate the centrality of original sin and threaten a genuinely religious view of life. They attempted, therefore, to reassert outer authority over humans' souls. In the Catholic Church, the Jesuits, for example, developed a Christian educational program that "tends to stress submission to outer authority at the expense of inwardness and individuality." At the same time, "each important Protestant group worked out its creed or convention and knew how to make it very uncomfortable for any one of its members who rebelled against authority."[29]

Babbitt argued that by the time Christian leaders moved to rebut naturalistic ideas, they had already permeated the West during the Renaissance and were powerful enough to inspire a backlash against both Catholic and Protestant attempts to restore the outer authority of Christian churches. Babbitt said that the growth in the prestige and moral authority of science was a decisive obstacle that prevented the reimposition of Christian authority in the West: "All these attempts, Protestant as well as Catholic, to revive the principle of authority, to put the general sense once more on a traditional and dogmatic basis," were defeated by the "spirit of free scientific enquiry in the Renaissance" that had inspired "great naturalists like Kepler and Galileo" and "had been adding conquest to conquest."[30]

The outer authority of religion was defeated, Babbitt argued, because "science has won its triumphs not by accepting dogma and tradition but by repudiating them, by dealing with the natural law, not on a traditional basis but on a positive and critical basis." The result of the triumph of science was to obscure "the very notion that man is subject to two laws." Human nature would now be seen through the prism of the laws of science and "treat man as entirely the creature of the natural law."[31]

The rise of scientific authority led at first to theological Deism. While maintaining the traditional theological belief in an "Unmoved Mover," Deism proclaimed that God had set the scientific and material laws in motion but does not participate in the inner life of individual humans "and that inwardly man may be guided aright by his unaided thoughts and feelings (according to the predominance of thought or feeling the deist is rationalistic or sentimental)."[32] The denial of the inner life embodied in Deism led to what Babbitt called "the application of scientific method to the soul." And "under this accumulation of outer influences the free agency of the individual tends entirely to disappear."[33]

Babbitt argued, however, that a purely scientific outlook could not satisfy the spiritual longings found in the human soul. When the problem of the soul was simply banished by Bacon and his followers, the result was a cold rationalistic view of human life that appeared a spiritual dead end. Babbitt pointed to the coldness and spiritual emptiness of scientific naturalism in the nineteenth-century writings of Hippolyte Taine, who "compares the position of the human family in the midst of the blind indifferent powers of nature to that of a lot of field-mice exposed to the tramplings of a herd of elephants; and concludes that the 'best fruit of our science is cold resignation which, pacifying and preparing the spirit, reduces suffering to bodily pain.'"[34]

Such an extreme weakening of the traditional understanding of the soul and the elimination of the struggle "between a higher and lower self" was problematic because, Babbitt insisted, this internal struggle is a fact of human existence.[35] Many writers and intellectuals, among them Charles Augustin Sainte-Beuve, came to conclude that "doubtless . . . you shall never be able to proceed for man exactly as for plants or animals. . . . He has what is called *liberty*."[36]

The scientific naturalist had denied the uniquely divine quality in human beings and reduced them to subrational animals. For example, Babbitt said that Taine's unwillingness to recognize that there is an "inner check that may restrain the *élan vital* and direct it to some human end" had led Taine to some preposterous conclusions about how to analyze human beings:

> He has endless comparisons to suggest how inevitably human faculties unfold and how little they are a matter of individual choice or volition. At one time he compares men to the lower animals; his only aim as an historian, he says, is to be a student of moral zoölogy. "You may," he says again, "consider man as an animal of superior species who produces philosophies and poems about as silk-worms produce their cocoons and bees their cells." He is going to study the transformation of France by the French Revolution as he would the "metamorphosis of an insect."[37]

Babbitt saw particular danger because scientific humanitarianism was weakening the obligation that individuals felt to improve their character while simultaneously increasing the material power available to society.

> What is monstrous in this age is not that it possesses mechanical efficiency, in itself an excellent thing, but that this mechanical efficiency has no sufficient counterpoise in spiritual efficiency. It would seem, therefore, that the first step in clearing up the present imbroglio is to call the humanitarians to a stern reckoning for the flabbiness they have encouraged on the human and spiritual levels of man's being; for having sought to discredit all traditional restraints and failed at the same time to establish any new centre and principle of control; for having, on the contrary, belittled in a thousand ways intellect, insight, self-control, everything, in fact, in comparison with sympathy.[38]

With the carnage that resulted from the advancements in firepower that were brought to bear during the Great War, Babbitt's concerns about science seem to have taken on a greater urgency in his later, post–World War I writings: "Now in the absence of ethical discipline the lust for knowledge and the lust for feeling count for very little, at least practically, compared with the third main lust of human nature—the lust for power. Hence the emergence of that most sinister of types, the efficient megalomaniac. The final use of science that has thus become a tool of the lust for power is in Burke's phrase to 'improve the mystery of murder.'"[39]

Babbitt pointed out that scientific humanitarianism obscured the looming danger of the Great War because leaders in the West wrongly assumed that progress and enlightenment followed scientific discovery: "An age that thought it was progressing toward a 'far-off divine event,' and turned out instead to be progressing toward Armageddon, suffered, one cannot help surmising, from some fundamental confusion in its notion of progress."[40] Regarding science without ethical self-control, Babbitt insisted, "A terrible danger thus lurks in the whole modern programme: it is a programme that makes for a formidable mechanical efficiency and so tends to bring into an ever closer material contact men who remain ethically centrifugal."[41] Science had made significant progress since Bacon, but with the growth in humanity's knowledge of the natural world, no corresponding growth had occurred in wisdom or virtue. Babbitt believed that mechanical power without self-control was pernicious.

The problems that have been engaging more and more the attention of the Occident since the rise of the great Baconian movement have been the problems of power and speed and utility. The enormous mass of machinery that has been accumulated in the pursuit of these ends requires the closest attention and concentration if it is to be worked efficiently. At the same time, the man of the West is not willing to admit that he is growing in power alone, he likes to think he is also growing in wisdom.[42]

The rise of scientific and sentimental humanitarianism elevated "altruism" as the great virtue of Western elites. Science had made awesome power available to human beings, and sentimental humanitarianism had then told them that such power should be brought to bear on humanitarian causes. The need for restraint and self-mastery faded from memory. "One is tempted to define the civilization (or what we are pleased to term such) that has been emerging with the decline of the traditional controls as a mixture of altruism and high explosives."[43] The cult of science had given birth to a world in which power and pleasure were the highest goals. Babbitt wrote that Diderot, one of the chief propagandists of the cult of science, came to view life as "a universal scramble for power and pleasure. The prizes go to the strong and cunning, and the fools and weaklings pay for all the rest. Rationalism has undermined the traditional foundations of society, and is impotent to put anything in their place."[44]

Babbitt's warnings on the dangers of an unchecked science were remarkably prescient, including his very early warnings about the potential dangers of the atom bomb as well as dangers to liberty and privacy. Of the atom bomb, he wrote, "Occidental man is . . . reaching out almost automatically for more and more power. If he succeeds in releasing the stores of energy that are locked up in the atom—and this seems to be the most recent ambition of our physicists—his final exploit may be to blow himself off the planet."[45] Of the emerging communications technologies, Babbitt cautioned, "With the development of inventions like the radio and the wireless telephone, the whole world is becoming, in a very literal sense, a whispering-gallery. It is hardly necessary to dilate on what is likely to follow if the words that are whispered are words of hatred and suspicion."[46]

While Babbitt wrote extensively about scientific humanitarianism, his background in French literature and Romanticism led him to even more extensive critiques of sentimental naturalism of the Rousseauistic type. But he insisted that the two forms of naturalism were intellectually compatible: "Up to a certain point the rationalistic and sentimental deists worked together; they were both arrayed against supernatural religion, against revelation and miracles. Rousseau himself appears as one of the keenest rationalists in his attitude toward miracles. Voltaire, as we know from his annotated copy of the *Profession*, took satisfaction in all this portion of Rousseau's argument."[47] In fact, Babbitt argued that Rousseau would not have been possible without Bacon.

Babbitt's argument was that the success of the natural sciences helped to discredit the authority of the church and therefore to discredit the obligation that church-following individuals might feel to engage in ethical concentration. Once Bacon, the Encyclopedists, and other advocates of salvation through data accumulation had shifted the foundations of ethics away from the human soul, Rousseau's emotional naturalism was the next logical step, as an overflowing emotionalism could fill the void left in the soul by the cold sterility of science.

While Bacon had cleared the path for Romanticism by repudiating the human law, Babbitt did see some truth in the analysis of Romanticism as a clear reaction against the cold, scientific rationalism of the Enlightenment: "Now it has been a constant experience of man in all ages that mere rationalism leaves him unsatisfied. Man craves in some sense or other of the word an enthusiasm that will lift him out of his merely rational self."[48] Scientific naturalism had set aside or denied all the great questions of existence, of virtue and character, of happiness and anxiety. With science, there was no telos of human existence for individual souls. There was only cold reason, with individual human beings left utterly exposed to the cold machinations of the scientific world.

Yet the reaction of Romanticism against science sometimes obscured their intellectual linkages. Because Rousseau had attacked science, most prominently in his *First Discourse*, that attack, Babbitt said, had obscured the natural progression from scientism to Romanticism. The accumulation of scientific knowledge had created a conceit about human nature, Babbitt pointed out, that led Western culture to embrace the ethics of Romanticism. "If men had not been so heartened by scientific progress they would have been less ready, we may be sure, to listen to Rousseau when he affirmed that they were naturally good."[49]

Babbitt maintained that scientific naturalism therefore served as the intellectual midwife for emotional naturalism because it had loosened humans from traditional obligations and from the need to focus on the restraints on their passions. The logical next step was that virtue was what came "naturally" to human beings.

All the nobler aspirations of man, all his notions of conduct, had clustered around the old-time conception of the soul, and the struggle between the higher and lower self. The weakening of the traditional belief has been followed by such an unsettling of all fixed standards, by such intellectual and moral chaos, that we are inclined to ask whether the modern man has not lost in force of will and character more than an equivalent of what he has gained in scientific knowledge of life.[50]

Romanticism had, Babbitt argued, accepted one all-important premise of Baconian rationalism: the lack of dualism of human nature. Emotional or sentimental naturalism shared with scientific rationalism the belief that there was no need for individuals to perform ethical work and access the human law. This shared premise represented the bridge between Rousseau and Bacon.

For Babbitt, however, scientific naturalism and sentimental naturalism also had important distinguishing characteristics. For example, the most important doctrine of emotional naturalism was the affirmation of "natural" spontaneity as the redefinition of virtue. For the sentimental Romantic, "religion itself thus becomes in Blake the mere sport of a powerful and uncontrolled imagination, and this we are told is mysticism."[51] The hollowness and sterility of scientific naturalism created an attraction to Romanticism based in the assertion that the unfiltered impulses of human beings should not be controlled through ethical effort; rather, they must be affirmed as spontaneous virtues and could provide religious feeling.

Babbitt viewed Rousseau as the most influential Romantic and sentimental humanitarian. Rousseau's view of human nature was an inversion of the classical Greek understanding of civilized persons as having effectively mastered their passions. To Rousseau, virtue was rooted in instinct, not self-mastery. Babbitt pointed out that Rousseau's elevation of instinct was the culmination of an intellectual trend that was at least two hundred years old: "One should note as far back as the sixteenth century an incipient glorification of instinct that was later to culminate, in one of its most characteristic expressions, in the cult of the noble savage."[52]

Simply put, Rousseau redefined virtue. "Virtue is no longer to be the veto power of the personality, a bit and bridle to be applied to one's impulses, and so imposing a difficult struggle. These impulses, Rousseau asserts, are good, and so a man has only to let himself go."[53] Once instinct and emotion were raised on the ethical pedestal as forming the core of "virtue," any checks on impulse would be seen as vices, not virtues. "According to Rousseau, the state of nature is not a state of reason. On the contrary, the man who thinks is already highly sophisticated, or, in Rousseau's phrase, 'a depraved animal.'"[54] Rousseau's ethics were the laws of the animal kingdom: one should operate on pure instinct. The human proclivity for thought, deliberation, and conscience are all unnatural, artificial hindrances to true virtue.

Babbitt quoted Sir John Hawkins's critique of the novelist Henry Fielding as criticism that could be also leveled against Rousseau: Fielding's "morality, in respect that it resolves virtue into good affections, in contradiction to moral obligation and sense of duty, is that of Lord Shaftesbury vulgarized. He was the inventor of that cant-phrase, 'goodness of heart,' which is everyday used as a substitute for probity, and means little more than the virtue of a dog or a horse."[55]

Rousseau's particular genius, however, was in disguising his revolution in ethics by using classical and Christian language. Babbitt argued that Rousseau's terminology masked the fact that he had turned Western ethical understandings on their head: "No writer is more lavish in his praise of virtue and conscience. But he gives to these words entirely new meanings. . . . Conscience, instead of being, as it has always been traditionally, an inner check on impulse, becomes itself an expansive emotion."[56]

Babbitt pointed out that Shaftesbury, who also deserves great credit for the humanitarian concept of social service, heavily influenced Rousseau:

> The sentimental movement was already well under way when he began writing. As an originative force in this movement the third Earl of Shaftesbury is perhaps more important than Rousseau. For Shaftesbury conscience is felt, not as an inner check, but as a passion for doing good to others, for what we should call nowadays social service. No one who wishes to trace the rise of humanitarianism can afford to neglect Shaftesbury.[57]

Rousseau's glorification of instinct logically led, Babbitt believed, to a revolt against the institutions of civilization that are designed to restrain disorderly impulses. As Babbitt summarizes Rousseauistic ethics, "The old dualism put the conflict between good and evil in the breast of the individual, with evil so predominant since the Fall that it behooves man to be humble; with Rousseau this conflict is transferred from the individual to society. . . .

The guiding principle of his writings, he says, is to show that vice and error, strangers to man's constitution, are introduced from without, that they are due in short to his institutions."[58]

Rousseau's view of human nature would create a new form of Western religion without a focus on fallen human nature and with no requirement for cultivating conscience. Religious feeling would become an aesthetical sentimentalism. "Instead of adjusting his temperament to religion, he adjusts religion to his temperament. One may set up as religious without having to renounce one's ordinary self."[59]

Rousseau's repudiation of ethical self-mastery, Babbitt said, required him to look outside of the soul for the source of evil in human society. The institutions of society, especially those surrounding religion and private property, became for Rousseau and his followers the corrupting influence on human nature, leading humans away from the natural and virtuous instincts that were exhibited in the state of nature prior to the formation of societies.

Rousseau therefore served as an inspiration to modern revolutionaries, including the French Jacobins, and there is a clear line from Rousseau to Marx to Kropotkin and to other revolutionary critics of traditional institutions. Rousseau was highly influential in propagating the notion that destroying the hierarchy of society's institutions such as the church, the monarchy, and private property would lead to a return to nature, freedom, and equality. The French revolutionaries' attack on the monarchy, the clergy, and the wealthy was a near perfect transformation of Rousseau's ideas into a program of political action.

Babbitt believed that the political manifestation of Rousseau's sentimental humanitarianism had broader and deeper appeal than a worship of science and that Rousseau's sentimental humanitarianism had achieved such popularity and lasted through so many centuries not because it was true but because it was flattering. According to Babbitt, "It is not only very flattering itself; it seems to offer a convenient escape from the theological nightmare. Above all, it flattered those at the bottom of the social hierarchy. Christianity at its best had sought to make the rich man humble, whereas the inevitable effect of Rousseauistic evangel is to make the poor man proud, and at the same time to make him feel he is the victim of a conspiracy."[60] Rousseau invented an ingenious new form of ethics that "was perhaps the most alluring form of sham spirituality that the world has ever seen—a method not merely of masking but of glorifying one's spiritual indolence."[61] Freed from the necessity of controlling its own appetites, the Romantic soul "may indulge in the extreme of psychic unrestraint and at the same time pose as a perfect idealist or even, if one is a Chateaubriand, as a champion of religion."[62]

So while the scientific humanitarian avoided the issue of ethical concentration, the sentimental humanitarian took the issue head-on and redefined true virtue as the affirmative rejection of ethical concentration. What Rousseau had jettisoned, Babbitt said, was "the presence in man of a restraining, informing and centralizing power that is anterior to both intellect and emotion."[63] Rousseau was the foremost modern example of a philosopher who constructed an ethical system wholly designed around the attempt to justify moral laxity. Babbitt argued that Rousseau's entire system is an evasion of the central problem of ethics: "It has been said that a system of philosophy is often only a gigantic scaffolding that a man erects to hide from himself his own favorite sin. Rousseau's own system sometimes strikes one as intended to justify his own horror of every form of discipline and constraint."[64]

Political order could not be built, Babbitt insisted, on Rousseauistic ethics because it replaced the traditional virtues with a worship of an impulsive emotionalism. Without inner restraints, human beings would not unite in peaceful communion because their temperamental selves would drive them to conflict. "Now to be spiritually inert, as I have said elsewhere, is to be temperamental, to indulge unduly the lust for knowledge or sensation or power without imposing on these lusts some centre or principle of control set above the ordinary self. The man who wishes to fly off on the tangent of his own temperament and at the same time enjoy communion on any except the purely material level is harboring incompatible desires."[65] Babbitt viewed the loosening of temperament and the lack of inner self-control as leading not to peace among human beings but to conflict. "The ugly things that have a way of happening when impulse is thus left uncontrolled do not, as we have seen, disturb the beautiful soul in his complacency. He can always point an accusing finger at something or somebody else. The faith in one's natural goodness is a constant encouragement to evade moral responsibility."[66]

Rousseauistic ethics had turned upside down the traditional hierarchy of human values. For example, this inverted scale of values actually led Rousseau to exhibit greater affection for animals than for his own children. Babbitt pointed to a genuine spiritual disease in Rousseau: "Medical men have given a learned name to the malady of those who neglect the members of their own family and gush over animals (zoöphilpsychosis). But Rousseau already exhibits this 'psychosis.' He abandoned his five children one after the other, but had we are told unspeakable affection for his dog."[67]

In another example, French Romantic novelist Victor Hugo, Babbitt said, "declares in the 'Legend of the Ages' that an ass that takes a step aside to avoid crushing a toad is 'holier than Socrates and greater than Plato.'"[68] The elevation of animals found in Romantic ethics was not random; it was, Babbitt pointed out, "at once a protest against an unduly squeamish decorum, and a way of proclaiming the new principle of unbounded expansive sympathy."[69]

This inverted scale of values involved more than animals. In fact, when it came to human beings, sentimental naturalism of the Rousseauistic type created an inverted ethics that elevated reprobates who, after all, were operating on the level of natural instinct. "The Rousseauist is ever ready to discover beauty of soul in anyone who is under the reprobation of society."[70] In *Rousseau and Romanticism*, Babbitt cited many examples from Romantic literature in which "rascals," "vagabonds," and "convicts" were considered truly virtuous simply because "the virtues that imply self-control, count as naught compared with the fraternal spirit and the readiness to sacrifice one's self for others."[71]

No Romantic novelist, Babbitt said, carried the spirit of Rousseau into literature more than Victor Hugo.

> In "Les Miserables" Hugo contrasts Javert who stands for the old order based upon obedience to the law with the convict Jean Valjean who stands for the new regeneration of man through love and self-sacrifice. When Javert awakens to the full ignominy of this role he does the only decent thing—he commits suicide. Hugo indeed has perhaps carried the new evangel of sympathy as a substitute for all the other virtues further than any one else and with fewer weak concessions to common sense.[72]

Elsewhere, in Hugo's poem "Sultan Murad," the principal character, "after committing every imaginable crime of unrestraint, is pardoned at last by the Almighty because on one occasion he brushed away the flies from the wounds of a dying pig."[73] In Romantic ethics, an emotional and ostentatious sympathy emerges as the replacement for every other virtue.

To Babbitt, who was steeped in Aristotle and Buddha, the lack of moral strenuousness in Rousseau's ethics made this philosophy a kind of parody of ethics. As Babbitt scholar Peter Stanlis has explained, "A sentimental conception of the moral nature of man, which makes emotion a feeling identical with conscience, and bases its whole value system in things spiritual upon subjective feelings, is not Christian but Rousseauistic and humanitarian."[74]

Babbitt's analysis of scientific and sentimental humanitarianism was developed in his first book, *Literature and the American College* (1908), and he continued with similar themes in one of his last books, *Democracy and Leadership* (1924). His discussion of the two types of humanitarianism are important to understanding his view of democratic imperialism from the French Revolution to modern times.

Both scientific and sentimental humanitarianism placed the emphasis not on the reform of oneself but on reform of society at large. But as social movements, the two pointed in different directions of reform. Scientific humanitarianism became the inspiration for sociology and modern government bureaucracies that seek to manipulate citizens into orderliness using incentives (or worse) offered up by various sociological studies. Scientific humanitarianism is not inherently hostile to traditional institutions as long as they do not pose obstacles to research and appear to have some social utility.

In contrast, sentimental humanitarianism as a social movement is revolutionary and corrosive to traditional institutions. The reform of society can be accomplished only by deconstructing traditional institutions that represent the chief obstacle to the flowering of the natural goodness of human beings. In its benign form, sentimental humanitarianism can be found in the residents of the peaceful commune who eschew all the traditional institutions of private property, marriage, religion, and law so that they can live "naturally." In its less benign form, sentimental humanitarianism can be found in the modern revolutionary butchery inflicted on the religious, the wealthy, or anyone representing traditional institutions. From the Jacobins to Pol Pot, the merciless destruction of traditional society as part of a plan of political action is rooted in the sentimental humanitarian's belief that the destruction of those institutions will unleash the natural goodness of human beings that has been choked off by civilization.[75]

Because sentimental humanitarianism was destructive of both traditional institutions and traditional ethics, the lion's share of Babbitt's opprobrium was directed toward that philosophy. If scientists were dropped into a culture of moderation, restraint, and good sense, Babbitt believed that their inventions would likely be directed toward worthy goals. But if society had become unmoored from traditional standards, decadent, and unrestrained, then the inventions of science would become not only a nuisance but also a mortal threat because the power that they created would be directed toward pernicious ends. For Babbitt, therefore, the particular danger at the turn of the twentieth century was that science was unleashing exceptional power at the same time that Romantic sentimentalism was discrediting every form of ethical control and restraint.

For Babbitt, Rousseau therefore was a towering, ingenious, and brilliant figure whose ideas instigated a transformation in the self-understanding of the West. Babbitt argued that Rousseau's "influence so far transcends that of the mere man of letters as to put him almost on a level with the founders of religions."[76] One could not understand modern politics, ethics, and culture without an understanding of Rousseau: "Among the men of the eighteenth century who prepared the way for the world in which we are now living, I have, here as elsewhere in my writings, given a preeminent place to Rousseau."[77] A more specific discussion of Babbitt's critique of Rousseau helps shed light on his ideas as the influential source of contemporary sentimental humanitarianism.

For Rousseau, the traditional Christian notion of conscience or the Hindu concept of an "inner check" needed to be discarded as artificial, since these internal voices of restraint would interfere with humanity's natural virtuosity. Babbitt saw the influence of Diderot on his friend Rousseau: Diderot puts the underlying thesis of the new morality almost more clearly than Rousseau: "Do you wish to know in brief the tale of almost all our woe? There once existed a natural man; there has been introduced within this man an artificial man and there has arisen in the cave a civil war which lasts throughout life."[78] Babbitt described this as Rousseau's attempt to rid human beings of the civil war in the cave: "Everything, then, that restrains 'nature' is to be dismissed as empty convention.... Diderot would therefore turn away from the 'war in the cave,' that is the struggle between good and evil in the breast of the individual, and fix his attention on the progress of mankind as a whole in knowledge and sympathy."[79]

Rousseau's ethics had transformed religiosity from an ethical discipline to a sentimental assertion of emotion. "Virtue, for example, according to Rousseau, is not merely an impulse, but a passion, and even an intoxication.... Now Joubert says that whereas virtue before Rousseau had been looked upon as a bridle, Rousseau turned it into a spur."[80] In Babbitt's analysis, Rousseau had retold the biblical account of the fall of man. In the Old Testament, humans fell away from God because of evil in their hearts. In Rousseau's myth, evil was introduced into human nature by society as a foreign element. "Rousseau's expedient for getting rid of man's sense of his own sinfulness on which fear and humility ultimately rest is well known. Evil, says Rousseau, foreign to man's constitution, is introduced into it from without."[81]

With Rousseau's Romanticism, Babbitt argued, Western institutions were transformed from sacred representations that reflected the divine order, as they had been viewed in medieval Europe, into artificial and pernicious restraints that suppressed the natural goodness of human beings who would flower if they could operate solely on natural impulse.

> The whole movement from Rousseau to Bergson is, on the other hand, filled with the glorification of instinct. To become spiritual the beautiful soul needs only to expand along the lines of temperament and with this process the cult of pity or sympathy does not interfere. The romantic moralist tends to favor expansion on the ground that it is vital, creative, infinite, and to dismiss whatever seems to set bounds on expansion as something inert, mechanical, finite.[82]

Rousseau transformed bohemian indecency into the highest virtue and, Babbitt said, "also declares war . . . in the name of what he conceives to be his true self—that is his emotional self—against decorum and decency."[83]

A social order built on Rousseauistic ethics does raise a central problem of political philosophy: If human beings are acting on selfish impulse, how is it possible to have an orderly society? Babbitt said that Rousseau, ever the creative genius, did not shirk from the problem, answering cleverly that the highest "natural" virtue, the one implanted into human beings from the beginning, is that of pity or sympathy. In Rousseau's state of nature, all human beings have an instinct for self-preservation and self-love. However, "natural man has another instinct, namely, an instinctive dislike of seeing his fellow creatures suffer, which is alone a sufficient counterpoise to the love of self."[84] The soul who exhibits great pity—or sentimental humanitarianism—need not worry about developing other virtues.

Babbitt's argument was that Rousseau's redefinition of virtue was formed by his reaction against two intellectual and religious trends. First, he recoiled from the Christian religious doctrines that had emphasized humanity's total depravity and offered the opposite extreme: humanity's thoroughgoing goodness. "But other Catholics, notably Jansenists, as well as Protestants like the Calvinists, were for insisting to the full on man's corruption and for seeking to maintain on this basis what one is tempted to call a theological reign of terror. One whole side of Rousseau's religion can be understood only as a protest against the type of Christianity that is found in a Pascal or a Jonathan Edwards."[85] The theological position that humanity's fate was wholly determined by an arbitrary concept of Christian grace brought an inevitable counter reaction in Rousseau.

The second trend from which Rousseau recoiled, Babbitt argued, was the artificial decorum of the court of Louis XIV. That court, with its unending formalism, claimed to represent the pinnacle of Christian morals, manners, and propriety. "The members of the French aristocracy, and that as far back as Richelieu and Louis XIV, had largely ceased to perform the work of an aristocracy. They had become drawing-room butterflies and hangers-on at court."[86] The historical reality was that the court was a place where the courtiers "set up as personages in the grand manner and at the same time behind the façade of conventional dignity to let their appetites run riot."[87] For Rousseau, this artificial modesty of the French aristocracy discredited the very idea of decorum itself. Would not humans be more virtuous outside of such a corrupt civilization?

Babbitt pointed out that the decadence of the French aristocracy represented the perfect opportunity for Rousseau to promulgate a theory of morals that abandoned propriety and restraint. "It would have been perfectly legitimate at the end of the eighteenth century to attack in the name of true decorum a decorum that had become the 'varnish of vice' and the 'mask of hypocrisy.' What Rousseau actually opposed to pseudo-decorum was perhaps the most alluring form of sham spirituality that the world has ever seen—a method not merely of masking but of glorifying one's spiritual indolence."[88]

For Rousseau, the ersatz modesty of the royal court was living proof of his position that impulse was the truest virtue. Impulse, temperament, and instinct were to be glorified as the true nature of nobility:

> He puts the blame of the conflict and division of which he is conscious in himself upon the social conventions that set bounds to his temperament and impulses; once get rid of these pure artificial restrictions and he feels that he will again be at one with himself and "nature." With such a vision of nature as this it is not surprising that every constraint is unendurable to Rousseau, that he likes, as Berlioz was to say of himself later, to "make all barriers crack." He is ready to shatter all forms of civilized life in favor of something that never existed, of a state of nature that is only the projection of his own temperament and its dominant desires upon the void. His programme amounts in practice to the indulgence of infinite indeterminate desire, to an endless and aimless vagabondage of the emotions with the imagination as their free accomplice.[89]

As a social movement, Rousseau's sentimental humanitarianism was a primary philosophical inspiration for the French Revolution. Among the revolutionaries, there was no religious or humanistic outlook; virtue was found in reforming society, particularly in overthrowing the priests and aristocrats that had constructed the artificial institutions of civilization that suppress the goodness of natural man.

The anticlericalism and murder of the clergy were not simply part of a power struggle between different factions in revolutionary France. The denial of the spiritual substance of human beings *required* the destruction of the clergy, who were a living symbol of a false ethics.

> In Robespierre and other revolutionary leaders one may study the implications of the new morality—the attempt to transform virtue into a natural passion—not merely for the individual but for society.... Both Rousseau and his disciple Robespierre were reformers in the modern sense,—that is they are concerned not with reforming themselves, but other men. Inasmuch as there is no conflict between good and evil in the breast of the beautiful soul he is free to devote all his efforts to the improvement of mankind, and he proposes to achieve this great end by diffusing the spirit of brotherhood.[90]

The institutions of civilization and their representatives must be destroyed because they are conspiring against the natural goodness of human beings and thwarting universal comity. When the monstrous artificial complex of civilization is overthrown, the preeminent human virtue—pity—will rise to the surface, inspiring a brotherhood not seen since the state of nature.

> All the traditional forms that stand in the way of this free emotional expansion [Rousseau] denounces as mere "prejudices" and inclines to look on those who administer these forms as a gang of conspirators who are imposing an arbitrary and artificial restraint on the natural goodness of man and keeping it from manifesting itself. With the final disappearance of the prejudices of the past and those who base their usurped authority upon them, the Golden Age will be ushered in at last; everybody will be boundlessly self-assertive and at the same time temper this self-assertion by an equally boundless sympathy for others, whose sympathy and self-assertion likewise know no bounds.[91]

Babbitt insisted forcefully that Rousseau's advocacy for the destruction of the institutions of civilization to unleash the "natural" soul would promote "the reality of strife that it is supposed to prevent." The revolution, it could have been predicted, ended in an orgy of violence.

Anyone who rejects the humanitarian theory of brotherhood runs the risk of being accused of a lack of fraternal feeling. The obvious reply of the person of critical and experimental temper is that, if he rejects the theory, it is precisely because he desires brotherhood. After an experience of the theory that has already extended over several generations, the world would seem to have become a vast seething mass of hatred and suspicion. What Carlyle wrote of the Revolution has not ceased to be applicable: "Beneath the rose-colored veil of universal benevolence is a dark, contentious, hell-on-earth."[92]

The French Revolution had, in Rousseauistic fashion, repudiated Christian civilization with its emphasis on original sin and personal humility. The "citizens" of France did not feel that they were flawed sinners who needed to reform their souls; they were instead proud reformers of society armed with the "rights of man." Babbitt pointed out, however, that this Rousseauistic influence did not create peace and brotherhood: "The only brotherhood the Jacobinical leaders had succeeded in founding was, as Taine put it, a brotherhood of Cains."[93]

Rousseau's assertion of humanity's natural goodness represented a revolutionary change in the traditional Western understanding of human nature and would lead to a new theory of democracy predicated on the natural goodness of the popular will. In contrast, *The Federalist* had an entirely different view of human nature and democratic theory. Its authors' view of human nature, with its potential for good and evil, caused them to attempt a system that would bring to power leaders of strong moral character and to construct a constitutional republic that would limit the influence of popular passions and force the "will of people" to run a gauntlet of constitutional constraints before popular desires could become law. These two conflicting views of democracy, Babbitt believed, represented two of the greatest opposing forces found in American history.

CHAPTER 3

Two Types of Democracy

> A main purpose to my present argument is to show that genuine leaders, good or bad, there will always be, and that democracy becomes a menace to civilization when it seeks to evade this truth. The notion in particular that a substitute for leadership can be found in numerical majorities that are supposed to reflect the "general will" is only a pernicious conceit.
>
> —Irving Babbitt, *Democracy and Leadership*

If we are to understand the root of Irving Babbitt's theory of imperialism, we must first understand which qualities in a democracy Babbitt felt would make it conducive to peace and which qualities would make it warlike. Over the course of his many writings, Babbitt consistently argued that there are two types of democracy. The first type, reflected in the American Constitution, is based on an implicit understanding of the dualism of human nature and of the need to cultivate a political order that represented the sober and considered judgment of the people, not their emotional, selfish, or impulsive desires. This type of constitutionalism assumes the importance of leaders who have developed a level of moral character sufficient to make them restrained and temperate. The second type of democracy, Rousseauistic democracy, denies the dualism of human nature and asserts that the general will of the people needs no bit or bridle to help direct or restrain its judgment. The will of the people is not to be checked or impeded even by the nation's leaders, whose role is not to deliberate and to cool popular passions but to serve as their handmaiden.

Claes G. Ryn characterizes Rousseauistic democracy as plebiscitary: "Plebiscitary democracy aspires to rule according to the popular majority of the moment. To ensure the speediest implementation of their wishes, it seeks the removal of representative, decentralized, and decentralizing practices and structures that limit the power of the numerical majority."[1] For Babbitt, the pure democracy of Jean-Jacques Rousseau was a menace to be feared by both its citizens and its neighbors because the popular will is not subject to any higher moral authority.

Babbitt believed that Rousseau's fundamental errors in diagnosing human nature had led to his flawed concept of democracy. One of Babbitt's fiercest critics, H. L. Mencken, called Babbitt's views on Rousseau "absurd" and particularly criticized Babbitt's attempt to integrate Rousseau's various ideas into a relatively coherent political philosophy. Mencken wrote, "I doubt, indeed, that Jean-Jacques was the inventor of most of our current curses, or even that he gathered them together and made a system of them. His actual system, as a matter of fact, was full of contradictions, and large portions of it were old when he adopted them."[2] It is not clear that Mencken had read Babbitt's entire body of work on Rousseau because Babbitt seems in fact to have pulled the many divergent strands of Rousseau's ideas into a very coherent political philosophy. A more systematic review of Babbitt's writings seems to demonstrate that he was able to explain a logically ordered progression in Rousseau's ideas, first from his views on human nature and education leading upward to his ideas on democracy, revolution, and imperialism.

As with most intellectuals, Rousseau did have contradictions in his thought, but he noticed internal contradictions and worked openly to resolve them. One of the leading contradictions in Rousseau's thought was found in his differing theories of education, first in *Emile*, where he discussed how to educate a child, and later in his *Considerations on the Government of Poland*, where he discussed how to educate a citizen. Resolving this seeming contradiction on educational theory is important because it helps to create a bridge from Rousseau's ideas on education to his views on democracy.

Babbitt's writings on education were prolific and opinionated, and he jousted with prominent university leaders, including presidents of Harvard (which may indeed have set back his academic career). Babbitt's thought shared similarities with Aristotle in the understanding that a regime's theory of education provided a window into its understanding of human nature and therefore formed the foundation of the regime type and the nature of the political order.

Babbitt also agreed with Aristotle that education is an indispensable tool in the formation of political leaders, as it tends to influence whether future leaders will be just or unjust, enlightened or tyrannical.

According to Aristotle,

> That education should be regulated by law and should be an affair of state is not to be denied, but what should be the character of this public education, and how young persons are to be educated, are questions which remain to be considered. As things are, there is disagreement about the subjects. For mankind are by no means agreed about the things to be taught, whether we look to virtue or to the best life. Neither is it clear whether education is concerned with intellectual or with moral virtue.[3]

Babbitt was concerned that the leaders of his time, including Mencken, could not see the connection between an unsound education system and an unsound democracy. In 1917, for example, Babbitt reviewed C. E. Vaughan's recently published *The Political Writings of Jean-Jacques Rousseau*. While praising Vaughan's "important contribution to the desideratum" of Rousseau's writings, Babbitt nonetheless criticized the editor for omitting passages that were not explicitly political but that formed the foundation of Rousseau's political thought: "There is danger in studying the political writings of Rousseau apart from his other writings, and especially in separating the passages which are supposed to be political from those which are not."[4]

Babbitt went on to say that Rousseau's book on education, *Emile*, might be the most important guide to understanding his political thought, yet Vaughan had not excerpted key passages from that work: "For example, the book which had most influence in preparing the Revolution was not, as Professor Vaughan seems to think, the 'Discourse on Inequality,' but 'Emile.'"[5] Babbitt in fact insisted that Rousseau was the "father of modern education."[6] In this regard, given the political results that modern education was producing in the early twentieth century, Babbitt saw it as imperative that we understand Rousseau's educational theory.

Babbitt captured the education theory of *Emile* in one concise idea: Rousseau had "sought to discredit habit . . . 'The only habit the child should be allowed to form,' says Rousseau, 'is that of forming no habit.'"[7] For Babbitt, it seemed obvious that Rousseau's theory of education was precisely the opposite of Aristotle's. "One of the ultimate contrasts that presents itself in a subject of this kind is that between habit as conceived by Aristotle and nature as conceived by Rousseau."[8] Aristotle's understanding was, of course, that the formation of good habits in children is the indispensable center of education; children's good habits will become their virtue.

For the ancient Greeks, this virtue was found not in spontaneity or impulsiveness but in ethical work. For the Aristotelian, the goal of education was to help children discover the law of measure, not to act on impulse. As Babbitt described it, "This gradual conversion the Aristotelian hopes to achieve by work according to the human law."[9] Babbitt described education as the formation of right habits in children to carry virtue and therefore civilization from one generation to the next. "For civilization (another word that is sadly in need of Socratic definition) may be found to consist above all in an orderly transmission of right habits; and the chief agency for the transmission must always be education, by which I mean far more of course than mere formal schooling."[10]

Babbitt called Rousseau's worship of the spontaneity in children "chimerical" because the real challenge in education is deciding which habits should be passed down and instilled into children, which traditions and conventions in civilization are worthy of transmission and which are not.

> The trait of the child to which the sensible educator will give chief attention is not his spontaneity, but his proneness to imitate. In the absence of good models the child will imitate bad ones, and so, long before the age of intelligent choice and self-determination, become a prisoner of bad habits. Men, therefore, who aim to be civilized must come together, work out a convention in short, regarding the habits they wish transmitted to the young. A great civilization is in a sense only a great convention.[11]

Rousseau, in contrast, denied this central mission of education and advocated freeing children from convention. He asserted that an education system based on the principles of *Emile* would allow citizens to get in touch with their "natural" instincts and eschew their own self-interests. In contrast, Babbitt insisted that when education fails to pass along civilizing traditions, the results for politics are pernicious, as proper traditions might temper leaders from operating on the basis of the law of the jungle. A temperamental child, denied sound habits and civilizing traditions, might very well become a temperamental adult and as such would likely not be fit to lead a democracy.

Rousseau's theory of education, Babbitt said, illuminated a larger political philosophy and provided a window into the intellectual endowment Rousseau provided to Machiavellian revolutionaries from Robespierre to Lenin. Denied the conventions of civilization, the law of force would come to the fore in a society based on Rousseau's naturalism. Babbitt said that those raised in the world of nature—that is, the jungle—would not find themselves constrained by any warrants of civilization; they would not find their behavior circumscribed; and they would soon learn to trust only in cunning and force. To describe the law of the jungle, Babbitt quoted from a Wordsworth poem about the roguish and somewhat lawless Scottish rebel Rob Roy MacGregor: "The good old rule, the simple plan: That they should take who have the power, And they should keep who can."[12]

For the political order, Babbitt insisted, Rousseau's redefinition of education as spontaneity also invited anarchy in the relations between nations because it jettisoned the moral and ethical dimension of learning for future leaders. "But why should an Emile who has learned the lesson of force from nature herself not be ready to pass along this lesson to others, whether to his fellow-citizens or to the citizens of some other state? It remains to consider more fully this latter point—the implications of Rousseauism for international relations." Babbitt pointed out that on occasion, even Rousseau himself would emerge from his idyllic Romanticism and recognize that the world of nature was indeed a world without restraint on force. Because "Rousseau has no notion of any such spiritual discipline . . . [i]n spite of his talk of natural pity, he saw that what prevails on the naturalistic level is the law of force."[13]

In his first book, *Literature and the American College*, Babbitt argued that Rousseau's influence was beginning to dominate American higher education. In his later review, Babbitt continued this theme, lamenting that a Baconian worship of science, already present for generations in American education, would be combined with Rousseauistic humanitarianism. "There has thus grown up gradually that singular mixture of altruism and high explosives that we are pleased to term our civilization."[14] Babbitt believed that modern American universities were jettisoning their mission to shape moral character and evolving into institutions designed merely for the acquisition of scientific knowledge and its deployment in humanitarian causes.

Thomas Nevin has argued that the social changes wrought by the massive industrialization of the United States in the fifty years after the Civil War led Harvard president Charles W. Eliot to adapt higher education to two humanitarian goals: utilitarian organization and service to humankind. The economy needed to be organized, Eliot believed, with a view toward harnessing the great power of industry, while the plight of a growing and vocal class of industrial workers had to be mitigated. The primary goal of higher education was, according to Eliot, efficiency and sympathy. As Nevin summarized Eliot's view, "In collegiate education, too, there was a move toward collective order. President Eliot's ethic of training for service and power was a formula for direct accommodation of newly rising social and industrial conglomerates."[15] Nevin continued, "In Eliot, then, a Baconian ethic of utility fused with the Rousseauist assumption of individual spontaneity."[16]

Babbitt was highly critical of Eliot's outlook. *Literature and the American College* was a direct response to Eliot's installation of an elective system and the elimination of certain required courses such as classical languages. Babbitt believed that both Bacon and Rousseau had heavily influenced Eliot in arguing that the curriculum of higher education needed to both serve the vocational needs of the economy as well as the spontaneous liberty of the student.[17]

Eliot, in fact, hinted at his rejection of the moral dimension in education when he acknowledged Rousseau's personal behavior as reprehensible, particularly in sending all his children to orphanages and to a likely death, but this behavior was not relevant to Rousseau's philosophy. These actions, Eliot said, could be excused by Rousseau's devotion to "the great doctrine of human liberty." Regarding Rousseau's children, Babbitt quoted Eliot as saying in a speech, "Verily, to have served liberty will cover a multitude of sins."[18]

For Babbitt, the elective system instituted by Eliot had a very personal aspect. In 1889, Babbitt had graduated from Harvard's Department of Classics with high honors. When he returned to teach in that department in 1894, Babbitt found that it had been significantly diminished as a consequence of President Eliot's elimination of the classical languages requirement for undergraduates.[19] The classics, of course, were the first great ethical teachings of the West, and to put them on par with other less profound subject matter was an important error, Babbitt believed.

Babbitt predicted that with Eliot's weakening of educational standards, students would make course selections with "no general norm, no law for man" and that selections would be "entirely with reference to [the students'] own temperament and its (supposedly) unique requirements. The wisdom of all the ages is to be as naught compared with the inclination of a sophomore." The educational establishment had adopted the advice of *Emile* and denied the obligation to pass down certain conventions, traditions, or habits of civilization.

Babbitt critically quoted Eliot as saying, "a well-instructed youth of eighteen can select for himself a better course of instruction than any college faculty."[20]

Babbitt's earlier views on education therefore seemed to have shaped his democratic theory because of his belief that severing the ethical dimension from education and democratizing the curriculum would lead to a decline in standards (conventions, if you will) and a weakening of the natural aristocracy that a democracy requires. For Babbitt, the two forms of humanitarianism that actively undermined the cultivation of civilization had corrupted education's primary goal of transmitting right habits. "Self-expression and vocational training combined in various proportions and tempered by the spirit of 'service,' are nearly the whole of the new education. But I have already said that it is not possible to extract from any such compounding of utilitarian and romantic elements, with the resulting material efficiency and ethical inefficiency, a civilized view of life."[21]

For Babbitt, the specific danger of the humanitarian education was that it substituted "sympathy" and the "scientific method" for "high and objective standards of excellence." Humanitarianism would weaken what should be the primary outcome of a college education: the creation of a genuine aristocracy that would infuse the democratic body politic with high standards. Babbitt believed that refined and civilized elites were the essential feature of a sound democracy. "As formerly conceived, the college might have been defined as a careful selection of studies for the creation of a social elite. In its present tendency, it might be defined as something of everything for everybody." The university was being infused with a "democratic spirit" that entails a "democracy of studies to meet the needs of a student democracy."[22]

In education, Babbitt viewed the pure democratic spirit as generating a mediocre equality: "With the progress of democracy one man's opinion in literature has come to be as good as another's."[23] Babbitt insisted that the curriculum necessary for a formative education would be found in works such as "the Greek and Latin classics" that have "survived for centuries after the languages in which they are written are dead, the presumption is that these books are not dead, but rather very much alive—that they are less related than most other books to what is ephemeral and more related to what is permanent in human nature." The curriculum for an aristocratic education must be selected by accessing Burke's "wisdom of the ages" so "as to register the verdict and embody the experience of a large number of men extending over a considerable time."[24]

Babbitt insisted throughout his writings that a sound and orderly democracy required a class of elites whose education had been "formative."[25] This failure of educational institutions to cultivate a set of ethical, aristocratic leaders was a particular danger to the politics of a democracy because "in one sense, the purpose of the college is not to encourage the democratic spirit, but on the contrary to check the drift toward pure democracy. If our definition of humanism has any value, what is needed is not democracy alone, nor again an unmixed aristocracy, but a blending of the two—an aristocratic and selective democracy."[26]

For Babbitt, the particular danger for politics was that the new education would breed leaders who were of no particular use and were even dangerous to a democracy. Democracies required a "permanent element of judgment, whether in an individual man or in a body of men," that stands as a counterpoise to the "impulse of the moment."[27] In democracies, Babbitt argued, this aristocratic element was indispensable because of the constant pressure of public opinion regularly inflamed by an irresponsible media.

Therefore, Babbitt's theories about the implications of a Rousseauistic education were at the root of his insistence that Rousseau's non-political writings were the most insightful passages in understanding his political theory. In this regard, Babbitt pointed to one of the most important passages in Rousseau, cataloged in book VIII of his *Confessions*. Rousseau's friend Diderot had been imprisoned in the city of Vincennes. Rousseau, short on money, decided to take the long walk from Paris to visit his friend. Along the way, he was reading a French journal, *Mercure de France*, in which he noticed the Dijon Academy's essay contest for the next year's prize: "Has the progress of the sciences and arts done more to corrupt morals or improve them?"

Upon reading this, Rousseau had a vision, Babbitt says, "comparable to that of Saint Paul's vision on the road to Damascus."[28] As Rousseau wrote,

> The moment I read this I beheld another universe and became another man.... [W]hen I reached Vincennes, I was in a state of agitation bordering on delirium.... All my little passions were stifled by an enthusiasm for truth, liberty, and virtue; and the most astonishing thing is that this fermentation worked in my heart for more than four or five years as intensely perhaps as it has ever worked in the heart of any man on earth.[29]

This vision on the road to Vincennes, of course, was the inspiration for his *Discourse on the Arts and Sciences*, which won the Dijon Academy's prize in

1750. Babbitt summarized the core of that vision: "Among the multitude of 'truths' that flashed upon Rousseau in the sort of trance into which he was rapt at the moment, the truth of overshadowing importance was, in his own words, that 'man is naturally good and that it is by our institutions alone that men become wicked.'"[30]

In the vision that inspired the *Discourse*, traditional education was viewed as corrupting morals and artificial to true human nature; civilization itself was destructive to human virtue. Rousseau's vision was a revolution in the West's understanding of human nature and education, a "new dualism . . . that between man naturally good and his institutions."[31] Babbitt said that this moment was decisive for Rousseau because this "first effect" of a new dualism "was to discredit the theological view of human nature, with its insistence that man has fallen" and that the "true opposition between good and evil is in the heart of the individual."[32] Rousseau's vision at Vincennes and the resulting *Discourse*, Babbitt believed, were one of the most powerful inspirations for purging character formation as a goal of education. Rousseau then built on the Vincennes vision when he composed the *Discourse on the Origins of Inequality*, in which he begins laying out the characteristics of natural humanity uncorrupted by civilization.

Babbitt pointed to a passage in the *Confessions* in which Rousseau's uncontrolled idealism about human nature serves as the basis of his political philosophy. "We can trace even more clearly perhaps the process by which the Arcadian dreamer comes to set up as a seer. . . . He goes off on a sort of picnic with Thérèse into the forest of Saint Germain and gives himself up to imagining the state of primitive man." There in the forest, Rousseau invented an imaginative world that explained human existence.

Babbitt quoted Rousseau:

> I sought and found there the image of primitive times of which I proudly drew the history; I swooped down on the little falsehoods of men; I ventured to lay bare their nature, to follow the progress of time and circumstances which have disfigured it, and comparing artificial man (*l'homme de l'homme*) with natural man, to show in his alleged improvements the true source of his miseries. My soul, exalted by these sublime contemplations, rose into the presence of the Divinity.[33]

This new imaginative creation, of course, was Rousseau's vision of the "noble savage" who was not corrupted by private property and other societal institutions and was animated only by the virtue of pity. In the world of the noble savage, uncorrupted by the institutions of society, human beings lived in peace and harmony because they lived in precivilizational environs.

Babbitt pointed out that Rousseau's world of "natural men" was an imaginative invention. There was never a historical period in which humanity found itself in a "state of nature" with noble savages lounging under shade trees. Babbitt said that Rousseau's political theories were built on flights of fancy: "Now the most salient trait of the sentimentalist is that he always has some lovely dream that he prefers to the truth.... He took flight on the wings of his imagination into some 'land of chimeras,' as he said, or, as we should say, into some tower of ivory. He built up a world of pure fiction alongside the real world and called this world of fiction the ideal. In the name of his ideal he refused to adjust himself to the real."[34]

The superstructure of Rousseau's political theory, Babbitt said, was built on a fanciful narrative that began with the worship of spontaneity in *Emile* and proceeded to the political conclusion that civilization itself was the source of corruption in human souls. Humanity had been brought low by its institutions. If the institutions of civilization, including the arts and sciences, represented major obstacles to the flowering of human goodness, then the political program must entail destroying these institutions and those who administer them. In actual practice, the human representatives of civilization become the targets of political action. "Practically, the warfare of the Rousseauistic crusader has been even less against institutions than against those who control and administer them—kings and priests in the earlier stages of the movement, capitalists in our own day." As Babbitt pointed out, Rousseau's anticivilizational philosophy tended to flatter the radical: "[A]s a result of the superior imaginative appeal of the new dualism based upon the myth of man's natural goodness, the rôle he has actually played has been that of arch-radical."[35]

The revolutionary implications of Rousseau's political ideas are discussed in later chapters, but Rousseau's theory of education and human nature, embodied in the idea that spontaneity and impulse were naturally good, represented a revolution in political theory. These ideas repudiated the great Western religious and ethical traditions that were rooted in an understanding that human beings must conform their own selfish wills to higher divine or humanistic order. That older tradition assumed that religion, education, and other institutions of civilization were essential supports to assist human beings in overcoming the weaknesses in their natures.

In his political writings, Rousseau then began the process of explicitly linking his views on human nature to a democratic theory that would recommend specific societal reforms. Yet because of his views on human nature, he faced a formidable challenge and contradiction in constructing a political and social order. For how can one build the institutions of a democratic polity when one's view of human nature is highly individualistic and asserts that all political and social institutions are unnatural and corrupting?

Rousseau's reply to this contradiction was that only by completely abdicating individuality and immersing oneself in the collective general will could the individual achieve freedom and equality. As Babbitt explained Rousseau's resolution of the contradiction, "From the unflinching individualism of the *Second Discourse*, where man is conceived as a sort of isolated and unrelated particle, he passes to the no less unflinching collectivism of the *Social Contract*."[36] What was required to create a just social order, said Rousseau, was "divesting man as completely as possible of his natural virtue in order that he may acquire the virtue of the citizen."[37]

The only way to square the circle of Rousseau's radical individualism with his radical collectivism, Babbitt argued, was to assert that complete freedom and equality would emerge only when citizens had given up every shred of their individuality to the collective. "The only free and legitimate government is founded upon a true social compact" in which individuals freely subsume their individuality under the "general will" of the community. Babbitt explained the key passage from Rousseau: "Only, under the social contract, these virtues no longer reside in the individual, but in the general will. All the clauses of the social contract 'reduce themselves to one: the total alienation of every associate with all his rights' (including his right to property) 'to the whole community.'"[38]

For Rousseau, this subjugation of the individual within the nation represented true democracy and equality, not a tyranny. In Rousseau's *Social Contract*, the individual disappears into the collective will, and this submission, Rousseau surmised, would naturally protect liberty because no organism would harm its own component parts. As Babbitt explained, "The use that Rousseau makes of the parallel is to argue that the community cannot will the harm of any of the individuals that compose it any more than the single person can will the harm of one of his own members."[39]

Rousseau's extreme collectivism was highlighted when he posed the question of whether the love of his fellow humans or the love of country was greater. He answered this question in his *Considerations on the Government of Poland*.

Babbitt explained, "On this point, no doubt is possible. The love of country [Rousseau] takes to be the more beautiful passion. The virtuous intoxication of the internationalist seems to him pale and ineffectual compared with the virtuous intoxication of the citizen."[40] When he becomes a citizen, the natural human, subsumed by the state, becomes "free."

Therefore, for Rousseau, the education of *Emile* was essential to break down individuals' attachments to civilization and prepare them for the day when they could subsume their individual will into that of the collective, assuming the mantle of true patriotic citizens. For Rousseau, when this collective was formed, law, tradition, or other constitutional barriers could not limit popular sovereignty because citizens in the collective would now be unencumbered by competing loyalties to any institutions other than the nation. Babbitt pointed out that with Rousseau's democracy, "the individual is to have no rights against the numerical majority at any particular moment because this majority expresses the general will and the general will is ideally disinterested."[41]

For Babbitt, Rousseau's collective regime entailed the end of liberty. The idea of individuals subsuming their personalities into the community implied the destruction of human diversity. Basing popular sovereignty and political legitimacy on this type of general will, Babbitt believed, would lead to tyranny: "Democracy in the sense of direct and unlimited democracy is, as was pointed out long ago by Aristotle, the death of liberty."[42]

Babbitt argued that Rousseau's version of democracy, with its firm belief in the wisdom of the collective will, tended to ignore the necessity of sobriety, deliberation, and a disinclination to act impulsively. "The will of the popular majority at any particular instance should be supreme—this is the pseudo-democracy of Rousseau. We may safely trust the democratic spirit, if by democracy we mean selective democracy of the sober second thought, and not the democracy of the passing impression."[43]

Babbitt argued that the lack of a check on popular will was, writ large, akin to freeing individuals from any check or restraint on their own passions: "[H]is method, in spite of the usual cautions and reservations, is that which has been adopted by so many of his disciples—to seek to discredit the veto power in the state in favor of popular impulse."[44] Rousseau's definition of popular sovereignty had, of course, inspired a commonly held view that constitutional checks or procedural obstacles to popular passions are inherently antidemocratic. Babbitt contrasted Rousseau's understanding of popular sovereignty with the English tradition in which a system of checks and balances is designed "to bestow a little sovereignty here and a little there and absolute sovereignty nowhere; and then set up a judiciary sufficiently strong to put a veto on any of these partial sovereignties that tend to overstep their prescribed limits."[45]

While Rousseau's influence on imperialistic nationalism is discussed in forthcoming chapters, Babbitt maintained a philosophical connection between Rousseau's theory of popular sovereignty and radical nationalism, where human beings believe that they can recover their true selves only by a total submission to the state. For Rousseau, one did not discover one's true self by the practice of Aristotelian virtue or by acting on the callings of conscience. Instead, the very idea of conscience was denied so that natural humans could assume their roles as citizens. The pull of conscience within an individual, in fact, would only create divided loyalties for the citizen.

Babbitt believed, therefore, that Rousseau was the prime influence on the German intellectual tradition of *Kultur*:

> By his corruption of conscience Rousseau made it possible to identify character with temperament. It was easy for Fichte and others to take the next step and identify national character with national temperament. The Germans according to Fichte are all beautiful souls, the elect of nature. If they have no special word for character it is because to be a German and have character are synonymous. Character is something that gushes up from the primordial depths of the German's being without any conscious effort on his part.[46]

Babbitt argued that German nationalism derived inspiration from the Rousseauistic vision of loyal citizens possessing no divided loyalties and lacking fidelity to any institutions other than the state. "The tendency to set country over all (Deutschland über alles), to make a religion of country, is not mediaeval, but Rousseauistic. . . . The God to whom the Hohenzollerns make such frequent and fluent appeal is, far more than the God of the Middle Ages, a tribal God."[47]

German *Kultur*, in fact, combined a virulent strain of nationalism with an emphasis on scientific progress that tended to worship not only the nation but also its military power. *Kultur* represented the combination of both modern forms of naturalism. "When one analyses in depth German *Kultur*, one finds that it encompasses two rather distinct elements: first, the utilitarian element, the cult of science and efficiency and second the nationalistic enthusiasm which uses scientific efficiency to achieve its ends. It is obvious that if there is Rousseauism in *Kultur*, it exists mostly in the second of the two elements that I have identified, i.e. in the national enthusiasm."[48] It was Rousseau's advocacy for an undisciplined emotional outpouring, Babbitt argued, that formed the heart of modern nationalism: "One might suppose that Rousseau would seek to retain in some form or other this spiritual bond that is set above nationality. But the whole conception has the drawback of being disciplinary, and what Rousseau wants is not discipline, but emotional expansion, especially in the nationalistic form—the intoxication of patriotism."[49]

Rousseau's thought therefore represented an important precursor to German idealism and in turn to German nationalism, where, Babbitt said, "a whole national group may thus flatter one another and inbreed their national 'genius' in the romantic sense, and feel all the while that they are ecstatic 'idealists'; yet as a result of the failure to refer their genius back to some ethical centre, to work, in other words, according to the human law, they may, so far as the members of other national groups are concerned, remain in a state of moral solitude."[50]

While in several places Babbitt pointed to Rousseau's influence on *Kultur* and in turn to *Kultur*'s role in the lead-up to the Great War, Babbitt wrote even more extensively about the influence of Rousseau's democratic theory on the French Jacobins, who adopted not only his view of human nature but also his views on popular sovereignty. "In Robespierre and other revolutionary leaders one may study the implications of the new morality—the attempt to transform virtue into a natural passion—not merely for the individual but for society."[51]

The adoption of a Rousseauistic concept of democracy and popular sovereignty by the French Jacobins had two sets of implications, one for domestic and one for international politics. Domestically, any institution that created divided loyalties or unequal citizens had to be destroyed. To restore natural rights and bring equality, the king and queen and many members of the aristocracy, the wealthy classes, and the clergy would be sent to the guillotine.

For international affairs, Rousseau's version of popular sovereignty was rightly seen as a threat to the perceived legitimacy of the monarchical and aristocratic nation-states surrounding France because the Jacobins had declared that the only legitimate forms of government were those that had adopted Rousseau's restoration of democratic "natural rights." As Simon Schama described the European war crisis of 1791 and 1792, "Against the higher moral law of self-determination embraced by the Revolution, even the language of treaties between princes had no standing. How could the Pope claim to be sovereign of Avignon, or some German princes of the Empire claim property rights in Alsace, when the citizens of those places had never consented to the alienation of their territory?"[52]

As Schama pointed out, all other European governments, no matter the historical richness and legacy of their monarchies, were declared outlaws by the Rousseauistic revolution: "The Declaration of the Rights of Man and Citizen and the assertions of natural rights on which the constitution was based were, by definition, universally applicable. How could men be born to freedom in equality in one patch of the world but not another?"[53] (This point will be discussed in more detail in chapter 5.)

Babbitt, on the contrary, saw in the Jacobin-style assertion of abstract and universal "natural rights" a debauched form of democracy because it avoided the central requirement of liberty, "the need of a veto power either in the individual or in the state."[54] Babbitt, like Burke, maintained that liberty is earned, not declared, and its origin is rooted in ethical work by individuals over generations. Communities and nations achieve liberties when their citizens and leaders become self-ordered and therefore lessen the need for outer control and authority. It is quite simple to proclaim liberty, Babbitt said, but much harder to actually devise a system that protects it. "The liberty of the Jeffersonian . . . makes against ethical union like every liberty that rests on the assertion of abstract rights."[55]

Babbitt believed that the Romanticism undergirding theories of natural rights was artificial because it "encourages a total or partial suppression of the true dualism of the spirit and of the special quality of working it involves." A conception of liberty that merely allowed individuals to do as they please would be a false liberty, inviting anarchy. "For true liberty," Babbitt said, "is not liberty to do as one likes, but liberty to adjust oneself, in some sense of the word, to law. . . . [G]enuine liberty is the reward of ethical effort; it tends to disappear if one presents liberty as a free gift of 'nature.'"[56]

Edmund Burke, of course, heavily influenced Babbitt's view of liberty; Babbitt's very terminology echoed Burke. In Burke's worldview, duties take precedence over and give birth to rights and liberties. Liberties do not simply appear because they are declared abstractly in a political document; they are the result of work over generations. As Burke wrote, "In the famous law of the 3d of Charles I. called the *Petition of Right*, the parliament says to the king, 'your subjects have *inherited* this freedom,' claiming their franchises not on abstract principles 'as the rights of men,' but as the rights of Englishmen, and as a patrimony derived from their forefathers."[57]

Rights, Burke insisted, flow from the mastery of one's passions:

> Government is a contrivance of human wisdom to provide for human *wants*. Men have a right that these wants should be provided for by this wisdom. Among these wants is to be reckoned the want, out of civil society, of a sufficient restraint upon their passions. Society requires not only that the passions of individuals should be subjected, but that even in the mass and body as well as in the individuals, the inclinations of men should frequently be thwarted, their will controlled, and their passions brought into subjection.[58]

Without coupling rights with duties, Babbitt argued that there is a "tendency of the doctrine of natural rights to weaken the sense of obligation, and so to undermine genuine liberty."[59]

Babbitt further pointed out how a theory of natural rights tends to justify a meddling and expansive domestic government. Babbitt argued that a political spirit based solely on "rights" tends to produce individuals who, in asserting their liberty, fail to live up to their responsibilities and create disorder in society. Faced with disorder, leaders of this society recognize the challenges created by this type of problematic individual but can solve the problem only by counterpoising an alternative theory of the "rights of society." When the rights of society are asserted against the individual, social utility for the greater number tends to override personal liberty—that is, individual assertions of right tend to be trumped by the needs of society. Under these theories of abstract right, therefore, the nation's leaders tend "not only to ascribe unlimited sovereignty to society as against the individual, but also to look upon [themselves] as endowed with a major portion of it, to develop a temper, in short, that is plainly tyrannical."[60] Babbitt concluded, therefore, that when the traditional ethical controls break down in individuals, "humanitarian crusaders" offer detailed reforms for society that end up becoming genuine threats the liberty of individuals because there is "under cover of their altruism, a will to power."[61]

Babbitt viewed a legalistic culture as an outgrowth of this humanitarian outlook. "The result of the attempt to deal with evil socially rather than at its source in the individual, to substitute an outer for an inner control of appetite, has been a monstrous legalism, of which the Eighteenth Amendment is only the most notable example.... The multiplication of laws, attended by a growing lawlessness—the present situation in this country—is, as every student of history knows, a very sinister symptom."[62]

Babbitt argued that Rousseau's absolutist conception of popular sovereignty and his assertions of abstract natural rights were the hallmark of radical democracy and the opposite of the constitutionalism of *The Federalist*. In fact, these two divergent forms of democratic theory, he believed, had been competing in the politics of the United States since its inception. "In this country the contest can be traced in the authors of *The Federalist*, for example, on the one hand, and the representatives of the Jeffersonian and Jacksonian democracy on the other."[63]

Babbitt argued that the French Revolution and American constitutionalism did not share a common theory but instead were in opposition to each other, representing two divergent views of human nature and two fundamentally different types of democracy. Although elements of Rousseau's thought had been present throughout American history, the Framers of the Constitution adopted a distinctly anti-Rousseauistic view of human nature and popular sovereignty. "If we go back, indeed, to the beginnings of our institutions, we find that America stood from the start for two different views of government that have their origin in different views of liberty and ultimately of human nature." The tradition of natural rights and of direct democracy was best represented by Jefferson, while "[t]he view that inspired our Constitution, on the other hand, has much in common with that of Burke" and "has its most distinguished representative in Washington."[64]

In his clearest enunciation of the differences between the two versions of democratic theory, Babbitt said,

> The contrast that I am establishing is, of course, that between constitutional and direct democracy. There is an opposition of first principles between those who maintain that the popular will should prevail, but only after it has been purified of what is merely impulsive and ephemeral, and those who maintain that this will should prevail immediately and unrestrictedly. The American democracy has, therefore, from the outset been ambiguous, and will remain so until the irrepressible conflict between a Washingtonian and a Jeffersonian liberty has been fought to a conclusion.[65]

At its core, American constitutionalism in the tradition of *The Federalist* required two essential features that shared a common view of human nature. First and foremost, democracy could not survive without leaders of strong moral character; this is the primary argument in Babbitt's *Democracy and Lead-*

ership. Rousseau's concept of popular sovereignty had obscured the centrality of ethical leadership in a democracy, Babbitt insisted. "One's choice may be, not between a democracy that is properly led and a democracy that hopes to find the equivalent of standards and leadership in the appeal to a numerical majority, that indulges in other words in a sort of quantitative impressionism, but between a democracy that is properly led and decadent imperialism."[66]

The American constitutional tradition encouraged leaders with an aristocratic temperament who would assist in preventing the triumph of a pure democracy and could steer popular opinion toward choices that were in their truest long-term interest. Rousseau's direct democracy, in contrast, was inspired by a Romantic sentimentalism that no one person was better than the next and that aristocrats, as a general matter, were illegitimate rulers who had achieved their superior position by cunning and deception. Rousseau sought leaders who were not true leaders but rather mere servants of the popular will.

Babbitt's contrasting of Rousseau's view of leadership and that of *The Federalist* was the single most essential distinction in his democratic theory. The success of the American republic flowed from the aristocratic temperament of George Washington and the insistence by *The Federalist* that an orderly democracy required not popular but representative government whose leaders might elevate and refine popular desires. Based on their reading of the history of ancient democracies, the American Framers did not believe that democracy could survive without representatives who possessed the requisite character and virtue and who would serve as checks on popular passions. As Babbitt explained, "A democracy that produces in sufficient numbers sound individualists who look up imaginatively to standards set above their ordinary selves, may well deserve enthusiasm. A democracy, on the other hand, that is not rightly imaginative, but is impelled by vague emotional intoxications, may mean all kinds of lovely things in dreamland, but in the real world it will prove an especially unpleasant way of returning to barbarism."[67]

In *Federalist 71*, Alexander Hamilton pointed to the paramount importance of leadership in cooling the popular passions of democracy:

> When occasions present themselves, in which the interests of the people are at variance with their inclinations, it is the duty of the persons they have appointed, to be the guardian of those interests; to withstand the temporary delusion, in order to give them time and opportunity for more cool and sedate reflection. Instances might be cited, in which a conduct of this kind has saved the

people from very fatal consequences of their own mistakes, and has procured lasting monuments of their gratitude to the men who had the courage and magnanimity enough to serve them at the peril of their displeasure.[68]

The Federalist's emphasis on a representative republic provides an obvious contrast with Rousseau's concept of popular sovereignty.

The second salient characteristic of American constitutionalism that contrasted with Rousseau, Babbitt argued, was institutions arranged in a manner that would check popular passions and force deliberation in the body politic. These institutional checks, Babbitt said, parallel the "higher will" that individuals must impose on their own impulses. "Just as man has a higher self that acts restrictively on his ordinary self, so, they hold, the state should have a higher or permanent self, appropriately embodied in institutions, that should set bounds to its ordinary self as expressed by popular will at any particular moment."[69]

In the United States, the traditional reverence for the Constitution and its institutional safeguards had created stability, with popular respect for checks on the popular will. Babbitt maintained that the success of this constitutional tradition derived from its sound view of human nature, the ethical insight that "the state should have a permanent or higher self that is felt as a veto power upon its ordinary self" and that "rests ultimately upon the assertion of a similar dualism in the individual."[70] Babbitt's essential argument was that the entire structure of the American Constitution, with its representative government and elaborate mechanisms to thwart the spontaneous popular will, assumed that the impulsive desires of the people might very well be arbitrary and selfish—precisely the opposite of Rousseau's views on human nature. As James Madison wrote, certain constitutional structures were put in place "as a defense to the people against their own temporary errors and delusions." Because the people could be "stimulated by some irregular passion," the system should be designed to allow the "cool and deliberative sense of the community" to prevail.[71]

From his earliest to his last books, Babbitt expressed his belief that a healthy democracy would be home to leaders and institutions that could both resist the fleeting emotions of the moment and access a more timeless standard of judgment.

> Why then, it may be asked, should not democracy select without restraint? The answer is, that democracy should not be restrained in its judgments, but only in its impressions. Three institutions in this country—the Senate, Constitution,

and Supreme Court—were especially intended to embody the permanent judgments and experience of democracy and at the same time serve as a bulwark against popular impulse. Attacks on these institutions are usually inspired by the rankest Rousseauism.[72]

Babbitt was consistent in his view that the Senate, the Constitution, and the Supreme Court were the three most important institutional checks on the tendency of American democracy to accede to popular passions. In *Democracy and Leadership*, published sixteen years after *Literature and the American College*, Babbitt continued to maintain the connection between sound education and sound constitutionalism: "There is a real relation between the older educational standard that thus acted restrictively on the mere temperament of the individual and the older political standard embodied in institutions such as the Constitution, Senate, and Supreme Court, that serve as a check on the ordinary or impulsive will of the people."[73]

In particular, according to Babbitt,

> John Marshall deserves special praise for the clearness with which he saw the final center of control in the type of government that was being founded, if control was to have an ethical basis and not be another name for force, must be vested in the judiciary, particularly in the Supreme Court. This court, especially in its most important function, that of interpreting the Constitution, must, he perceived, embody more than any other institution the higher or permanent self of the state.[74]

In the opening paragraphs of his one book devoted to democratic theory, *Democracy and Leadership*, Babbitt proclaimed that "[t]his book in particular is devoted to the most unpopular of tasks—a defense of the veto power." He carefully chose the word *veto*. In the context of the paragraph in which he used the word, he was clearly referring to the inner veto within the soul of the individual, to "a certain quality of will, a will that is felt in relation to his ordinary self as the will to refrain."[75] Of course, use of *veto* also carries the overtone of the presidential veto, or the prerogative to override popularly enacted legislation.

A recognition of the importance of the veto power, Babbitt maintained, was the key difference between Jeffersonian democracy and Washingtonian constitutionalism: "The Jeffersonian liberal has faith in the goodness of natural man, and so tends to overlook the need of a veto power either in the individual or the state. The liberals of whom I have taken Washington to be the type are less expansive in their attitude toward the natural man."[76] For Babbitt, understanding the difference between a Jeffersonian liberal and a Washingtonian constitutionalist was "the key that unlocks American history."[77]

In his recounting of the opprobrium heaped on Washington for eschewing an alliance with the French Jacobins, Babbitt emphasized the requirement in a democracy for "an enlightened minority" because "the notion that wisdom resides in a popular majority at any particular moment should be the most completely exploded of all fallacies."[78] In his most powerful broadside against popular majorities in general and referenda in particular, Babbitt pointed out that "[i]f the plain people of Jerusalem had registered their will with the aid of the most improved type of ballot box, there is no evidence that they would have preferred Christ to Barabbas. In view of the size of the jury that condemned Socrates, one may affirm confidently that he was the victim of a 'great and solemn referendum.'"[79]

Washington's personal character and decorum exemplified the traits that Babbitt thought required for leaders in a healthy democracy. In viewing life's challenges, Washington took precisely the opposite of Rousseau's view. Virtue was not natural; it was the omnipresent struggle within oneself. As one recent Washington scholar wrote of the first president's character, "The theory of behavior that Washington and his peers knew and attempted to live by did not view any virtue as natural.... While fortifying their own self-esteem is an activity that individuals gladly beaver away at, self-mastery, the seemly control and direction of the *amour-propre*, is a much harder slog—and needs all the props of morality and religion that society can muster."[80]

For Babbitt, there were two poles of democracy, one sound and disposed to personal liberty, one unsound and a threat to personal liberty. The first, rooted in a dualistic view of human nature, was embodied in the American Constitution, with its many safeguards preventing the popular passion from imposing itself with any immediacy. The second form of democracy, inspired by Rousseau, denied the "civil war in the cave" and worshipped "natural" impulse, both in individuals and in the popular will. This second form of democracy was fully on display in Jacobin France, first with anarchy, next with the Terror, and finally with the imposition of a militaristic order from above. The first form of democracy was punctuated by an ordered liberty and was led by leaders of an aristocratic temperament who possessed strong character and high standards. The second was punctuated by revolutions and anarchy and led by demagogues who flattered the fluctuating popular will while amassing power around themselves.

In distinguishing between the two forms, Babbitt argued that there was one symptom that could help diagnose the slide into the decadent form of democracy: class warfare. "The egoistic impulses that are not controlled at their source tend to prevail over an ineffectual altruism in the relations of man with man and class with class."[81] In a decaying democracy, the members of the propertied class, because they are not sufficiently aristocratic, tend to believe in conserving property for "its own sake . . . not like Burke," who believed in defending private property "because it is an almost indispensable support of personal liberty, a genuinely spiritual thing."[82] A decadent elite had no credible response to complaints about their wealth when class warfare arrived on their doorstep.

Class warfare, Babbitt argued, would always be the mark of a declining democracy and a sign that it had entered a radical and decadent phase. "Every student of history is aware of the significance of this particular symptom in a democracy."[83] Income inequality for Babbitt was not necessarily the cause of class warfare, and schemes to confiscate wealth, therefore, were not a true solution. "Every form of social justice, indeed, tends toward confiscation and confiscation, when practiced on a large scale, undermines moral standards and, in so far, substitutes for real justice the law of cunning and the law of force."[84]

The envy of wealth that drove class warfare, Babbitt said, could be corrected only by elites of an aristocratic temperament who are enlightened and self-disciplined rather than rapacious and grasping. "The only remedy for economic inequality, as Aristotle says, is 'to train the nobler sort of natures not to desire more'; this remedy is not in mechanical schemes for dividing up property; 'for it is not the possessions but the desires of mankind that need to be equalized.'"[85]

Babbitt pointed out that in the United States, a sometime counterweight to the demagogues of class warfare could typically be found in the "great unionist tradition," which embodied "the idea that state should have a permanent or higher self."[86] Yet Babbitt believed that this tradition was waning and that under the influence of humanitarianism, the emerging culture was simultaneously engaging in class warfare and worshipping the acquisition of material goods and wealth. "The type of individualism that was thus encouraged has led to monstrous inequalities and, with the decline of traditional standards, to the rise of a raw plutocracy." The decline of the elite class away from an aristocratic temperament and into self-indulgence would, he said, lead to class warfare: "People will not consent in the long run to look up to those who are not themselves looking up to something higher than their ordinary selves. A leading class that has become Epicurean and self-indulgent is lost."[87]

Finally, Babbitt pointed out that when radical democracy had reached a point when significant intermediate institutions were being undermined by the popular passion to equalize all things, its pretension to popular sovereignty was ultimately illusory. A small, ruthless minority would inevitably dictate the political order of a radical democracy. "No movement, indeed, illustrates more clearly than the supposedly democratic movement the way in which the will of highly organized and resolute minorities may prevail over the will of the inert and unorganized mass."[88]

Babbitt's democratic theory was ultimately rooted in his assertion of a human law that creates ethical obligations for individuals. Successful democracy would be found, he believed, only where leaders and in turn citizens had acquired good habits, checked their impulses, and engaged in the ethical work that is the only route to a sound political order. Leaders in a democracy, in particular, needed to possess this quality of self-mastery, or they would not display the kind of temperament that makes for an orderly democracy. The Romantic notion that unleashing popular passions would bring justice, Babbitt said, was a chimera. Unleashing popular passions and destroying traditional habits and institutions would have one inevitable political result: class warfare and anarchic revolution.

CHAPTER 4

Democracy as Revolution

> In the words of Madame de Staël, he invented nothing, but set everything on fire.
>
> —Irving Babbitt, *Democracy and Leadership*

> Every atrocity the time could imagine was meted out to the defenseless population. Women were routinely raped, children killed, both mutilated.
>
> —Simon Schama, *Citizens: A Chronicle of the French Revolution*

> The murder of a king or queen, or a bishop, or a father, are only common homicide—and if the people are by any chance or in any way gainers by it, a sort of homicide much the most pardonable, and into which we ought to not make too severe a scrutiny.
>
> —Edmund Burke, *Reflections on the Revolution in France*

The two opposing democratic theories described by Babbitt have existed side by side in the American polity. The first was articulated in *The Federalist* and was embodied in the political restraint and personal reserve of George Washington, while the second was the direct democracy of Jeffersonianism and was embodied in a populist president such as Andrew Jackson. *The Federalist* tradition was not much influenced by Rousseau but instead bore the imprint of the British tradition of constitutionalism. Cognizant of the history of the ancient world, the authors of *The Federalist* warned that popular opinion was, like human beings themselves, sometimes inclined toward impulsive, destructive, and disorderly behavior but nonetheless possessed the potential for measured and reflective judgment.

The Framers knew that popular governments in ancient Greece and Rome were plagued by revolutions, civil wars, coup d'états, assassinations, and other civil disorders, and this historical knowledge motivated them to develop constitutional safeguards to mitigate the effects of popular passions. As Claes G. Ryn has explained, the authors of *The Federalist* understood the historical dangers of decadent democracies: "To understand the Framers' conception of good government it is necessary, however, to remember that they had a very low opinion of what they called 'democracy' or 'pure democracy'. They associated it with demagoguery, rabble-rousing, opportunism, ignorance and general irresponsibility."[1]

In contrast, there was far less skepticism about democracy in the Jeffersonian tradition, which was profoundly influenced by Rousseau. Rather than being cautious about popular passions, Jeffersonians saw wisdom in unfiltered popular sentiment. They were always concerned that constitutional checks on the popular will could create obstacles to "the people's agenda." This tradition of populism has gained greater currency in modern American politics. For instance, it seems unproblematic to many that our legislators regularly make decisions about complex questions of public policy on the basis of public opinion polls. Likewise, many erroneously consider the American constitutional tradition to be one of simple majority rule. Jeffersonian populism has adherents on both the left and right side of the American political spectrum.

Irving Babbitt believed, however, that an unvarnished Rousseauistic populism should carry an important warning for democracies: it tends to breed violent revolution. Thomas Jefferson famously praised revolution in a letter to James Madison:

> Even this evil is productive of good. It prevents the degeneracy of government, and nourishes a general attention to the public affairs. I hold it that a little rebellion now and then is a good thing, and as necessary in the political world as storms in the physical. Unsuccesful rebellions indeed generally establish the incroachments on the rights of the people which have produced them. An observation of this truth should render honest republican governors so mild in their punishment of rebellions, as not to discourage them too much. It is a medecine necessary for the sound health of government.[2]

In the American context, a Rousseauistic admiration for rebellion has always been in competition with the constitutional tradition of *The Federalist*, although popular reverence for the Constitution has created a US political order that has been buffeted but never overcome by waves of popular unrest.

Babbitt argued that the influence of Rousseau's philosophy not only had bred revolution and violence in eighteenth-century France but had even contributed to the radicalism of the early twentieth century. In a 1910 review of a book on Pascal, Babbitt remarked that the contemporary intellectual interest in Rousseau was not a coincidence: "The return to Rousseau evidently bears a close relation to the great wave of radicalism that has been sweeping over the world."[3] Despite Rousseau's "timid" personal nature, Babbitt said that Rousseau's writings contained the seeds of violent revolution. As Babbitt observed, "In his theories Rousseau is a wild revolutionary dreamer, but timid and circumspect in the last degree in everything that relates to practice. His genius, however, appears only in the stormy orchestration of the sentiments of revolt."[4]

On the surface, Rousseau's role in inspiring revolt seems counterintuitive because of his fondness for seemingly peaceful and solitary reveling in pastoral nature. In Plato's *Phaedrus*, for example, Socrates is lured to the woods and expresses admiration for the beauty of nature, causing Phaedrus to ask Socrates why he does not come more often. Socrates replies that the "fields and trees do not teach me anything but men in the city do."[5] Rousseau, on the other hand, seems happiest when strolling through the forest and finds the most profound wisdom in the simplest peasant. However, Babbitt argued, Rousseau's flattery of the peasant has a darker side: a rebellious hatred of civilization.

Rousseau's dream of pure uncorrupted democracy that would return society to an aboriginal condition was based on his observations of Swiss peasants going about their business in an orderly and sensible way. He noticed that they cordially lived their lives with efficiency and good cheer and seemed to have little need of leadership. Rousseau persuaded himself that these peasants were so orderly and placid because, in their simplicity, they had been uncorrupted by civilization and its institutions. As Babbitt quoted Rousseau, "When you see ... in the happiest people in the world bands of peasants regulate the affairs of state under an oak-tree and always behave sensibly, can you keep from despising the refinements of other nations which make themselves illustrious and miserable with so much art and mystery?"[6]

Babbitt pointed out, however, that Rousseau was viewing these peasants through an idyllic imagination, "through the Arcadian glamour." In fact, Rousseau saw these peasants "[I]n much the same way Emerson saw proof of the consonance of democracy with human nature in the working of the New England town-meeting. But both Rousseau's Swiss and Emerson's New Englanders had been moulded by generations of austere religious discipline and so throw little light on the relation of democracy to human nature itself."[7]

Admiration for the political order of the Geneva peasants, Babbitt noted, did not prevent Rousseau from writing down the most inflammatory and seditious thoughts about the council of twenty-five patrician families that actually ruled Geneva through the Petit Conseil. Rousseau could, when approaching Geneva, embrace lofty idyllic images of the pacific peasants simultaneously with a seething passion for revolution against their leaders.

> Even in regard to Geneva, Rousseau is capable of passing, after the fashion of the radical, from the fairest visions to the darkest suspicions. The Petit Conseil which is presented in the introductory letter to the Second Discourse as ideally subservient to the general will appears in the "Lettres la Montagne" . . . as a gang of conspirators who are seeking to thwart this general will. Rousseau is here seen fomenting an actual revolution; his method, in spite of the usual cautions and reservations, is that which has been adopted by so many of his disciples—to seek to discredit the veto power in the state in favor of popular impulse.[8]

Babbitt argued that Rousseau's misleading diagnosis of the peasants' happy and orderly lives provides a key insight into his larger political philosophy. Rousseau simply avoided or denied the fact that the peasants were peaceful largely as a consequence of a rigorous religious tradition, not because they had eschewed the trappings of civilization. According to Babbitt, Rousseau's idyllic imaginings on these peasants contain an inkling of the revolutionary personality who believes that political order will come only through the destruction of the institutions of civilization, not through religious or humanistic discipline.

One also sees the darker side of the Rousseauistic imagination in his accusation that the very existence of institutions of civilization and their leaders was evidence of a conspiracy. Babbitt explained,

> The guiding principle of [Rousseau's] writings, he says, is to show that vice and error, strangers to man's constitution, are introduced from without, that they are due in short to his institutions. Now institutions mean in practice those who administer them. A small group at the top of the artificial hierarchy, kings and priests and capitalists, sit on the lid, as it were, and keep man's native goodness (as in Shelley's "Prometheus Unbound") from gushing forth torrentially.[9]

Rousseau had given birth, Babbitt believed, to the conspiratorial outlook of the modern revolutionary who is eager to destroy those conspirators through violence.

Under Rousseau's assumptions, with civilization and its institutions as the enemy of democracy, the heroes of the revolutionary mind-set become the rascals, vagabonds, and reprobates who are willing to destroy the institutions of the established order, with the means less important than the ends. Babbitt quoted extensively from a passage of Pierre Lasserre's *Le Romantisme Français* to describe how the revolutionary breaks down society into two groups: "sublime" criminals and assorted crooks, who are willing to destroy civilization, and the "wicked," who seek to protect the retrograde institutions of civilization:

> "Sublime convicts" says M. Lasserre, "idlers of genius, angelic female poisoners, monsters inspired by God, sincere comedians, virtuous courtesans, metaphysical mountebanks, faithful adulterers, form only one half—the sympathetic half of humanity according to romanticism. The other half, the wicked half, is manufactured by the same intellectual process under the suggestion of the same revolutionary instinct. It comprises all those who hold or stand for a portion of any discipline whatsoever, political, religious, moral or intellectual—kings, ministers, priests, judges, soldiers, policemen, husbands and critics."[10]

For the revolutionary Romantic, political violence against civilization was the essence of personal virtue and explained the tendency for revolutions to lionize rogues and criminals who were devoted to the "cause." In revolutions, as in some Romantic literature, the scoundrels became the heroes and the heroes became scoundrels.

Rousseau's view of human nature and his belief in the natural goodness of man led him to attack civilization's institutions as well as their leaders. Evil, for Rousseau, was found in the institutions of civilization and their representatives, not in the souls of individuals. As Babbitt concisely summarized this view, "Thus according to Rousseau, man is 'naturally good.' If evil appears, it is to be referred not to a failure on the part of the individual to control himself but to 'institutions.'"[11]

Rousseau's ideas on the natural goodness of man, Babbitt believed, led in turn to the view that the people would become sovereign only when historically rooted institutions, traditions, and conventions were drained of authority. Rousseau's concept of popular sovereignty, for example, had achieved such prominence in late-eighteenth-century France that even Louis XVI, who represented a Bourbon dynasty extending back to the sixteenth century, was under its spell. Louis was paralyzed by the thought that the violent outbursts of the Parisian mob might actually represent the true spirit of the French people and therefore took no action to put down the growing rebellion. Louis developed what Babbitt described as a "monomaniacal" inability to act that was "not unrelated to the growing belief not only that the will of the people is sovereign but is identical with its shifting caprice, for example, with the will of the Parisian mob. If the King and his counselors had not been thus touched by the new philosophy, the 'whiff of grapeshot' would not have come before 1790 at the latest and there would have been no reign of Terror."[12]

Indeed, Babbitt viewed the French Revolution as a highly representative political expression of Rousseau's philosophical Romanticism: "If we wish to see the psychology of Rousseau writ large we should turn to the French Revolution. That period abounds in persons whose goodness is in theory so superlative that it overflows in a love for all men, but who in practice are filled like Rousseau in his later years with universal suspicion."[13] Revolutions based on Rousseauistic principles, Babbitt argued, would entail attacks on whole classes of individuals and institutions that are viewed as impediments to the vox populi. The revolutionary attacks in France, intended to bring freedom and democracy, would instead target important intermediate institutions such as the church and would result, finally, in a tyrannical dictator who would be legitimized as the "true voice" of the popular will.

The leaders of the revolution had expressed all of Rousseau's loftiest idealism—*liberté, égalité, fraternité*—yet would produce the Terror. Babbitt thought the Terror should not be understood as an excess of a revolution that had spun out of control or had drifted from its earlier noble intentions; it was, he believed, a logical result of Rousseauism. In Babbitt's words, "By setting up his chimerical contrast between some 'natural' or 'ideal' state in which men are peaceful, benevolent, and happy without any genuine moral effort, and an actual society in which they are oppressed and corrupted by their institutions and those who administer them, Rousseau opened the way for more convulsions and breaches of peace than all the cynics from Machiavelli to Hobbes down."[14] An idealism that had escaped reality gave the revolution a simultaneous aura of lofty humanitarianism mixed with the most brutal realism, a reflection of the idealism and realism found in Rousseau's ideas. Babbitt offered his analysis of this contradictory character of revolutions: "The soft temperamentalists are overflowing with beautiful professions of brotherly love, and at the same time the hard temperamentalists are reaching out for everything in sight; and inasmuch as the hard temperamentalists operate not in a dreamland, but in the real world, they are only too plainly setting the tone. Very often, of course, the same temperamentalist has his hard and his soft side."[15]

Ryn points out that after centuries of bloody and violent revolutions inspired by lofty idealistic dreams, political idealism nonetheless continues to enjoy immunity against condemnation despite its link with massive brutality.

> Some of the biggest idealists, championing a vision of universal brotherhood—Lenin, Trotsky, Mao—were also among the greatest killers and murderers. They caused enormous suffering. Yet the Western world seems to have learnt very little about idealism from this horrifying experience. Idealists *still* expect, and often receive, admiration for their allegedly noble visions. The *idealism* cannot be blamed for the homicidal mania, the idealists tell others.[16]

In this regard, Ryn's view implies some mild criticism of Babbitt for his characterization of Rousseau's imagination as "idyllic," since this term does not precisely capture the dark moral import of many forms of political idealism. "Imagining and advocating unattainable goals," Ryn says, "is from the point of view of traditional morality not admirable, but perverse and dangerous."[17]

Simon Schama's monumental history of the French Revolution, *Citizens*, chronicles this perversity and takes historians of the French Revolution to task for soft-pedaling the brutality of the Terror and in particular for claiming that the violence and bloodshed represented an "aberration" from the otherwise noble goals of the revolution. "Confronted with the evidence of an apocalypse, it does historians no credit to look aside in the name of scholarly objectivity."[18] The Romantic historical accounts of the French Revolution, Babbitt claimed, had airbrushed the Terror: "In Heaven's name, let us have the cold facts, unembroidered by these arabesques of a disordered fancy, and undistorted by the hallucinations of a revolutionary temperament!"[19]

For Schama as for Babbitt, the violence of the revolution was not an excessive aberration but a predictable result of the revolution's principles. "The exterminations practiced there were, in fact, the logical outcome of an ideology that progressively dehumanized its adversaries and that had become incapable of seeing any middle ground between total triumph and utter eclipse." Rather than lamenting the violence or complaining that some revolutionaries had taken things too far, "Robespierre had rejoiced that 'a river of blood would now divide France from its enemies.' That river was now swelling its banks; the current was flowing fast but it remained obscure, except to the intimates of the Incorruptible, where it was taking the Republic."[20]

One of Babbitt's favorite French authors and a critic of Romanticism, Joseph Joubert, had written, "Philosophers fall into unreality from 'confounding what is spiritual from what is abstract.'"[21] Yet after living through the Terror, Joubert had remarked that the sheer brutality of the revolution made him wish to flee reality, not face it squarely. "Joubert's shrinking from *l'affreuse réalité* is also to be connected to the fact that he lived through the Reign of Terror. 'The Revolution,' he says, 'drove my spirit from the real world by making it too horrible for me.' 'Revolutions are times when the poor man is not sure of his probity, the rich man of his fortune, and the innocent man of his life.'"[22]

There was a direct intellectual line, Babbitt felt, from Rousseau's democratic theory to the Terror, a line that continued to flame radicalism long after 1789:

> "We are approaching," Rousseau declared, "the era of crises, and the age of revolutions." He not only made the prophecy but did more than any other one man to insure its fulfillment.... In one of the best-balanced estimates that have appeared, the French critic Gustave Lanson, after doing justice to the various minor trends in Rousseau's work, sums up accurately its major influence: "It exasperates and inspires revolt and fires enthusiasms and irritates hatreds; it is the mother of violence, the source of all that is uncompromising; it launches the simple souls who give themselves up to its strange virtue upon the desperate quest for the absolute, an absolute to be realized now by anarchy and now by social despotism."[23]

This revolutionary outlook swept France after Rousseau published *The Social Contract* in 1762. As Ryn explains,

> In France, Rousseau's view of man and his vision of a new society spread quickly and soon became a powerful political force. It was espoused with increasing militancy by the Jacobin clubs, which saw themselves as incorruptible guardians of universal principles.... They were ushering a new way of life, a society of equality and democracy, a glorious goal that permitted no mercy for those who stood in the way. Jacobinism inspired the French Revolution's murderous hatred of traditional elites, its reign of terror, and its messianic ambitions.[24]

Babbitt quoted Robespierre extensively because he was "probably a more thoroughgoing Rousseauist than any other of the Revolutionary leaders."[25] Like Rousseau, Robespierre explicitly redefined virtue by associating it with overflowing feeling rather than self-control. As Babbitt quoted Robespierre,

> Doubtless virtue is a natural passion.... Yet virtue exists as you can testify, feeling and pure souls; it exists, that tender irresistible, imperious passion, torment and delight of magnanimous hearts, that profound horror of tyranny, that compassionate zeal for the oppressed, that sacred love for one's country, that still more sublime and sacred love for humanity, without which a great revolution is only a glittering crime that destroys another crime.[26]

Virtue was for Robespierre an overflowing patriotic emotion, and once the patriot was captured by this emotion, he would turn his attention to political action that would usher in the utopian vision of the revolution. The idealistic vision *bred* the violence; they were not separate phenomena. As Babbitt described Robespierre's outlook, "If one wishes to enter into the psychology of the later stages of the Revolution, one should devote special attention to avowed disciples of Rousseau like Robespierre. He adopts a rather uncompromising form of Rousseau's view of 'virtue,' and so is led to set up an 'ideal' France over against the real France, and this 'ideal' France is largely a projection of what I have termed the idyllic imagination."[27] Robespierre possessed a monumental conceit about his natural virtue and that of the other Jacobins, and as Babbitt quoted, Robespierre told his fellow Jacobins that their natural virtue was "at this moment burning in your souls. I feel it in mine. But how could our vile calumniators have any notion of it?"[28] Other, less worthy, souls must be killed because the *fraternité* of society, Robespierre believed, *depended* on such killings and murders.

Robespierre drew inspiration from Rousseau's wayward imagination and his willingness to impose, through violence if necessary, that Romantic dream on society. As Babbitt pointed out regarding the French Revolution and Romanticism generally, when one acts in politics on the basis of unreality, on the basis of a dream, the result is a messianic revolution.

Babbitt cited Aristotle's definition of Romanticism as things that are "wonderful rather than probable."[29] Rousseau, Babbitt believed, preferred living in a fantasy world: "The creative imagination is thus for Rousseau a means of escape into a land of heart's desire, a world of sheer unreality."[30]

Babbitt conceded that imaginative Romantic literature and occasional escapist daydreaming might have a perfectly healthy place in the busy life of human beings who often face a grinding reality. However, when revolutionaries declared it to be a political requirement to actually create and live in a world that is more "wonderful" than "probable," one begins to see the strong influence of Rousseauistic imagination on the modern revolutionary mind-set. As Babbitt explained, "Thus alongside the real world and in more or less sharp opposition to it, Rousseau builds up a fictitious world, that *pays des chimères*, which is alone, as he tells us, worthy of habitation."[31] This type of imagination becomes madness when Romantics cannot distinguish the Arcadian dream world from the real world and proceed to act as if they are living in the dream rather than in reality.

Babbitt pointed to one incident in which Rousseau's imagination tipped over into a kind of madness: "It was, for example, natural for a youth like Rousseau who was at once romantic and musical, to dream that he was a great composer; but actually to set up as a great composer and to give the concert at Lausanne, shows an unwillingness to discriminate between his fictitious and his real world that is plainly pathological. If not already a megalomaniac, he was even then on his way to megalomania."[32] As Babbitt said of Rousseau's imagination, "The striking fact is that, far more than Wordsworth, he held fast to his vision. He refused to adjust it to an unpalatable reality."[33] Babbitt said that Rousseau "is ready to shatter all forms of civilized life in favor of something that never existed, of a state of nature that is only the projection of his own temperament and its dominant desires upon the void."[34]

When Robespierre faced the reality of prerevolutionary France and concluded that it did not comport with his imaginary France, he was forced to adopt the position—one held by so many modern revolutionary movements—that certain elements in society had corrupted the virtue of the nation and must be purged. Society would be divided into the virtuous and vicious not on the basis of character but on the basis of class. Babbitt explained Robespierre's outlook: "The opposition that he established between the virtuous and the vicious is even less an opposition between virtuous and vicious individuals than between whole classes of individuals. The judging of men by their social groupings rather than by their personal merits and demerits, that seemed to Burke so iniquitous, has, as a matter of fact, been implicit in the logic of this movement from the French to the Russian Revolution."[35]

For the revolutionaries, the natural goodness of humanity could only be restored when those "calumniators" who were standing in the way were destroyed. Schama explained the revolution's justification for the Terror: "Inheriting from Rousseau (albeit in garbled form) the doctrine that government was a form of educational trust, the guardians of the Revolution meant to use every means possible to restore to a nation corrupted by the modern world the redemptive innocence of a presocial child. On the ruins of the monarchy, aristocracy and Roman Catholicism would sprout a new natural religion: civic, domestic and patriotic."[36] Babbitt quoted Danton, who explained the logic of the Terror in a pithier way: "These priests, these nobles are not guilty, but they must die, because they are out of place, interfere with the movement of things, and will stand in the way of the future."[37]

Rousseau's democratic theory, with its elimination of any the intermediate institutions that might divide the loyalties of citizens, Babbitt insisted, inevitably led to violent revolutions that targeted a "whole social strata that seemed to be made up of parasites and conspirators, in order that they may adjust this actual France to the Sparta of their dreams."[38] Babbitt argued that these types of revolutions consistently displayed conspiratorial tendencies because of the failure of their unrealizable dream world to emerge. The entire progression of Rousseau's Romanticism, Babbitt said, "lends color to the assertion that has been made that the last stage of sentimentalism is homicidal mania."[39]

The historical record, in fact, corroborates Babbitt's position that the revolutionary purging was not random violence or simply the targeting of political opponents. What was on display in revolutionary France was the systematic targeting of certain populations who, by the nature of their positions, were considered conspirators against the popular will. For example, 1,905 people were executed in the city of Lyon alone after a rebellion had taken place against the revolutionary government. These deaths were not the arbitrary result of people "caught up" in the violence but occurred because classes of people were systematically targeted because of the tenets of Jacobin ideology. As Schama explains, "They included, of course, many of the Lyonnais notability. . . . Aristocratic army officers, members of the rebel department of Rhone-et-Loire, federal magistrates and priests were all high on the list, as was anyone who could be associated with the capacious category 'the rich,' with 'merchants' or with any tradesmen or manufacturers accused by sans-culottes of economic crimes."[40]

Rousseau had embraced the dream of a democracy with an undifferentiated mass of citizens, none better than others. He rejected any aristocracy based on either lineage or merit. As Babbitt stated, "Rousseau is very hostile not only to any aristocracy in particular, but to the aristocratic principle in general. Humankind is made up of the people and what is not the people consists of so few that they do not count."[41] This rejection of the very idea of leadership creates a particular problem during revolutions, which by their nature must be led by someone. Therefore, in very Rousseauistic fashion, the leaders of the French Revolution declared that they were not influencing events but only acting as servants of the popular will. Robespierre, Babbitt said, "is not a real leader at all—only the people's 'hired man.' But at critical moments, in the name of an ideal general will, of which he professes to be only the organ, he is ready to impose tyrannically *his* will on the actual people."[42]

Yet, Babbitt argued, this denial of the need for leadership actually generated resentment in the lower classes of society, whose members suddenly viewed themselves as not deserving of their inferior position. Babbitt contrasted Rousseau's views on leadership in a democracy with classical philosophy: "Leadership of some kind Plato and Aristotle felt there must be, so that everything in the art of government hinges on getting the right quality of leadership. The total tendency of what they urge is to restrain the passions and appetites of the most intelligent members of a community, the tendency of what Rousseau urges is to inflame the passions and appetites of its least intelligent members."[43]

While Rousseauistic revolution rejected the idea of aristocratic leadership, religion also served as a particularly troublesome obstacle to the goals of the revolution, providing a reminder that citizens might well retain loyalties to something higher than the state. The Jacobins who sought the murder of priests and nobles as well as the de-Christianization of France to replace the old civilization with a new "civil religion" and "cult of reason" were simply good Rousseauists. For Rousseau, Christianity represented a threatening set of imaginative symbols that would divide the loyalties of human beings away from their duties as citizens. Rousseau's new civil religion, his new "creed," must replace any traditional religion, and that new civil religion, which would be imposed by the sovereign, was not tolerant of dissent. The spiritual substance of Christianity, which is the struggle between good and evil in the soul of the individual who is reaching for something eternal, had vanished in Rousseau. All that was left was religion as a deterrent force to keep order in society and support the sovereign state. Babbitt found the last chapter in Rousseau's *Social Contract* "in the highest degree hostile to Catholicism, inasmuch as even the aesthetic Catholic is unwilling to subordinate himself entirely to the state."[44]

Rousseau, Babbitt believed, had created a bastardized form of religion that served as a mere prop to the political order:

> The remedy is to get rid of historical Christianity, and not only to make the state supreme, but also to set up a state religion—a religion that was not to be, properly speaking, religious, but merely an "aid to sociability." . . . Rousseau would banish fear from religion entirely, and everything that is form and discipline being, as he holds, not the essence of religion, he would turn over to the state. The essence of religion he sees in a fluid emotionalism, and this a man may indulge in without having two fatherlands, without dividing his allegiance between the spiritual and the temporal order, as he must do if he remains a Christian in the traditional sense.[45]

The hostility toward religion among the French revolutionaries helped to foster Burke's strong distaste for the revolution, as he believed that civilization itself was not possible without true religion: "Nothing is more certain, than that our manners, our civilization, and all the good things which are connected with manners, and with civilization, have, in this European world of ours depended for ages upon two principles; and were indeed the result of both combined; I mean the spirit of a gentleman, and the spirit of religion."[46]

Rousseau's hostility to traditional Christianity was the philosophical antecedent to the anticlericalism and the systematic murder of the clergy during the French Revolution, Babbitt argued: "One immediately relates Rousseau's hostility to Christianity as a form of discipline quite apart from the state to the anticlericalism that has prevailed in France from the Revolution to the present day; and the connection of Rousseau's religious ideas with those of Robespierre, for example, is close and indubitable."[47] Robespierre was the revolution's enforcer of the civil religion. "Few facts are more certain, for example, than that the passage in the 'Contrat Social' on civil religion as interpreted by Robespierre sent many persons to the guillotine."[48]

In addition to purging aristocracy and Christianity, Rousseau also took particular aim at the wealthy. Babbitt linked Rousseau with modern egalitarian radicals and class warfare:

> One need scarcely be surprised that this and similar passages of the *Second Discourse* should still be a direct source of inspiration to the bomb-throwing anar-

chist. What one hears throughout this treatise, as elsewhere in Rousseau, is the voice of the angry and envious plebeian, who in the name of love is actually fomenting hatred and class warfare.... The crusader against social inequalities on Rousseauistic lines may easily become not merely an enthusiast but a fanatic.[49]

Revolutionary violence based on class warfare was an essential and oft-overlooked element of Rousseau. Rousseau's objection to property did not parallel Marx, although there certainly are intellectual linkages. Rousseau did not have a full-blown theory of dialectical materialism, but he did view the institutions of civilization as creations of a wealthy class that used them as mechanisms to suppress the natural goodness of the peasantry. A return to simple nature would be impossible when there existed a class of people who enjoy such largesse; a return to nature necessitated an attack on the wealthy. Babbitt explained the class warfare imperative at the heart of Rousseau:

> Now it is in the man of the plain people that the lively native impulse is least sicklied o'er by the pale cast of thought. "Love had he found in the huts where the poor men lie." As one ascends in the social scale, love diminishes, and as one approaches the top, it gives way to the opposite. As for the rich, Rousseau compares them to "ravening wolves, who having once tasted human flesh, refuse every other form of food, and henceforth desire to devour only men."[50]

Babbitt pointed out that Rousseau is quite clear in his writings that private property was one of the key institutions that destroyed the blissful state of nature:

> Just as in the old theology everything hinged on man's fall from God, so in Rousseau everything hinges on man's fall from nature. The first and decisive step in this fall and the source of social evils was, according to Rousseau's familiar account, the invention of private property in the form of property in land. With the invention of property, "equality disappeared" ... slavery and wretchedness were soon to spring up and grow with the crops." Misery, in short, is the result of industry.[51]

Not only was this class warfare the logical result of Rousseau's political philosophy, but, as Babbitt pointed out, it happened to be politically effective given that the rich never outnumber the poor and that Rousseau's ideas flattered and emboldened the poor. "The man at the bottom of the existing social order is flattered by being told that he is more virtuous, more fully possessed, in other words, of the spontaneous goodness of the state of nature than the man at the top. [Rousseau] owes no small part of his amazing influence to his flattery of the popular head as well as of the popular heart."[52]

Babbitt's analysis was that the revolutionary mind-set was connected to Rousseau's ethical philosophy because both encouraged humans to shed any check on their temperamental selves and to direct their ire at the traditions and conventions of civilization:

> Usually the brake on temperament is supplied by the ethos, the convention of one's age and country. I have tried to show elsewhere that the whole programme of the eccentric individualist is to get rid of this convention, whatever it may be, without developing some new principle of control. The eccentric individualist argues that to accept control, to defer to some centre as the classicist demands, is to cease to be himself. But are restrictions upon temperament so fatal to a man's being himself?[53]

Babbitt pointed to Edmund Burke as the most prescient analyst of this revolutionary psychology. Burke was often portrayed as a reactionary defender of tradition, almost a mountebank, who defended the old order for nefarious but unsaid reasons. But for Babbitt, "Burke was no mere partisan of the *status quo*. He was not opposed on principle to revolutions."[54] Babbitt understood that Burke was instead fundamentally opposed to the core philosophical principles of Rousseauistic Jacobinism.

Babbitt saw Burke's assault on the French Revolution as a profound philosophical critique of the Jacobin's view of human nature and of the dangerous mind-set of the revolutionary personality, not simply as a political polemic. If Burke "refused, therefore, to compromise with the French Revolution, the reason is to be sought less in the field of politics than in general philosophy, and even of religion. He saw that the Revolution did not, like other revolutions, seek to redress specific grievances, but had universal pretensions. France was to become the 'Christ of nations' and conduct a crusade for the regeneration of mankind."[55]

Babbitt argued that Burke saw that the revolutionary mind-set was fundamentally "subversive of the existing social order of Europe."[56] Revolutionaries would not stop when a handful of grievances were addressed; they would see all of the institutions that were the basis of European civilization as fundamentally illegitimate. Rousseau's revolutionary was not motivated by a naked power grab or a desire to steal. His was an ideological outlook that was the logical result of Rousseau's philosophical premises.

> The new revolutionary evangel was the final outcome of the speculations that had been going on for generations about a state of nature, natural rights, the social contract, and abstract and unlimited sovereignty. Burke is the chief opponent of this tendency toward what one may term metaphysical politics, especially as embodied in the doctrine of the rights of man. "They are so taken up with the rights of man," he says of the members of this school, "that they have totally forgotten his nature." Under cover of getting rid of prejudice they would strip man of all the habits and concrete relationships and network of historical circumstance in which he is actually implicated and finally leave him shivering "in all the nakedness and solitude of metaphysical abstraction."[57]

The revolutionary would weaken the historical bonds that unite citizens in a common civilization and, with anarchy and violence, make true community impossible. Babbitt argued that Burke had put his finger on the revolutionary nature of Rousseau's concept of the general will. If the fleeting impulses of popular opinion were the guide to the polity, men would lose their common inheritance and their sense of community: "By an unprincipled facility in changing the state such as is encouraged by Rousseau's impressionistic notion of the general will, the generations of men can no more link with one another than the flies of a summer."[58]

Burke emphasized that the institutions and traditions of civilization and religion were mechanisms to mitigate the human tendency toward disorderliness because they provided each citizen with conventions to revere that were above the ordinary self. "When antient opinions and rules of life are taken away, the loss cannot possibly be estimated. From that moment we have no compass to govern us; nor can we know distinctly to what port we steer."[59] As Babbitt concisely stated, "A man's first need is to look up to a sound model and imitate it."[60]

Burke argued that the atomistic and abstract concepts embodied in social contract theory pushed the human imagination to invent worlds that did not exist and represented a revolt against the institutions that are more grounded reminders of the reality of the human condition. This Romantic imagination was not "moral" but was so romanticized that it led to ruthless rebellions against institutions based on a false picture of reality. Human beings, Burke pointed out, never existed as unsociable and isolated noble savages who made abstract decisions about the legitimacy of society, contemplated the existence of natural rights, or decided whether to participate in society. Rather, he believed that human nature was and would always be sociable and that humans' thoughts, habits, and worldview could not and should not be abstractly ripped away from culture and tradition. According to Babbitt, "Burke is antiindividualistic in that he would not set the individual to trading on his own private stock of wit. He would have him respect the general sense, the accumulated experience of the past that has become embodied in the habits and usages that the superficial rationalist would dismiss as prejudice."[61]

Babbitt pointed out that Rousseau's form of liberty encouraged social anarchy as it sought to free individuals from any form of control, be it the outer control of law or the inner control of conscience.

> Rousseau, as he never tires of telling us, has a horror of every constraint upon his emotional impulse. He does not spurn merely certain barriers and limitations, but all barriers and limitations whatsoever. When he speaks of liberty, he does not mean, as a typical Englishman (let us say Burke) would mean, liberty defined and limited by law, but an undefined liberty that is tempered only by sympathy, which in turn is tempered by nothing at all. An undefined liberty and unselective sympathy are the two main aspects of the movement initiated by Rousseau—the poles between which it oscillates.[62]

Burke stated the problem quite simply: "The effect of liberty to individuals is, that they may do as they please: We ought to see what it please them to do, before we risque congratulations, which may be soon turned into complaints."[63] Babbitt added that this lack of limits was part and parcel of the imagination of the revolutionary: "A liberty that means only emancipation from outer control will result, I have tried to show, in the most dangerous form of anarchy—anarchy of the imagination."[64]

Rousseau insisted, of course, that unbridled liberty would not lead to anarchy because the overriding human passion was pity and sympathy for others. However, Babbitt warned, sympathy was not enough to restrain the dangers inherent in human nature: "Unfortunately, a formidable mass of evidence has been accumulating (the Great War was for many a convincing demonstration) that, in natural man as he exists in the real world and not in some romantic dreamland, the will to power is more than a match for the will to service."[65] Therefore, the loosening of every restraint through a licentious form of liberty would unleash revolutions. Babbitt warned, "This conception of love and liberty may very well cease to be a virtue and become a disease."[66]

Babbitt described the revolutionary disease born of Rousseau as "eleutheromania," which was defined "as the instinct to throw off not simply outer and artificial limitation, but all limitations whatsoever."[67] A lack of limits in the political order would by definition constitute anarchy and revolution. "For over a century the world has been fed on a steady diet of revolt. Everybody is becoming tinged with eleutheromania, taken up with his rights rather than his duties, more and more unwilling to accept limitations."[68]

Rousseau felt that just as temperamental individuals would be softened by natural pity, a disinterested general will would pacify temperamental democracies. Babbitt argued that Rousseau's desire to emancipate democracies from healthy constraints would not bring community but would unleash an unrestrained ego and a lust for power.

> The preliminary to achieving either of these ideals is that the traditional checks on human nature should be removed. But in exact proportion as this programme of emancipation is carried out what emerges in the real world is not the mythical will to brotherhood, but the ego and its fundamental will to power. Give a bootblack half the universe, according to Carlyle, and he will soon be quarreling with the owner of the other half. He will if he is a very temperamental bootblack.[69]

Babbitt argued that even "moderate" social contract theorists such as Locke had paved the way for the revolutionary. Social contract theory was based on the fanciful notion that individuals provide their consent to participate in society. This idea, Babbitt said, was corrosive to liberty. "The final superficiality of Locke is that he granted man abstract natural rights anterior to his duties, and then hoped that it would be possible to apply this doctrine moderately. But it has been justly said that doctrines of this kind are most effective in their extreme logical form because it is now in this form that they capture the imagination."[70]

Burke's concept of a moral imagination meant that unlike the revolutionary or even the moderate social contract theorist, human beings were not free to invent metaphysical worlds of the imagination that were unmoored from the reality of human existence. Reality imposed obligations. Burke said: "But I cannot stand forward, and give praise or blame to any thing which relates to human actions, and human concerns, on a simple view of the object, as it stands stripped of every relation, in all the nakedness and solitude of metaphysical abstraction. Circumstances (which some gentlemen pass for nothing) give in reality to every political principle its distinguishing colour, and discriminating effect."[71] And, human beings were, Burke insisted, particularly proscribed from actually carrying out a political program designed to bring these imaginary metaphysical worlds into existence through revolutionary action.

For Rousseau, in contrast, the invention of these metaphysical worlds and political action based on them was desirable and noble. As Babbitt explained, "Now the most salient trait of the sentimentalist is that he always has some lovely dream that he prefers to the truth. 'There is nothing beautiful,' Rousseau was fond of saying, 'save that which is not.'"[72]

Babbitt argued that Burke wanted imagination rooted in the reality of tradition since he "saw how much of the wisdom of life consists in an imaginative assumption of the experience of the past in such fashion as to bring it to bear as a living force in the present. The very model that one looks up to and imitates is an imaginative creation. A man's imagination may realize in his ancestors a standard of virtue and wisdom beyond the vulgar practice of the hour; so that he may be enabled to rise with the example to whose imitation he as aspired."[73]

However, neither Burke nor Babbitt blindly supported tradition and aristocracy. Innovations in the social order were indispensable to its health, but those innovations should be made slowly and with the utmost care because the institutions of society may have a latent wisdom that is not readily apparent to each new generation. Revolutions simply tear down institutions that may be indispensable supports to society's health. Babbitt insisted that Burke "would admit innovations in the social order only after a period of severe probation. He is no partisan of an inert traditionalism."[74]

Babbitt argued that traditions must be refreshed by each generation through vibrant and virtuous leaders who display a sound vision for society that would foster community and prevent revolution. In his analysis of the French Revolution, he pointedly criticized the hollow formalism of the French aristocracy, who failed to keep imaginative traditions alive. He believed, for example, that the court of Louis XIV was possessed by an artificial and unimaginative pomp and was not a worthy aristocracy. "It cannot be said that the decorous reserve of the French aristocracy that had been more or less imitated by other European aristocracies was in all respects commendable. According to this decorum a man should not love his wife, or if he did, should be careful not to betray this fact in public. It was also good 'form' to live apart from one's children and bad form to display one's affection for them."[75]

In the neoclassical theater enjoyed by the French aristocracy, "only the aristocracy had the right to appear in tragedy, whereas the middle class was relegated to comedy and the man of the people to farce."[76] The hollow formality and detachment of the French aristocratic culture, Babbitt argued, created a reaction in the form of emotional Romanticism, particularly in drama. "At no time have there been so many persons who, with streaming eyes, called upon heaven and earth to bear witness to their innate excellence.... [I]t had become almost a requirement of good manners to weep and sob in public."[77] What was lacking in the new Romantic drama was an ethical dimension. Great drama, said Babbitt, does not engage in "explicit moralizing" but provides a "scale of ethical values, or what amounts to the same thing, a sense of what is normal and representative and decorous, and the quality of the characters is revealed by their choices good or bad with reference to some ethical scale."[78]

There were neoclassical critiques of the Romantic revolt in art and literature, but the reaction against Romanticism failed to produce an imaginative defense of tradition. Babbitt argued that some of the French anti-Romantic writings defending the late Ancien Régime were, for example, totally inaccessible to foreigners, a sure sign that they were not sufficiently imaginative and did not portray anything with universal appeal. "What the foreigner objects to, on the other hand, may be summed up in the word artificiality, a pervading suggestion of the somewhat hollow pomp and grandiosity of the court of Louis XIV—an element, in short, that is pseudo-classic rather than truly classical."[79] In short, Babbitt agreed with Burke that an unimaginative defense of tradition would not be effective. There was always an obligation on the part of the defenders of civilization to remake the traditions in each generation in a new imaginative light. Without this, traditions become opaque, and societies would undermine their moral authority and risk revolution.

Leaders' role was to utilize the moral imagination to constantly renew society by preserving what is valuable in the past, not by wholesale renovations. Babbitt pointed to two famous quotes from Burke's *Reflections*: "'By preserving the method of nature in the conduct of the state, in what we improve we are never wholly new; in what we retain, we are never wholly obsolete.' 'The disposition to preserve, and ability to improve, taken together, would be my standard of a statesman.'"[80]

Babbitt contrasted Burke's thought with Rousseau's political philosophy, rooted in an affirmation of abstract equality and without reverence for anything higher. "The world of the *Social Contract*, no less than that of the Second *Discourse*, is a world without degree or subordination; a world in which no one looks up to anyone else or expects anyone to look up to him; a world in which no one (and this seems to Rousseau very desirable) has either to command or to obey."[81]

Some observers have commented that both Rousseau and Burke have what might be described as an anti-intellectual strain. Burke saw a latent wisdom in tradition that could not be fully understood even by the sharpest intellect, while Rousseau saw the deployment of the intellect as downright pernicious. Yet Babbitt argued that the "resemblance is, however, only superficial. The wisdom that Rousseau proclaimed was not *above* reflection but *below* it."[82] Rousseau's anti-intellectualism derived from his Romanticism and his desire to find "emancipation of temperament" that welcomes the "vital, dynamic and creative." So, "in direct proportion as he turns his attention to the infinite manifoldness of things he experiences wonder."[83] The Rousseauist, Babbitt said, was not seeking unity, not looking for a common center. The Rousseauist objected to anything that "interferes with the creative impulse of genius as it gushes up spontaneously from the depths of the unconscious. The whole movement is filled with the praise of ignorance and of those who still enjoy its inappreciable advantages—the savage, the peasant, and above all the child."[84]

For Babbitt, the difference between Rousseau and Burke was the "contrast between the superrational and the subrational."[85] Babbitt described the difference: "As a man grows religious, awe comes more and more to take the place in him of wonder."[86] What is distinctly human is the ability to experience awe and the superrational, not Rousseau's return to the natural world and the suppression of those institutions and traditions that bring an experience of something larger than self.

Babbitt theorized that a philosophy based on the worship of what is temperamental and impulsive in human nature would not serve as the basis of order and community but would bring revolt. Rousseau's Romantic idealism, his discounting of tradition, and his hostility to the intermediate institutions tended to foster resentments in the populace and revolutions, not orderly communities. Yet Babbitt also argued that even when democracies do not engage in full-blown revolutions, Rousseauistic characteristics might be apparent. Babbitt's list provides an interesting cultural commentary on the contemporary United States. The culture of this type of democratic society, Babbitt said, would exhibit contempt for tradition, especially traditions that encourage moderation and personal probity. In this type of democratic culture, personal virtue was a matter of indifference and even scoundrels would be feted as long as they expressed support for a sympathetic "cause," their moral indolence notwithstanding. In the law of this culture, society would ignore traditional legal precedents and legal rulings and would pander to popular fads and opinions, with laws proliferating wildly as a substitute for personal self-control. In politics, the goal of this society's politicians and their operatives would be to inflame popular opinion against adversaries, not to encourage thoughtful deliberation or moderation. In arts and letters, this society would produce art and literature dedicated to the expansive emotions and self-expression, not to classical balance and decorum; the arts would be simultaneously wonderful and trivial.

Babbitt highlighted the presence of these features in American society as a warning about the influence of Rousseau and the struggle within the American polity between two views of human nature and democracy. These features, if they continued to gain broader saliency, would cause the internal decomposition of American society.

The next task to consider is how such Rousseauistic democracies treat their neighboring nations. When Rousseau proclaimed in the *Social Contract* that "man is born free and he is everywhere in chains,"[87] he followed this sweeping proclamation with the question of how any government could be made "legitimate." The less-than-subtle implication was that all governments not based on Rousseauistic principles were illegitimate. If heartily embraced, Rousseau's ideas would, Babbitt argued, move democracies to imperialism.

CHAPTER 5

Democracy as Imperialism

> The humanitarian would, of course, have us meddle in foreign affairs as part of his program of world service. Unfortunately, it is more difficult than he supposes to engage in such a program without getting involved in a program of world empire.
>
> —Irving Babbitt, *Democracy and Leadership*

Rousseau's democratic theory, rooted in an emotional expansionism and a worship of the impulsive spirit, would inspire the French revolutionaries. In the domestic politics of France, their outlook fostered the belief that traditional institutions of civilization were an impediment to the flowering of the virtuous general will and would need to be destroyed. So the French revolutionaries went about destroying those institutions with brutal attacks on members of the royalty, aristocracy, clergy, and wealthy.

The Rousseauistic outlook also had important implications for the foreign policy of the revolutionary nation. For the revolutionaries, the conspirators against the flowering of popular will were not limited those within France. Other peoples and nations, the revolutionaries believed, were by definition enslaved everywhere that a Rousseauistic revolution had not occurred. By late 1791, the revolution in France had taken its logical turn—toward the conspirators against the rights of man not just within France, but abroad. As historian of the French Revolution Simon Schama said, "With these kinds of moral criteria in mind, nothing was easier than to represent the Declaration of Pillnitz as a direct affront to the sovereignty of the people, the first state of a counterrevolutionary warfare. 'A huge conspiracy against the liberty not only of France but of the whole human race' was being planned, said Hérault de Séchelles, ex-Parlementaire and eager Jacobin. But the brilliant light thrown by the Revolution would penetrate even the veil of obscurity which tyrants had thrown over their machinations."[1]

To the inflammatory speakers in the Jacobin Clubs, the foreign kings, priests, and aristocrats were as much the enemy as similar domestic conspirators. Schama pointed out that "the Declaration of the Rights of Man and Citizen and the assertions of natural rights on which the constitution was based were, by definition, universally applicable," and speakers in the assembly began to create new concepts of international order based on the "polarity between the free and the 'enslaved' nations."[2] With the discovery of the rights of man, Maximin Isnard, a prominent member of the assembly, declared that "[t]he French had become the foremost people of the universe, so their conduct must now correspond to their new destiny. As slaves they were bold and great; are they to be timid and feeble now that they are free?"[3] To the revolutionaries, the new democracy of France had transformed it into the exceptional, indispensable nation.

France therefore would not limit its ambitions to domestic revolution. Any monarch who did not submit to popular rule was, by Jacobin definition, a tyrant and despot, and these nations were declared to be enemies of the revolution. On Christmas Day 1791, Elie Guadet dramatically proclaimed to his colleagues in the assembly, "If the Revolution has already marked 1789 as the first year of French liberty, the date of the 1st of January 1792 will mark this year as the first year of universal liberty."[4] Only a handful of Jacobins, such as those immediately surrounding Robespierre, were skeptical of these internationalist ambitions. Schama captured Robespierre's prescient remarks about the dangers of international democratic crusading, thoughts that are quite relevant today: "'No one,' he stated prophetically, 'loves armed missionaries.'"[5] As war fever swept France, Robespierre's reservations would subside.

Faced with an increasingly tenuous grip on power and the rising call for an international crusade against tyrants, Louis XVI tried to save his throne by riding the wave of patriotic and imperialistic fervor and declaring war on Prussia and Austria. In early 1792, addressing the assembly "[i]n a flat, faltering voice Louis XVI then read the formal declaration of war as though it were a death sentence upon himself. Which indeed it was."[6]

And so began more than a decade of wars growing out of the revolution, conflagrations that at first were limited to Central Europe but that spread far beyond the Continent and brought the rise of an ambitious young military officer, Napoleon Bonaparte. The reign of Napoleon should be interpreted not as a hijacking of an otherwise idealistic revolution but as its culmination. While no doubt an opportunist throughout his life, Napoleon was nonetheless a loyal Jacobin who eagerly participated in the Jacobin Clubs. He was firmly anticlerical, anti-Christian, and antimonarchy. Indeed, he was the man who saved the revolution from being crushed in Paris in 1793 when he mowed down hundreds of royalist counterrevolutionaries with artillery fire, the famous "whiff of grapeshot." One recent biographer of Napoleon has pointed out that he "idolized Rousseau"; the young Bonaparte had written "a paean to *On the Social Contract*" and had adopted "Rousseau's beliefs that the state should have the power of life and death over its citizens, the right to prohibit frivolous luxuries and the duty to censor the opera and theatre."[7] Napoleon, in the fashion of a Rousseauistic leader, promised to govern not as a dictator but only as the instrument of the popular general will. In his coronation oath, Napoleon committed "to govern only in view of the interest, the wellbeing and the glory of the French people."[8]

The culmination of the revolution, as might have been expected of one inspired by Rousseau, was a patriotic militarism. Schama points out that "[m]ilitarized nationalism was not, in some accidental way, the unintended consequence of the French Revolution: it was its heart and soul. It was wholly logical that the multimillionaire inheritors of revolutionary power—the true 'new class' of this period in French history—were not some *bourgeoisie conquérante* but *real* conquerors." Therefore, when he took power in 1799 in a coup d'état, Napoleon was said to have remarked, "the Revolution is completed."[9]

Crusading imperialism wrapped in patriotism was the predictable outcome of an ideology that claimed to represent the only genuine embodiment of universal abstract rights. The revolutionaries believed that no nation or people should be denied these rights. The revolutionaries did not see their liberties as rooted in the historical institutions or cultural inheritances of France; these universal rights were the birthright of all nations and peoples, and the revolutionaries had a moral responsibility to spread those rights through war.

The wars of the late eighteenth and early nineteenth centuries were sometimes initiated by the messianic Jacobins and sometimes by Napoleon, while at other times they were waged preemptively by foreign monarchs who were well aware of the threat to their legitimacy represented by revolutionary ideology. In each case, however, the source of these conflagrations was the same: the ideology and will to power of Rousseauistic ideas. While there are certainly advocates of abstract rights who are not warlike, militant advocates of abstract rights tend toward international meddling, imperialistic ambitions, and perpetual warfare because they believe those rights are being suppressed by illegitimate tyrants and feel a moral obligation to intervene.

Moreover, imperialistic ambitions tend in turn to transform the domestic political landscape of the crusading nation. While the French revolutionaries had conducted domestic massacres, purges, and crackdowns in between 1789 and 1793, the murderous Reign of Terror can be fully understood only in the context of the French Revolutionary Wars. The Terror was largely a wartime crackdown on dissent, so common in history, to strengthen the home front after a series of setbacks on the battlefield. The Committee on Public Safety was created on April 6, 1793, as a result of a series of French military defeats. After spectacular losses at Neerwinden, at Louvain, and in the Rhineland, the most radical members of the assembly—those members led by Robespierre who sat in the so-called Mountain—believed that "there could be only one explanation for this sorry trail of disasters: conspiracy." Deputies from the Mountain argued that the defeats were related to treasonous conspiracies launched both at home and within the French army itself. A consensus was reached that the domestic machinery of surveillance and punishment needed to accelerate to prevent these conspiracies. "On March 11, a special Revolutionary Tribunal was established in Paris to try suspects accused of counter-revolutionary activities. . . . If guilty, they were to be shot within twenty four hours."[10] Within a month, the Committee of Public Safety would be created, and beginning in the fall of that year, the machinery for the Terror was put into place.

As a scholar of the French Revolution, Babbitt was intensely aware of how events developed in France and how a populist revolution had transformed itself into a military dictatorship. Recalling Burke's prescient predictions about the course of the revolution, Babbitt concluded that democracies of the Rousseauistic type were likely to become meddling menaces abroad and domestic tyrannies at home. Their metaphysical politics and their inflated sense of their own virtues led to messianic crusades internationally and to a police state at home. Ideological revolution, a suppression of civil liberties, and international imperialism were fruits of the same tree.

This chapter explores the development of Babbitt's concept of imperialism from his earliest writings to his latest in a rough chronological format, diverging from the approach of previous chapters to highlight how contemporary events and intellectual influences shaped Babbitt's thought on this key subject.

Although he was intellectually very consistent throughout his life, Babbitt did not write explicitly about imperialism early in his career. He began publishing articles in 1897, and his first book appeared in 1908, yet not until 1915 did he systematically lay out his theory of imperialism. Previously, he had written largely about French literature and the importance of a classical and humanities education, only gradually forming opinions about the political implications of Romanticism through the intersection of his literary scholarship and what he noticed in Rousseau's influence on the French Revolution. Once the Great War arrived on Babbitt's doorstep, he finally felt compelled to write specifically about imperialism in a two-part essay in the *Nation* (1915). Finally, Babbitt provided his most systematic explication of imperialism in one of his final books, *Democracy and Leadership*, which he decided to write because he believed that the deeper philosophical issues related to imperialism could not be adequately addressed in a shorter essay.

In his earliest book, *Literature and the American College*, Babbitt addressed the issue of war and peace indirectly by pointing out that if education has no ethical center and is largely grounded in utilitarianism or expansive emotion, the long-term result will be a warlike temperament in a nation's leaders. "A man may be a prodigy of energy and yet spiritually indolent. Napoleon showed his energy by conquering Europe; he would have shown his will if at the critical moment he had been capable of curbing his own lust for power (*libido dominandi*)."[11] As the Buddha said: "If one man conquer in battle ten thousand times ten thousand men, and another man conquer his own self, he is the greatest of conquerors."[12]

In *Literature and the American College*, Babbitt also argued that self-expression, the highest value of the Romantic education, was intellectually linked with Rousseauistic nationalism and the worship of national self-expression and self-assertion. "According to Herder every nation is to cultivate to the utmost its own national genius, and then, as an offset to this self-assertion, have a comprehensive sympathy for other national originalities. Nationalism is to be tempered by internationalism."[13]

In this early book, Babbitt laid out several of the ideas about human nature that ultimately undergirded his theory of imperialism and that contrasted with the premises of Romanticism. For Babbitt, the temperamental self-expression of the Romantic tended to divide people, not unite them. Moreover, emotional pity and sympathy for one's fellow human beings would not be a sufficiently powerful sentiment to unite people in peace. Years before the League of Nations and United Nations, Babbitt predicted that an internationalism founded on sentimental Rousseauistic principles would fail to keep the peace.

Our modern cosmopolitanism is simply one form of Rousseau's attempt to substitute sympathy for restraint as the foundation of ethics. Any one who believes that the instincts for brotherhood are strong enough to prevail unaided over the egoistic instincts in the relations between man and man may readily believe in a similar altruistic triumph in international relations. But in the eyes of the old-fashioned moralist there is something chimerical in the underlying assumption of the Rousseauist.[14]

While he never formulated an explicit theory of democratic imperialism in this first book, Babbitt began to make the connection between the influence of Romantic ethics and military adventurism. In the closing paragraphs of *Literature and the American College*, Babbitt pointed to two character types Plato described in *The Statesman*. The first type is full of "motion and energy," whereas the second exhibits "rest and quietness." While no city can prosper "where either of these two types is wanting," there is greater danger from the energetic leader who has no ethical center. While Babbitt's contemporary educational theorists were worshipping the man of action, Babbitt said that: "It would seem that they might recognize the claims of the contemplative life without encouraging a cloistered seclusion or falling into the monastic abuses of the past." Plato laid out the danger of the focused man of action: "For strenuousness when it gains excessive mastery, 'may at first bloom and strengthen, but at last burst forth into downright madness,' and is especially likely, Plato adds elsewhere, to involve a state in wars with all its neighbors."[15]

Babbitt's theory of imperialism was further developed in his next book, *The New Laokoon*. Later in life, he described *The New Laokoon* as an attempt to "exhibit the anarchy that has supervened in literature and the arts with the progressive decline of standards. Superficially, this anarchy seems above all an anarchy of the emotions. On closer scrutiny, however, emotional anarchy itself turns out to be a sign of something subtler and more dangerous—anarchy of the imagination."[16] *The New Laokoon* was Babbitt's least political book and was largely dedicated to detailed discussions of literary criticism and aesthetics as well as aspects of Romantic literature and neoclassicism. Taking the position that tradition and creativity must be combined, Babbitt pointed to Mozart as finding the golden mean: he "obeys musical law spontaneously, being in this respect at the opposite pole from some of our modern artists who, under the pretext of being original and expressive, merely succeed in violating law laboriously."[17]

Babbitt's views on aesthetics in *The New Laokoon* provided hints of his rising concerns about the political influence of Romanticism. For example, Babbitt pointed to Romanticism's "subliminal uprush or overflow of emotion" as assuming "forms" such as the "German Storm and Stress" and "the French Revolution."[18] Babbitt's ethical critique of Romanticism as fostering a revolutionary outlook was a subtle theme throughout *The New Laokoon*.

Toward the end of the book, however, Babbitt addressed these political overtones more explicitly when he offered his view that the kind of decadent democracy produced by Romantic ethics would ultimately produce revolution and imperial ambition. The naturalistic ethics of Romanticism had bred the type of man who would "engage in miscellaneous expansion and back it up if need be with noisy revolt against all the forms of the past."[19] The danger for politics was that this "apostle of everlasting expansion . . . is rendering inevitable a concentration that will not be humane, but of the military and imperialistic type peculiar to epochs of decadence. When the traditional checks and inhibitions finally disappear and the *élan vital* gets under way on a grand scale, with no countervailing *frein vital*, the only law that can decide which nation or which individual is to expand vitally or unrestrained is the law of cunning or the law of force."[20]

In a footnote that captures his emerging theory of imperialism, Babbitt presciently tied his concerns about Rousseauistic ethics to contemporary events: "The humanitarian will of course reply that all this expansion will be sufficiently tempered by an increase in altruism. Unfortunately evidence is as yet rather scanty that the human nature of the future is going to differ so radically from the human nature of the past. To illustrate concretely, the growth of international good will does not seem to reassure the English entirely regarding the vital expansion of Germany."[21] By 1910, when this passage was written, with alliances forming in Europe in the lead-up to World War I, the emerging crisis undoubtedly caused Babbitt to begin thinking more carefully about questions of war and peace and the intellectual and moral origins of imperialism.

Babbitt's next book, *The Masters of Modern French Criticism*, was published in 1912.[22] In his later summary of *Masters*, Babbitt said he wanted to "carry a stage farther my defense of critical humanism."[23] He argued that when traditional standards are weakened, human beings do not have general rules of conduct to follow and thus face the task of finding right behavior on their own without guidance from society. The breakdown of traditional conventions leaves human beings without reliable guideposts. In this situation, the everyday ethical tasks for individuals become more challenging, and people find that they "must rely on the critical spirit in direct ratio to the completeness of his break with the traditional unifications of life."[24] In ethics, the weakening of outer standards of conduct obliges greater personal introspection.

In an important passage that contains one of Babbitt's foundational thoughts about imperialism, he said that the "special theme of *The Masters* is the problem of the one and the many and the failure of Saint-Beuve and other eminent French individualists to deal with it adequately and so to achieve standards in a modern fashion."[25] Babbitt was pointing to what he believed was a metaphysical error in Romanticism, with the practical result that the French Romanticists desired to shake off the rules of society without replacing them with standards that might point human beings back to a common ethical center.

In *Masters*, Babbitt offered one possible antidote to this Romantic societal anarchy: the Eastern religions, which offered human beings the opportunity to find common ground through ethical work performed within themselves and not given from the outside as a set of dogmas. Babbitt's scholarship on Eastern religions was important in shaping his theory of imperialism because of their simple doctrine that human beings come together and form a peaceful community only when they have controlled their will. Those who are not exercising their higher will, according to the Buddha, are "asleep" and are in need of being "Awakened."[26] "Men tend to come together in proportion to their intuitions of the One; in other words, the true unifying principle of mankind is found in the insight of its sages. We *ascend* to meet."[27]

Masters, like *The New Laokoon*, was generally little concerned with politics. In his third and final chapter on Saint-Beuve, however, Babbitt repeats the theme that naturalism in ethics would begin in idealism and end in imperialism.

> The culmination of the political Romanticism in the Revolution of 1848 was followed by sudden and violent disenchantment. The fairest millennial visions had collapsed at the first contact with reality. The "idealists" had had an abrupt descent from the clouds, and lay bruised and bleeding upon the earth. What really goes with the naturalistic view of life is imperialism. Those who would set up as idealists and at the same time live on the naturalistic level simply hasten the triumph of the opposite cause to that they are preaching.[28]

The popular uprising in 1848 in France had ended in the ascension and dictatorship of Louis Napoleon Bonaparte and the abolishment of the French Parliament, another popular government ended by an idealistic revolution.

Babbitt connected this rise in idealistic revolutionary fervor—followed by an imperialistic strongman in 1851—with similar events in 1789. "Saint-Beuve says that the example of Napoleon had done much to corrupt the nineteenth century and encourage the cult of mere force even in literature. But Napoleon himself is only the ironical reply of the Nature of Things to the Utopias of the French Revolution."[29]

At the end of *Masters*, Babbitt again linked naturalistic ethics with imperialism. "A naturalistic age, whatever it may set out to be, will end up by being imperialistic."[30] With the collapse of the church and other institutions that upheld outer standards of behavior, Babbitt argued, the best opportunity for the West to recover morality was to develop a sound individualism in which moral unity is found within the individual. Inner standards must replace the outer standards that had been lost. The situation facing the West, he argued, was akin to the situation faced by Socrates when the sophists had destroyed the outer standards of Greek culture: "the great effort of Socrates, we are told, was to recover that firm foundation for human life which a misuse of the new intellectual spirit was rendering impossible."[31] A culture that had lost its standards would, he argued, inevitably progress to decadent imperialism.

Babbitt regularly cited anecdotes about imperialism from ancient times, but he viewed modern imperialism as more dangerous because of the cult of emotionalism propagated by Rousseau. "To the excessive mental suppleness of the sophists there is often added to-day an undue emotional pliancy. If some remedy is not found the modern world will, like the ancient Greek world, become the prey of the sophists. It will progress, not as our humanitarians would have us believe towards 'some far-off divine event,' but towards a decadent imperialism. What principle can set the bounds to all this intellectual and emotional expansiveness?"[32]

After the publication of *Masters*, Babbitt penned several shorter works: a book review on Rousseau's writings, an essay on the "Bicentenary of Diderot," and a review of an essay on Romanticism by his friend Paul Elmer More.[33] These writings captured previous themes on scientific and humanitarian naturalism, on the threat to civilization by abstract assertions of equality, on Rousseau's concept of that state of nature, and on the revolutionary nature of Rousseau's writings. He did not, however, reference his concept of democratic imperialism.

He picked up on the theme of imperialism again as he was researching his most famous book, *Rousseau and Romanticism*, and as the war drums were beating loudly in Europe. Contemporary events seem to have influenced Babbitt to use the insights from his research on the book to draft an essay explicitly linking Romanticism and imperialism. The result was a very important two-part essay article in which he systematically argued that the breakdown of the contemporary international order was intimately related to the success of Romanticism in the West. According to historian Richard Gamble, the essay "spoke directly to the West's moral crisis that had culminated with such force in the Great War."[34]

In early 1915, he shared the drafts of that essay with More, who was a prolific essayist and philosopher. More did not approve of the early draft, writing that he was "pretty sure" that he would not "get it printed in its present form" because he had "sown the full sack, and thought more of what was in" his mind than what the "reader could take *and put together*." Babbitt, it seemed, had contemplated sending the essay to the *Atlantic Monthly*, whose editor, Ellery Sedgwick, was a friend of More's. More told Babbitt that "possibly Sedgwick will not agree with me, but I suspect he will. I feel pretty sure that he would demand an abridgement by a fourth or third."

More advised Babbitt to trim the piece back significantly and to focus on a handful of the most important ideas, such as nationalism, humanitarianism, and expansionism: "You will gather from these criticisms that I judge the essay as a whole very harshly. Well, in one way I do, in another I do not." More believed that the subject matter was very important, given current events: "The season is ripe for such a paper as you can make out of this, and I hope you can work it over. The idea of Nationalism, to my mind, is the special thing much considered today and gives you an admirable handle for your propaganda."[35]

Babbitt replied to More a month later, confessing that "your criticism of my own paper was so drastic that it has quite put me out of conceit with it." Despite More's criticism, however, Babbitt had not attempted to make any changes in the essay and was not certain how to proceed. The problem was that the essay was grappling with the issue of "putting conduct on a positive and critical basis," which Babbitt called "my plea for humanism"; cutting out "illustrative material" would not be difficult, but the important discussion of humanism "is less easy to correct." Babbitt seemed to then offer the thought that an adequate discussion of humanism "needs to be developed in a book rather than an article; it would require a pretty thorough review of the present situation in philosophy."[36] This self-suggestion was probably the basis for his later book, *Democracy and Leadership*.

But Babbitt did not give up on the essay. He submitted it to the *Yale Review*, whose editors asked that he trim the article significantly, to about a thousand words. On April 27, 1915, Babbitt told More that he was not willing to trim the paper but that he had the idea to break the essay into two parts and submit it to the *Nation*, where More had been an editor from 1909 to 1914.[37] More apparently did not offer to assist in placing the essay at the *Nation*: Babbitt wrote two months later that "I finally decided to withdraw my war paper from the *Yale Review* and give it to the *Nation*. Your criticism of it was so severe that for a time I had about determined to suppress it entirely and I am somewhat nervous about seeing it in print, as it is." According to Babbitt, the editor at the *Nation* seemed to have been "very nervous about accepting it, not apparently because of doubts about the intrinsic quality of the article itself, but of fear as to how it might be taken by" Oswald Garrison Villard, the *Nation*'s owner and publisher and the founder of the American Anti-Imperialist League, an organization that sought to roll back the US annexation of territories such as the Philippines.[38] The subject matter of Babbitt's piece must have been of great interest to Villard, a prominent antiwar activist.

Babbitt's essay was finally published in the *Nation* under the title "The Breakdown of Internationalism" on June 17 and 24, 1915. A comparison of the published essay and Babbitt's original draft manuscript indicates that despite More's concerns, the published essay had undergone only limited editing.[39] Outside of removing a couple of sentences and a paragraph with detailed statistics on US homicides, the *Nation* editors removed only one major section of the manuscript.

The excised section featured Babbitt's prognostications on the future of Russia. He speculated that the next Alexander the Great would likely come out of Russia, which "would seem, more than any other country, to be qualified for world empire."[40] In this excised section, Babbitt also coined the term *over-civilization*. The nations of Western Europe, he asserted, were displaying symptoms of over-civilization such as declining birth rates. He defined over-civilized nations as "those in whom the growth of character and self-control has not kept pace with the emancipation of the intellect and emotions."[41] The *Nation* editors likely deleted this section because Babbitt closed his discussion of Russia by declaring that "speculations of this kind are highly uncertain at best, and on the part of one like myself who can lay claim to no special knowledge of Russia, perhaps wholly unprofitable."[42]

Events in Europe and Babbitt's extensive knowledge of Romantic literature converged in this essay, which included many passages that eventually found their way verbatim into *Rousseau and Romanticism*.[43] The many phrases common to the *Nation* article and *Rousseau and Romanticism* are a clear sign that Babbitt's research on Romanticism was what generated his theories on international relations. The article contained all the themes about Romanticism that are found in his earlier works but had never been previously presented as a systematic theory.[44]

The essay's title, "The Breakdown in Internationalism," must be read in two ways. While a breakdown had occurred in the relations between nations, the more profound problem was that a Romantic view of life had caused a breakdown in the relations between individuals. "Every one, beginning with the Germans themselves, seems to be losing sight of the fact that, before being Germans, the Germans are human beings."[45]

Babbitt also made clear in his subtitle, "The Relation of the War to the Movement Initiated by the French Revolution," that there was a clear intellectual line from the French Revolution to the ongoing Great War.

> The cry of the revolutionary army, "Vive la nation," heard by Goethe in a pause of the cannonading at Valmy, was rightly taken by him to mark the dawn of a new era. The beginnings of the very type of warfare we are now witnessing in Europe, that is, the coming together of whole nations for mutual massacre (*la levée en masse*), go back to this period. This type of warfare is therefore the final outcome of a propaganda for the establishment of universal brotherhood. The new national enthusiasm supplied France with soldiers so numerous and so spirited that she not only repelled her invaders, but began to invade other countries in turn, theoretically on a mission of emancipation.[46]

Babbitt began the article by reminding the readers about the nature of Jacobin ideology. Unlike the English Revolution of 1688, he said, the French Revolution had international ambitions. The declaration of the heretofore undiscovered universal rights of man, Babbitt said, would in one stroke "practically put in question the legitimacy of all existing European governments [and] inspired in the revolutionary leaders a policy that was felt by these governments themselves as intolerable meddling."[47]

Rather than bringing peace and brotherhood, the Romantic assumptions about human nature turned out to be "violently centrifugal," producing first the Terror and then Napoleon. As Babbitt ironically pointed out:

The passion for humanity that marked the dawn of the French Revolution culminated not merely internationally, but nationally as well, in imperialism. The triumph of brotherhood over traditional control was symbolized by the Federation on the Champ de Mars, when a vast multitude embraced, not merely figuratively, but literally. But here again we are confronted with a strange irony. Many of the very men who had embraced were guillotining each other not many months afterwards.[48]

Babbitt linked the rabid nationalism on display during the Great War with the French Revolution. "'The sentiment of nationalities,' says Renan, 'is not a hundred years old.' And he adds that this sentiment was created in the world by the French Revolution."[49] Babbitt then pointed to German culture, or *Kultur*, as the penultimate expression of this Romantic nationalism. Under the influence of French Romanticism, German culture had decomposed from the age of Kant to the age of "nationalism" under Bismarck to the present "age of imperialistic aggression." In tracing the French-German intellectual connection, Babbitt pointed to Nietzsche, who "was under special obligation for his gospel of force to Stendhal and his cult of Napoleon, that more or less openly avowed model of all supermen."[50]

Babbitt specifically referenced a recent book on the influence of French Romanticism on German thought as he discussed the new "Teutonic temperament."[51] The denial of the "civil war in the cave" propagated by French Romanticism had later manifested itself in German culture in the belief that the German soul is naturally virtuous. "Fichte says that there is no special word for character in German, because to be German and to have character are synonymous; character is something that gushes up without any conscious effort on his part from the primordial depths of a German's being."[52] The "monstrous flattery of the Teutonic temperament" was a haunting reminder of the monstrous self-flattery of Romantic writers who gushed about their inspired and visionary natures.[53]

This expansive flattery of the German soul, Babbitt said, demonstrated a self-flattery and a lack of ethical concentration that would inspire enmity because, as Goethe said, "everything that emancipates the intellect without a corresponding growth in self-control is pernicious" and it is akin to "unstrapping the devil."[54] In the modern world, this unstrapping of the devil was an acute problem since in a nation such as Germany, there are "sixty-seven millions of highly vitalized people" who are "confined in a territory of moderate fertility about half the size of Texas."[55]

Babbitt argued that the rest of Western Europe had been under the spell of Romanticism, and he pointed to the futility of the humanitarian peacemaking schemes that were floated at the time. He added that all of these proposals for world peace were premised on the idea that nations would come together either on the basis of sympathy or for utilitarian reasons. Appeals for peace on these grounds were bound to fail. For an example of such a scheme, he pointed to a statistician, Roger W. Babson, later the founder of Babson College, who created a mathematical model to demonstrate the financial advantages of peace over war.

The philosophical flaw in these humanitarian plans, Babbitt said, was that it was not possible to find genuine unity on the basis of sympathy or material advantage. "The problem of adjusting the relations between highly expansive individuals and nationalities is indeed the modern problem *par excellence*. . . . According as the humanitarian is emotional or rationalistic he assumes that the clashes which occur between different individuals or different states can be sufficiently mitigated by an appeal either to the principle of sympathy or to that of enlightened self-interest."[56]

For Babbitt, appeals to sympathy and self-interest were not strong enough tonics to prevent war: "on supreme occasions they fail."[57] The humanitarian understanding of human nature was naive and shallow, failing to take into account the primordial emotions that rise to the surface when leaders of nations consider questions of war and peace. Leaders of nations must possess a strong countervailing ethic to avoid being overcome by warlike emotion. "On such occasion men are not governed by cool reflection as to what pays, but by their passions and imagination; and the appeal that the emotional pacifist can make to their passions and imagination in the name of humanity at large, turns out to be pale and unsubstantial compared with the appeal of nationality. That, no doubt, is why the record of the advocates of peace on humanitarian lines has been a long series of failures."[58]

To buttress his point about sympathy not representing a strong enough countervailing force to war, Babbitt pointed to historical examples of pacifistic schemes that were followed by brutal wars. The French philosophe Abbé de St. Pierre, for example, offered one of the first internationalist schemes in his *Project for an Everlasting Peace in Europe*, which called for European disarmament and a council to arbitrate disputes. As Babbitt pointed out, this proposal was soon followed by the wars of Frederick the Great. Likewise, the French Revolutionary and Napoleonic Wars almost immediately followed Kant's essay on

"Perpetual Peace." In Babbitt's era, pacifists also saw their advocacy fail and had to watch the unfolding of the Great War. Elsewhere, Babbitt later wrote that he did not see the philosophy of Gandhi as an antidote to the "mass production and mechanical efficiency" that were helping to bring so much death to the battlefields of the West. "There is much in the teaching of Gandhi, however, that is more suggestive of Tolstoy than of the genuine Oriental seer."[59]

This essay represents the first detailed connection that Babbitt made between the idyllic imagination of Romanticism and the conspiratorial mindset that is the hallmark of idealistic political movements.[60] When the idealistic dream world of the Romantic humanitarian meets reality, Babbitt said, the failure of the theory is blamed not on its unreality but on an opposing conspiracy. During the French Revolution, the failure of the Jacobins to achieve universal fraternity was blamed on priests and nobles. In contemporary Europe, the humanitarians had found a new conspirator who had prevented the flowering of peace: "Thus the arch-conspirators for the early humanitarians were the kings and priests who sat on the lid, as it were, and so kept the natural goodness and peacefulness of man from manifesting itself. For many contemporary humanitarians, Germany has become the traitor nation that France became, after her invasion of Switzerland, for the humanitarians of the eighteenth century."[61]

Humanitarians, he said, also pointed to another conspirator responsible for the Great War: "Another and extraordinarily naïve type of contemporary humanitarian thinks that there would be an end of war if we could only get rid of the 'Armament Trust.'"[62] The armaments industry, Babbitt believed, had developed from the worship of efficiency and material power; however, the industry itself was not the cause of war but merely an outgrowth of the general ethical confusion of the West. That moral confusion was a humanitarian worship of science and impulse with no countervailing ethic. In one of Babbitt's most famous turns of phrase, he said that the combination of naive idealism and utilitarian efficiency "seems too much like picnicking on a battlefield."[63] And "the present alliance between emotional romanticists and utilitarians is a veritable menace to civilization itself."[64] Babbitt insisted that the decisive philosophical event that had given birth to this picnicking on a battlefield was Rousseau's idyllic quest to return human beings to a blissful state of nature where man's natural goodness would return. These utopian fantasies ignored the human propensity to assert a will to power, and "[m]en were interrupted in their wanderings over fair Arcadian meads by a sudden explosion of hell-fire. In like manner the 'evangelical' Republic of 1848 gave way with disconcerting suddenness to a brutal imperialism."[65]

These humanitarian errors were rooted not in flawed theories of international affairs but at a deeper level in wholesale misunderstandings of human nature and the qualities that bring order to society. Humanitarian naturalism, which encourages personal expansionism, a kind of "Promethean individualism," does not succeed in bringing people together in community. A culture of Promethean individualism, in fact, is more likely to promote imperialistic leaders and create discord among nations. Babbitt explained this error using the classical anthropological principle: "The expansive view of life is plainly not the peaceful view. It does not establish peace and unity among different nationalities, it does not establish peace and unity among members of the same nationality, it does not establish peace and unity—and this is the root of the whole matter—in the breast of the individual."[66] If people were seeking a peaceful world, Babbitt said, the culture must "repudiate the spirit of Napoleon and recover the spirit of Christ."[67]

Toward the end of his *Nation* essay, Babbitt returned to the French Revolution and other historical examples of nations and cultures that had lost their moral bearings and become imperialistic. Ancient Greek civilization, despite its humanistic civilizational traditions, had become decadent when "the expansive instincts of the different states and of individuals in each state tended to run wild."[68] The Peloponnesian War Babbitt called "an unpardonable crime against this civilization."[69] The exhaustion of Greek civilization in an orgy of war had, for Babbitt, its strong parallel in Europe's own cultural suicide as embodied in the Great War: "There is a certain likeness between the present war and the Peloponnesian War—both wars of commercial and imperialistic expansion."[70]

Babbitt argued that the decline of Greek culture had begun with a similar Romanticism in the arts and letters embodied in thinkers such as Aristophanes. "'Whirl is king,' exclaimed Aristophanes, 'having driven out Zeus.' The worship of the god Whirl was indeed erected by some of the sophists into a philosophy."[71] Aristophanes, who worshiped "change and novelty and motion," was the predecessor of modern Romanticism.[72] Romantic thinkers such as Henri Bergson later paralleled Aristophanes by advocating a dive "into the everlasting flux."[73] Babbitt believed that decadence, ancient and modern, shared a similar "spiritual joy-riding" and "all these writers and thinkers were alike in their expansiveness, in their exaltation of vital impulse over vital control. The final drift of the modern world, if it follows such leaders, will be like that of the ancient Greek world, toward a decadent, or, if the reader prefers, an irrational imperialism."[74]

What marks epochs of decadence is not universal brotherhood but a "noisy revolt against all forms of the past" as well as the appearance of leaders "of the military and imperialistic type" who, without ethical concentration, operate "unrestrained" utilizing the "law of cunning or the law of force."[75] In the case of ancient Greece and Rome, the attempts at rehabilitation were not successful, and both democracies, Babbitt pointed out, were "swept . . . towards the abyss of decadent imperialism."[76]

Babbitt then moved to consider what might arrest this decadent imperialism. For him, it seemed certain that the only solution would be a "recovery of the disciplinary virtues, the virtues of concentration."[77] The larger question was "on what basis these disciplinary virtues should rest if they are to be successfully rehabilitated."[78] Should an appeal be made to older traditions in the nation? Would a religious revival or a resuscitation of Puritanism suffice to restore them? Babbitt replied that nostalgia would not suffice: "Do not dream of an impossible return to the past, Socrates said in substance."[79]

An imaginative recovery of these disciplinary virtues might, he argued, create a true "internationalism" in which people are united based on what they have in common "from a truly human point of view."[80] The disciplinary virtues could be recovered only through a new humanism that would assert a "special law for human nature as opposed to the natural law."[81] It seemed unlikely that modern humans would rely on the authority of religion or tradition, so a recovery of these virtues would have to be put on a "positive and critical basis." What would be required was a dramatic break from the current "convention," a break with the "organized common-sense of the community in which one lives" and the adoption of a "commoner sense."[82]

At the conclusion of the *Nation* article, Babbitt made the explicit link between Romantic ethics and imperialism. Failure to control the will had generated in modernity an undisciplined imagination, and in the process, reality and common sense were slipping away from contemporary politics. The Romantic "bohemian" had asserted that he would not submit the "free play of his imagination" to tradition or to anything "so philistine as common sense."[83] But, Babbitt retorted, the "great poets and sages" had exhibited "inspired and imaginative good sense. . . . The opposition between imagination and common-sense is one of the most vicious assumptions of the modern movement."[84] Babbitt believed that a revival was possible, but only through sound leaders who were willing to impose the disciplinary virtues and who then could, through an act of imagination, set a standard to which people would look up. Leaders possessing a sound imagination would be essential to restoring more sensible politics.

A central premise of the *Nation* essay was that restoring a sound understanding of human nature was an essential first step in reviving the West. The rehabilitation of the disciplinary virtues was not simply a process of persuading people to change their behavior by presenting facts that are unknown. "Right knowing does not always insure right doing, as Socrates seems to say, but it is surely an indispensable preliminary."[85]

As he had intimated to More, Babbitt developed his ideas in ethics, aesthetics, and politics and on the problem of an overreliance on reason in much greater detail in *Democracy and Leadership*. But Babbitt had reached the clear conclusion by 1915 that for the sake of the Western world, the proper roles of will and imagination needed to be restored. Humanitarian idealists, Babbitt said, would not confine their imagination to the world that actually exists but instead would reach out and create a world that they wished to have exist. And simultaneous with the creation of fantasy worlds, idealists would feel no obligation to control their appetites. "Under cover of working a great good, the elevating of society," he explained, humanitarian idealists were "in danger of working a still greater evil—the undermining, namely, of the individual's sense of responsibility and spiritual self-reliance."[86] This type of idealism had a direct relationship with Rousseau's ersatz definition of virtue as an expansive emotion. In the *Confessions*, for example, Rousseau "declares war . . . in the name of what he conceives to be his true self—that is his emotional self—against decorum and decency."[87]

Babbitt said that the humanitarian activists were conveniently exempting themselves from the laws of decency and decorum. In Christian terms, this Romantic idealism had an antinomian quality that would lead to national and international meddling. "A suffragette who pours acid into a letter-box or mutilates a masterpiece with a meat-cleaver is convinced, whatever else she may be in doubt about, that she is an idealist." However, this type of idealism, "if scrutinized Socratically, would turn out to mean not much more than a meddler or busybody or downright anarchist."[88]

A sound humanist, in contrast, recognized that "man attains to the truth of his nature only by imposing decorum upon his ordinary self."[89] The secular antinomian quality of the humanitarians was a genuine threat to civilization as "all the terms expressive of the higher values of human nature are in danger of being discredited."[90] The idealist who throws off restraint, even for the sake of social causes, inevitably moves to a desire to dominate others—to imperialism.

Babbitt concluded the *Nation* essay by laying out a theme that would dominate *Democracy and Leadership*: a democracy that has thrown off the disciplinary virtues will always be in danger of developing into an international menace. Babbitt saw a grave error in the view that democratic societies were inherently peaceful. In fact, democracies would become most menacing and imperialistic when their leaders viewed political legitimacy as based on the free expression of unchecked popular opinion; imperialism rooted in popular passions was no different from the imperialism of the tyrant. Just as individuals who acted temperamentally and impulsively would inevitably crash into those around them, the plebiscitary democracy would inevitably crash into neighboring nations. As Babbitt summarized,

> Take the word democracy itself. At the very sound of the word we are supposed to cease discriminating and fall into a state of vague emotional exaltation. Yet what is valuable in democracy can be saved only by the utmost keenness of discrimination. We are being told that a remedy for war will be found in more democracy. If by more democracy is meant more radical democracy, the obvious reply is that radical democracy has in the past proved to be anything but a peaceful form of government. It has been at least as prone to quarrel with its neighbors as any other form, and its citizens have been peculiarly prone to quarrel with each other. As a result of these civil convulsions, most experiments in democracy, ancient, mediaeval, and modern, have tended by stages very familiar to the student of history to pass over into imperialism.[91]

In this passage, Babbitt crystallized his argument about democratic imperialism. A democracy was not necessarily any more warlike than other forms of government, he said, but democracies, more than other forms of government, must feature leaders whose character served as a restraining influence on popular passions. "A democracy that would get rid of all veto powers and take popular sovereignty to mean the immediate putting into effect of the shifting will of a numerical majority simply reproduces on a larger scale the case of the individual who would get rid of the veto power in his own breast and follow impulse; except that a state can afford even less than an individual to live impulsively."[92]

American society, Babbitt argued, had more and more exhibited the ethics of the humanitarian idealist rather than the humanist, and this political culture portended a future of meddling both in the lives of fellow citizens and in the affairs of other nations. Muckraking journalism, for example, encouraged Americans to turn "away from themselves and . . . to point an accusing finger at nearly everybody else." Rather than an understanding that liberty was rooted in personal probity, popular American legislatures had sought to micromanage every aspect of human behavior: "This multiplication of laws seems to have been attended by a decrease in the law-abiding spirit."[93] Rather than religious or humanistic self-control, Babbitt pointed to "the humanitarian legalist who passes innumerable laws for the control of people who refuse to control themselves."[94] Babbitt pointed out that little of this humanitarian meddling had fostered domestic tranquillity: crime in the United States had exploded, American popular tastes were increasingly vulgar, and the American educational system had failed to establish "habits of sound reading and reflection" so that the entire "educational system sometimes strikes one as an immense whir of machinery in the void."[95]

In response to this increasing domestic chaos, Babbitt continued, American leaders had not responded with a call to return to the disciplinary virtues. Instead, there was the belief that the solution could be found in philanthropy or social crusades.

> The divergence is radical between those who tell us that our prime concern should be to raise the general level of society by philanthropic endeavor and those who tell us to make sure first that our society has leaders who have imposed upon their impulses the yoke of the human law, and so have become moderate and sensible and decent. In the last analysis, what a man owes society is not his philanthropy, but his good example; and he can set this example only by practicing the virtues in due proportion, and not, like many of our rich men, trying to make ten percent of the virtues serve as a substitute for the other ninety.[96]

The meddling domestic policy of the humanitarian was intimately related to the meddling that would occur in international relations by leaders focused on crusading rather than self-reform. Leaders of nations would not be capable of displaying a peaceful disposition toward their neighbors if they had not first exercised a level of personal self-mastery and ethical restraint. Any philosophy that wished to move the nation toward peace "must show its efficacy, first of all, by establishing peace in the breast of the individual. To suppose that men who are filled individually with every manner of restlessness, maddened by the lust of power and speed, votaries of the god Whirl, will live at peace either with themselves or with others, is the vainest of chimeras."[97] The world stage required leaders capable of self-control. Only such leaders would have hope "that they may get within hailing distance of one another, even hope that they may subordinate to some extent the private interests of their respective states to the larger interests of civilization."[98]

With the *Nation* essay, Babbitt had finally constructed the intellectual bridge connecting his analysis of the Romantic movement with historical and contemporary political developments. The Great War inspired Babbitt to draw out his first articulation of the concept of imperialism. This essay was, in fact, a distillation of the political ideas that would thread their way through *Rousseau and Romanticism*, and it represented Babbitt's most succinct explication of his theory of democratic imperialism prior to *Democracy and Leadership*.

In 1917, while still researching *Rousseau and Romanticism*, Babbitt penned another essay for the *Nation* that explicitly drew the connection between democratic imperialism and Rousseau's aesthetical and philosophical theories. The 1915 *Nation* essay had never referenced Rousseau directly, although it clearly made implicit allusions to his thought. The 1917 essay, "The Political Influence of Rousseau," laid many of the modern problems directly at Rousseau's feet: "Rousseau has perhaps had more influence than any single person since Jesus.... But Jesus is not, like Rousseau, an Arcadian dreamer. He faces the facts of life and he faces them with imaginative good sense."[99]

"The Political Influence of Rousseau" is an excellent summary of Babbitt's views on Rousseau's political philosophy, views that previously had to be gleaned from Babbitt's writings on other subjects. The essay emphasized that Rousseau's concept of a state of nature was a "mere fiction." The general will, as conceived by Rousseau, would not foster liberty because "the individual is to have no rights against the numerical majority at any particular moment."[100] Rousseau's ideas, Babbitt said, would foment revolution because they affirmed popular impulse without reference to some higher standard of justice.

One important aspect of this 1917 essay, however, was Babbitt's footnoted hint that he had been influenced in his development of this theory of democratic imperialism by Ernest Seillière, who in 1908 had published *Le Mal Romantique: Essai sur l'Impérialisme Irrational*.[101] Babbitt pointed out that Seillière's writings explored the "relationship between Rousseauistic living and what he terms irrational imperialism."[102] This footnote did not provide an extensive discussion of Babbitt's views on Seillière's theory. However, by the time *Rousseau and Romanticism* was published in 1919, Babbitt seems to have concluded that Seillière's theory was only partially adequate in capturing the true dangers of democratic imperialism. In *Rousseau and Romanticism*, he qualified his earlier references to Seillière: "His point of view is on the constructive side very different from mine"; "like other leaders of the crusade against romanticism in France, S. seems to me unsound on the constructive side."[103]

Later, in *Democracy and Leadership*, Babbitt further clarified that Seillière had had a clear influence on Babbitt's theory of imperialism, but only "on the negative side."[104] What Babbitt implied by this remark was that he agreed with Seillière's thesis concerning the connection between Rousseau's Romanticism and imperialism. However, Babbitt stipulated, "on the positive and constructive side, on the other hand, M. Seillière and I diverge sharply." Babbitt's concern was that what Seillière "opposes to an irrational imperialism is a rational imperialism; by which he means 'the social army on the march towards the conquest of power by the coordination of individual efforts.'"[105]

Babbitt believed that imperialism was unproblematic for Seillière as long as it was rooted in the right social cause. This meant, Babbitt said, that Seillière's "general position, as revealed in such utterances, . . . seems to me to strike back through the utilitarians to Hobbes and ultimately, in some respects, to Machiavelli."[106] Babbitt, in contrast, was most interested in the ethical dimension of imperialism that first manifests itself in the human heart. According to Babbitt, "The essential contrast for me is not, as for Mr. Seillière, that between a rational and irrational imperialism, but between imperialism and that quality of will in man which is, in every possible sense of the word, anti-imperialistic."[107]

Nonetheless, Seillière's influence on the formation of Babbitt's theory seemed to persist. In his final book, Babbitt referenced the fact that Seillière "has been developing in numerous volumes the thesis that Rousseau's doctrine of man's natural goodness, in theory fraternal, results practically in an 'irrational imperialism.'"[108]

Seillière influenced Babbitt by establishing in his mind the strong connection between Romanticism and imperialism as well as by providing the likely source for his expropriation of the term *imperialism*. *Literature and the American College* (1908), Babbitt's earliest book, was the only one of his major books not to use *imperialism*. In that book, when Babbitt described the tendency of Rousseauistic democracies to threaten their neighbors, he described it as "egoistic instincts . . . in international relations."[109] He characterized the influence of Rousseauism on nationalities as "a mixture of sympathy and self-assertion."[110] In these earlier passages, Babbitt was clearly describing the tendency of Rousseauism to breed imperialism in world affairs, but he failed to use the specific term.

Babbitt subsequently adopted Seillière's general concept of Romantic imperialism and began using the term in all major political writings. However, Babbitt certainly redefined the term to embrace the moral errors that he believed were at the root of imperialism. No theory of international relations could be adequate if it did not embrace an understanding of the dualism of human nature and of the potentialities within the human soul that might ultimately manifest themselves in combat on the world stage.

After years of research, Babbitt finally published *Rousseau and Romanticism* in 1919. The political ideas articulated in the book are a direct reflection of the essays he published in the *Nation* in 1915 and 1917. Those essays, in fact, represent a handy distillation of the political ideas found in *Rousseau and Romanticism*, a book that is dedicated not to politics but to the Romantic imagination.

In *Democracy and Leadership*, Babbitt described *Rousseau and Romanticism* as "a book that is closely connected in argument with *The New Laokoon*, because it is a book where the problem of the imagination receives special treatment."[111] Babbitt accurately characterized the theme of *Rousseau and Romanticism* as primarily concerned with the imagination; the book is probably one of the most important literary analyses of the psychology of the Romantic imagination. The implications of the Romantic imagination for politics were, as written in the *Nation* essays, that civilization requires a certain quality of imagination in its leaders. The freewheeling imagination of the Romantic is an invitation to anarchy and imperialism; only an imagination shaped by ethical self-mastery can bring peace and order.

While Babbitt had been writing sporadically for two decades about the connections among Romanticism, decadent democracies, and imperialism, with *Democracy and Leadership*, he finally devoted an entire book to the subject. Immediately after *Rousseau and Romanticism* was published, Babbitt began his research on *Democracy and Leadership*. On July 10, 1919, Babbitt wrote to Paul Elmer More that the rest of the Babbitt family would be soon traveling to New Hampshire for vacation, "but I am likely to be in Cambridge for some time yet collecting material for *Democracy and Imperialism*."[112]

Babbitt intended the book to have that title from the time he began his research. Only during final negotiations did his editor at Houghton Mifflin, Ferris Greenslet, advise against this title. At that time, Babbitt wrote to More, "The present plan is to have the book appear early next April. Greenslet does not seem to warm up especially to the title 'Democracy and Imperialism.' Two other titles occur to me as possible: 'Democracy and Civilization' and 'Democracy and Leadership.' I should very much appreciate your opinion on the matter."[113] It is not known if More influenced Babbitt's decision to rename the book *Democracy and Leadership*, as More's reply to Babbitt's letter makes no mention of the possible title. What does seem clear is that Babbitt preferred to use the term *Imperialism*, which he had been using throughout his writing since 1908.

Babbitt struggled to complete the book. In early 1923, he accepted a position as a visiting professor at the Sorbonne. When he returned from Paris that September, he complained to More that he was working hard to complete the book but that "my stay in Paris was so strenuous socially that I found it left no time for writing or for anything else except recuperating from numerous dinner parties and late hours. I had planned to get the book out of the way before going abroad. Under the circumstances, I feel that I have made a mistake in accepting the foreign job at all at this time."[114]

During his time in Paris, he gave a series of lectures on "Democracy and Imperialism" that encapsulated the arguments he had made in the 1915 *Nation* essay and in *Rousseau and Romanticism*.[115] The Sorbonne lectures do not contain significant original themes that go beyond the ideas that Babbitt had laid out earlier in the *Nation* articles and in *Rousseau and Romanticism*, and surprisingly, they generally do not offer more than bits and pieces of the more sustained and systematic argument that appears in *Democracy and Leadership* despite his contemporaneous research for that book. Instead, in his lectures, he stressed the historical link between radical democracy and imperialism, the roots of German *Kultur* in Rousseau, the importance of Rousseau's redefinition of virtue, the role of scientific and sentimental humanitarianism, the Rousseauism of the French Jacobins, and the decadence of the French aristocracy—themes that had been discussed in his earlier writings.

Democracy and Leadership goes further, and Babbitt was insistent that the book was ultimately a work of philosophy. More specifically, Babbitt implied that it contributed to epistemology. And, unlike *Rousseau and Romanticism*, which was an exploration of the human imagination, *Democracy and Leader-*

ship was primarily concerned with the problem of will and how it shaped other human faculties. In *Democracy and Leadership*, Babbitt merged his previous writings on aesthetics in such works as *The New Laokoon* and *Rousseau and Romanticism* with his political ideas, which are scattered through all his writings but are systematically laid out only in the *Nation* articles.[116]

In the early spring of 1923, Babbitt sent More a partial manuscript of the book. More responded that he felt the first chapter on "Types of Political Thinking" was the "weakest part of the book" and that he did not "see that your critical thesis of ethos and government was worked out clearly, and the construction, or partition of subjects, did not strike me as orderly or effective."[117]

Babbitt did not reply to this criticism until September 17, 1923, when he lamented, "I did not find the general tenor of your observations especially exhilarating." In particular, Babbitt sought to clarify what he felt was More's misreading of the first chapter. "My first chapter by the way does not primarily deal with the relation between ethos and government (I attempt to elucidate that point in my last chapter) but with the passage from the mediaeval emphasis on the divine will to the modern emphasis on the popular will. The whole book in fact is devoted to the problem of the will."[118] Babbitt was insistent that the book was primarily a work of philosophy, not government.

A careful reading of the first chapter does not leave the reader with a detailed account of the problem of will, although the chapter certainly discusses ethics, virtue, the human law, and other themes related to will. One might even be inclined to agree with More that this is the weakest chapter in the book because it does not add "much to [Babbitt's] argument."[119]

In September, Babbitt indicated that he had not yet finished the introduction to the book and that he would send that introduction and conclusion to More when they were complete. This exchange of letters probably prompted Babbitt to craft the introduction so that it would clarify the central theme of the book as the problem of will. His argument about the purpose of the book became quite explicit in the final introduction:

> This book in particular is devoted to the most unpopular of tasks—a defense of the veto power. Not the least singular feature of the singular epoch in which we are living is that the very persons who are least willing to hear about the veto power are likewise the persons who are most certain that they stand for the virtues that depend upon its exercise—for example, peace and brotherhood. As

against the expansionists of very kind, I do not hesitate to affirm that what is specifically human in man and ultimately divine is a certain quality of will, a will that is felt in relation to his ordinary self as a will to refrain.[120]

This statement, probably prompted by his exchange with More, is the most succinct encapsulation of Babbitt's argument in the book.

The modern problem, for Babbitt, was that the ethical standards and conventions of the West, traditionally supplied by Christianity, had broken down. In such an environment, individuals were forced to fall back on their own inner resources to find high standards in their own inner life.

> Though the basis of the inner life is the opposition between a lower and a higher will, the higher will cannot, after all, act at random. It must have standards. Formerly the standards were supplied by tradition. The man who accepted Christian tradition, for example, was in no doubt as to the kind and degree of discipline he needed to impose upon his lower nature. He thus achieved some measure of moral unity with himself and also with other men who accepted the same discipline. If the individualist, on the other hand, is to have standards, he must rely upon the critical spirit in direct ratio to the completeness of the break with the traditional unifications of life.[121]

The introduction to *Democracy and Leadership* not only explicitly raised the problem of will but neatly summarized Babbitt's view of human nature and how human beings are to make sense of reality. For if individuals are left to their own devices in trying to sort out right behavior, they are "confronted at the outset with the most difficult of philosophical problems—that of the one and the many."[122] Behavior is choice, and every individual's daily life constantly includes complex choices that even in the Christian era could not be neatly solved with reference to a series of rules. In a secular society, with fewer traditional standards for behavior, the choices are even more numerous and bewildering. "The failure of criticism to attain to any center of judgment set above the shifting impressions of the individual and the flux of phenomenal nature is a defeat for civilization itself, if it be true, as I have tried to show, that civilization must depend on the maintenance of standards."[123]

Babbitt repeated his theme from the 1915 *Nation* essay by emphasizing that the problem of morality was therefore wrapped up in a proper understanding of the different faculties of the soul. In a time of civilizational flux, when conventions and standards are eroding, human beings must depend on their own imagination to solve the problem of the one and the many. The imagination is that quality that can find the universal standard embedded in the ever-changing circumstances of life. "The imagination, in other words, holds the balance of power between the higher and lower nature of man."[124] Since the era of the ancient Greeks and through the modern age of Romanticism, when society had failed to solve this problem of the one and the many, it has fallen back on relativism. In the case of Rousseauistic Romanticism, one found an outright worship of the relative, the anarchic, and the impressionistic and an explicit rejection of any universal standard.

As in *Rousseau and Romanticism*, the central problem for Babbitt in *Democracy and Leadership* was that a well controlled will must take mastery over the imagination: "Superficially, this anarchy seems above all an anarchy of the emotions. On closer scrutiny, however, emotional anarchy itself turns out to be only a sign of something subtler and more dangerous—anarchy of the imagination."[125] As Babbitt explained the challenge of understanding a standard above our ordinary selves amid a wealth of diversity, "If we mean by imagination not merely what we perceive, but what we conceive, it follows inevitably that the problem of the imagination is closely bound up with that of the One and the Many and therefore with the problem of standards; for it is impossible, let me repeat, to achieve standards, at least along critical lines, unless one can discover in life somewhere an abiding unity with which to measure its mere variety and change."[126]

In life as it is actually experienced, Babbitt repeated throughout his writings, it is impossible "to eliminate the element of illusion."[127] Solving the problem of illusion would not be found in "right reason" because a proper view of life is found not in simply analyzing random facts but in sorting out the correct set of facts to analyze. Nor could one sort out the changing circumstances of life by merely allowing the imagination to run wild and to dream up a world that does not exist. "The final contrast is not between reason or judgment and mere illusion, but between the imagination that is disciplined to what abides in the midst of the changeful and the illusory, and the imagination that is more or less free to wander wild in some 'empire of chimeras.'"[128] Life as it is actually experienced is neither all unity nor all change; it is, in Babbitt's famous phrase, "a oneness that is always changing."[129]

As Babbitt pointed out, humans can be highly imaginative but exhibit an uncontrolled and undisciplined imagination, a central problem of Romanticism. "The critical observer is forced to agree with Napoleon that, not reason, but 'imagination governs mankind.' It does not follow that mankind need be governed, as it has been very largely during the past century, by the Napoleonic quality of imagination."[130] For Babbitt, an uncontrolled imagination was "an invitation to Nemesis," since one can construct a dream world, an imaginative idealistic society, that bears no relation to the facts of existence.[131] "We have all grown familiar with the type of person who is in his own conceit a lofty 'idealist,' but when put to the test has turned out to be only a disastrous dreamer."[132]

Babbitt emphasized more explicitly in *Democracy and Leadership* that human character was ultimately shaped by a higher will that is naturally antecedent to a superior quality of imagination. These two faculties, which work in combination and strengthen one another, allow individuals to choose correct behavior. If one wished civilization to reestablish high standards of behavior and good order, its leaders must first possess this higher quality of will.

The implications for politics were that leaders who had restrained their will and developed a moral imagination would tend to be peaceful souls, whereas leaders who had been unrestrained in their will and imagination would tend to be imperialistic souls. Rousseau's imagination, Babbitt said, provided a glimpse of the imperialistic soul: "The Nature to which he invites us to return is only a conceit. This conceit encourages one to substitute for the vital control, which is the true voice of man's higher self, expansive emotion. Ideally, this substitution is to be marked by a triumph of the fraternal spirit. Actually, as I have sought to prove, the outcome of yielding to a mere expansive conceit is not fraternity, but a decadent imperialism."[133]

Babbitt then sought to make a distinction between types and even phases of imperialism. Rome's conquest of most of the known world was, without doubt, a form of imperialism. Yet in its early stages, it was not yet a decadent imperialism. "The critical moment for Rome was the moment of triumph when the leaders of the state no longer felt the restraining influence of dangerous rivals like Carthage." With the defeat of Carthage, Rome began to "throw off the traditional controls" and declined into decadence. Babbitt quoted the Roman poet Juvenal, who satirized the corruption of the second century AD: "'Luxury,' says Juvenal, 'more cruel than the foeman's arms, fell upon us, and is avenging the conquered world.'" When Rome's leaders jettisoned all restraint in private matters, Rome's politics began to exhibit the consequences in the public realm: "A graver symptom, however, was the appearance of leaders who were ever more and more ruthless in the pursuit either of their personal advantage or that of some class or faction."[134]

While Babbitt's tone was far from sanguine about the future of the contemporary West, he reserved judgment about whether the United States had moved into a period of decadent imperialism akin to that found in the late Roman republic. The United States, he said, was at "the acme of our power" yet was "at the same time discarding the standards of the past." He also saw parallels between Roman politics and American politics in their "highly unethical leaders—leaders who seek to advance the material interests of some special group at the expense of the whole community." The parallels, he admitted, "may perhaps be exaggerated," but the only way to "get to the root of the matter" was not to analyze the parallels but to "turn from the merely peripheral manifestations of the push for power to the inner life of the individual."

Babbitt, of course, made the classical Greek argument that the individual was the most important unit of analysis necessary to measure the level of decadence or health in society and hence the nature of a society's imperialism. "The more one ponders either the modern American or the ancient Roman situation, the more surely will one be led from imperialism in the political, to imperialism in the psychological sense."[135]

While Babbitt was not certain that the United States had reached a level of decadent imperialism, he was certain that the current set of political leaders was not even aware of the problem. The progressives of his era, Babbitt said, avoided the entire ethical problem and focused on the reform of institutions rather than on the ethical concentration of individuals despite the fact that "immediate experience" demonstrated an "opposition" within the individual soul "between a law of the spirit and a law of the members."[136] Society, he feared, had become more concerned with "service to others" than with personal virtue. "The humanitarian is not, I pointed out, concerned, like the humanist, with the individual and his inner life, but with the welfare and progress of mankind in the lump. His favorite word is 'service.'"[137] So, the question that must be asked in politics is "not whether one should be a moderate humanitarian, but whether one should be a humanitarian at all."[138]

Babbitt's conclusion was that the humanitarian leadership of the West must be replaced with humanists or some form of genuinely religious leaders, as these two options represented the only possible methods of controlling a decadent imperialism. The West must find leaders who were willing to master their own selves: "On the appearance of leaders who have recovered in some form the truths of the inner life and repudiated errors of naturalism may depend the very survival of Western civilization."[139]

Babbitt argued that throughout history, society might assume the mantle of one of three possible political forms: "naturalistic, or humanistic, or religious."[140] For the religious outlook, Babbitt pointed to medieval Christianity, Hindu religion in India as embodied in the *Laws of Manu*, and Buddhism. For the humanistic and nontheocratic alternatives, he pointed to the similarities between Confucius and ancient Greek philosophy, especially Aristotle. The distinction he made between the religious and the humanistic outlook was that "Confucius is less concerned with the other world than with living to the best advantage in this. To live to the best advantage in this world is, he holds, to live proportionately and moderately; so that the Confucian tradition of the Far East has much in common with the Aristotelian tradition of the Occident."[141]

Babbitt pointed out that the religious and humanistic traditions of East and West are united in their affirmation of a human law, "a law, the acceptance of which leads, on the religious level, to the miracles and other-worldliness that one finds in Christians and Buddhists at their best, and the acceptance of which, in this world, leads to the subduing of the ordinary self and its spontaneous impulses to the law of measure that one finds in Confucianists and Aristotelians."[142] By denying a uniquely human law, Romanticism and naturalism would provide no restraint on an ambitious will to power. "Other animals have appetite, but within certain definite bounds, whereas man is, either in a good or bad sense, the infinite animal."[143] Human beings have the potential for great saintliness or unimaginable evil; naturalistic philosophies that fail to concede this point would be naive about the potential for war and conflict.

Therefore, Babbitt saw only two potential checks, one religious, one humanistic, on the human desire for dominion. In the West, "Christianity has actually done more to curb the expansive lusts of the human heart, and among its other lusts, the lust for power."[144] This naturalistic turn of the West was decisive in the rise of total war among nation-states because the political result was the destruction of the authority of the church and the cosmopolitanism it inspired. "One important outcome of this naturalistic trend has been the growth of the national spirit. The Protestant religion itself, if one takes a sufficiently long-range view, appears largely as an incident in the rise of nationalism."[145]

Rousseau had inspired nationalism by morally sanctioning an expansive national spirit unchecked by any higher authority. Rousseau correctly perceived that the church's claim of authority over spiritual matters and its admonition that Christian rulers must embody a certain humility toward the church had weakened state power and authority, as "to be humble was to be submissive." Yet for Rousseau, "[o]ne should . . . discard humility in favor a patriotic pride, of the kind that flourished in the great days of Rome and Sparta."[146]

In *Democracy and Leadership*, Babbitt pointed out that Rousseau's political theory has such a humanitarian overlay, stressing pity and sympathy, that readers must focus carefully to understand that his nationalism is one of cunning and force. Rousseau's nationalism embodied a Machiavellianism in which "the rules of ordinary morality may hold in the relations between man and man, but only have a secondary place in the relations between state and state."[147] Machiavelli's *virtù* shared a similarity with Rousseau's virtue of the citizen, in which "the ruler above all should have no conscience apart from the state and its material aggrandizement."[148]

Babbitt saw Machiavelli, Rousseau, Hobbes, and other political theorists since the Renaissance as sharing a naturalism that denied a specifically human law. While conceding that Machiavelli was an "extraordinarily shrewd observer," Babbitt argued that Machiavelli's naturalism nonetheless combined "a clear perception of the facts of the material order with spiritual blindness" that would lead to "imperialistic dreaming" about the "glories of ancient Rome."[149] Hobbes likewise denied a uniquely human law that would apply to all of humanity's affairs. Hobbes's political order was predicated on the sovereign assuming complete control, unchecked by any other institution or principle. "Hobbes's assertion of absolute and unlimited sovereignty recalls the medieval notion of sovereignty with a most important difference: it rests upon force and is in this sense imperialistic; it does not, like the sovereignty of the Middle Ages, have a supernatural sanction."[150]

At this point, Babbitt began to frame his argument that any philosophy of naturalism, whether Machiavellian or Hobbesian, could not and would not unite human beings in peace. Only a humanistic or religious outlook could unite human beings and bring "cohesion among men." In Christianity, humans were united not by fear of the sovereign or submission to a popular will but by submission to God's will, a common endeavor that formed the spiritual glue of the Christian community. "According to the true Christian, the final counterpoise to egoism, in virtue of which alone men may be drawn to a common center, is submission to the will of God, a submission that is conceived in terms of the inner life."[151]

With the decline of Christianity and the rise of the nation-state, the chief problem that had arisen was what could unite men across national boundaries. Babbitt's clear answer was that once a Rousseauistic understanding of popular sovereignty firmly took hold, nothing could provide unity. If nations were in a state of nature with one another, then the only law that applied was that of force. At least under the divine right theory of kings, which recognized a law higher than popular or royal will, the king was obligated to rule under a divine sanction. With the new doctrine of popular sovereignty, Babbitt said, no authority could limit the will of the people. "Within the bounds of each separate nationality, the essential aspect of this secular process is the passage from divine right to popular right, from the sovereignty of God to the sovereignty of the people."[152] While the king had ruled in the place of God and had to be cognizant of divine judgment, the Rousseauistic general will asserts popular rule without divine blessing or sanction.

A general will for each individual nation, unmoored from any higher authority or constraint, was an invitation to war between nations would share no foundation for unity. This new nationalism was undoubtedly responsible for the Great War. "The question of war becomes acute if Europe, and possibly the world, is to be made up of a series of states, each animated by what one is tempted to term a frenzied nationalism, without and countervailing principle of unity. That the new nationalism is more potent than the new internationalism was revealed in August 1914 when millions of socialists, in response to the call of country, marched away to the slaughter of their fellow socialists in other lands."[153]

Modern theorists of popular sovereignty, natural rights, and the social contract had not and in contemporary times have not recognized this strain of nihilism in modern democratic theory. Rousseau asserted on a number of occasions that the love of country is the most "beautiful passion" and "[t]he fact that the *l'invresse patriotique* may make the citizens of one country ruthless in their dealings with citizens of other countries seems to him a matter of small moment."[154]

Babbitt argued that recognition of this problem was also lacking in Locke, the father of modern popular sovereignty. "However moderately [Locke] himself may interpret the sovereignty of the people, it is not easy to discover in his theory anything that will prevent this sovereignty from developing into a new absolutism."[155] Babbitt characterized this nihilistic popular sovereignty as "the evils of an unlimited democracy."[156]

Here Babbitt began to move from his critique of Romanticism to a positive solution regarding the problem of conflict. Refuting Machiavelli and Hobbes required showing "that there is some universal principle that tends to unite men across even national frontiers."[157] That unifying principle differed little in the international community and in small communities such as families and towns. To describe what was essential to peace, writ large or small, Babbitt returned to his core principles of ethics. What was required was some "recognition . . . that moves in an opposite direction from the outer impressions and expansive desires that together make up his ordinary or temperamental self."[158]

The most acute modern political problem for the rising Western democracies was finding checks on the relativism of popular sovereignty—that is, finding countervailing forces that could prevent a democracy from submitting to "the irresponsible tyranny of the mob."[159] Yet modern theories of popular sovereignty made finding such checks difficult because their premise was that there was no higher principle than the popular will.

For Babbitt, the primary answer was found in the revised title of his book: leadership. Democratic societies would be orderly and peaceful only where their leaders possessed a true aristocratic bearing derived from a focus on their inner life. Babbitt's immediate concern was that leadership in the Western democracies had not been aristocratic but had been egalitarian. Politicians had promised the people all manner of material schemes that would "promote what is socially useful, the greatest good for the greatest number."[160] The people, he argued, would not respect politicians who operated merely on the material level: "The people, especially the people of the great urban centers, no longer look up with respect to representatives who are themselves so imbued with the utilitarian temper encouraged by Locke that they have perhaps ceased to be worthy of respect. If the aristocratic principle continues to give way to the egalitarian denial of the need for leadership, parliamentary democracy may ultimately become impossible."[161]

In an anonymous book review published in 1920 in the *Weekly Review*, Babbitt had begun to formulate the central theme of *Democracy and Leadership*: sound and elevated leadership provides the main bulwark against capricious popular opinion in a democracy.[162] In the book review, Babbitt was commenting on a recent history of the French Revolution in which the author had taken the position that the French people were victims of a sophisticated conspiracy that duped them into committing heinous acts.

Babbitt was unequivocal that the people were not the important actors in either the revolution or in democracies generally: "The truth is that neither the good nor the evil of a movement like the French Revolution emanates spontaneously from the people. It is all a question of leadership; and the one serious doubt about democracy is whether it can show sufficient critical discrimination in the choice of its leaders."[163] Rousseau had sought to discredit aristocratic leadership and replace it with popular will: "'The people,' he says, 'constitute the human race': all that is not the people is parasitic and 'scarcely deserves to be counted were it not for the harm it does.'"[164]

In *Democracy and Leadership*, Babbitt provided two significant chapters contrasting Rousseau and Burke on the issue of aristocratic leadership in particular. Rousseau was the spiritual father of egalitarian democracy, which denies the need for an enlightened leadership that may guide popular will. Burke "took up the defense of the traditional order" and argued that popular passions were subject to a higher law because all human beings had to submit to a "standard of virtue and wisdom that is beyond the vulgar practice of the hour."[165]

Babbitt's discussion of Rousseau and Burke in *Democracy and Leadership* revolved around the problem of imagination. Babbitt argued that Burke had made a unique contribution to Western philosophy and epistemology by emphasizing the importance of tradition in shaping a higher quality of imagination that would be essential to leadership in a democracy. Babbitt's conclusion, however, was that Rousseau's ideas, not Burke's, had carried the day in the West. Burke's battle for the necessity of "prejudice and prescription" had been lost, and the "history of modern Europe, during and since the Great Revolution" had been shaped by Rousseau, leading to "the two chief political problems of the present time, the problem of democracy and the problem of imperialism, both in themselves and in relation to one another."[166]

Along with his 1915 essay in the *Nation*, the fourth chapter of *Democracy and Leadership* was Babbitt's most important concise discussion of the problem of democratic imperialism. Titled "Democracy and Imperialism," this chapter drew together the many strands of Babbitt's writings on ethics and politics into his lengthiest discussion on imperialism. Babbitt asserted that Rousseau's brand of democracy and popular sovereignty had come to dominate Western opinion. Babbitt asked whether the results of Rousseauistic democracy in the West—based on a "new ethics" whereby "virtue is not restrictive but expansive, a sentiment and even an intoxication"—had been "a paradise of liberty, equality, and fraternity."[167] The answer was firmly in the negative. This form of popular sovereignty tended to tear apart human beings, and centuries of wars were the result.

The centrifugal nature of the French Revolution, for example, did not cause its leaders to turn inward, to appoint leaders of character and self-discipline, or to institute sensible reforms that might have corrected the administrative problems that had built up over the course of the Ancien Régime. Instead, the revolutionary leaders, impressed by their own beautiful souls, turned outward.

The revolution and Napoleon were a direct result of the Rousseauistic democratic outlook that the revolutionaries had adopted:

> I have been trying to make clear the relation between Rousseauistic democracy and imperialism in France itself. The same relationship appears if we study the Rousseauistic movement internationally. Perhaps no movement since the beginning of the world has led to such an inbreeding of national sentiment of the type that in the larger states runs over very readily into imperialistic ambition. I have said that the Revolution almost from the start took on the character of a universal crusade. The first principles it assumed made practically all existing governments seem illegitimate.[168]

Of course, as the Revolutionary Wars demonstrated, monarchies and other nations with more traditional forms of government rightly understood the universalistic ambitions of the revolutionaries as a threat to their stability. As Babbitt put it, "What followed is almost too familiar to need repetition. Some of the governments whose legitimacy was thus called into question took alarm and, having entered into an alliance, invaded France."[169]

The historical result was a decade of warfare of a type that had not been seen on Western battlefields, the wholesale mobilization of entire nations, and a mind-set of "total war" among their leaders. Babbitt then repeated some important lines that he had written in his 1915 *Nation* essay connecting the French Revolution and the Great War: "The cry of the revolutionary army—*Vive la nation*—heard by Goethe in a pause of the cannonading of Valmy—was rightly taken by him to mark the dawn of a new era. The beginnings of the very type of warfare we have recently been witnessing in Europe, that is, the coming together of whole nations for mutual massacre (*la levée en masse*), go back to this period."[170] A humanitarian movement that weakened the traditional religious, cultural, and humanistic mechanisms tempering selfish impulses "actually promotes the reality of strife that it is supposed to prevent."[171]

In his 1915 *Nation* essay, Babbitt had remarked that a number of historical expressions of pacifism had ironically been followed by large wars. In *Democracy and Leadership*, he went further, arguing that pacifists should be lumped into the category of humanitarian movements that would actually break down traditional controls. "It is possible to show that the pacifist is not only a materialist, but a very objectionable type of materialist. In the name of the fairest of virtues, he is actually engaged in breaking down ethical standards. It is a matter of common sense and everyday experience that there can be no peace with the unrighteous and the unrighteous always have been and are extremely numerous."[172]

The final result of the democracy of the Rousseauistic type, with its repudiation of ethical restraint and worship of unvarnished and unchecked popular sovereignty, would be militarism and imperialistic war:

> From a strictly psychological point of view, the movement we are studying had not only produced all its characteristic fruits over a hundred years ago, but also its two outstanding and truly significant personalities—Rousseau and Napoleon. If there had been no Rousseau, Napoleon is reported to have said, there would have been no Revolution, and without the Revolution, *I* should have been impossible. Now Rousseau may be regarded as being more than any other one person the humanitarian Messiah. Napoleon, for his part, may be defined in Hardy's phrase, as the Christ of War. So that the humanitarian Messiah set in motion forces that led to a process that I have attempted to sketch in rough general outline to the rise of the Christ of War.[173]

The will to power that marked the revolutionaries, in fact, attracted them to the "imperialistic superman" embodied in Bonaparte. "What became apparent, on the contrary, was the affinity that has always existed between an unlimited democracy and the cult of ruthless power. No one crawled more abjectly at the feel of Napoleon than some of the quondam Terrorists."[174]

Chateaubriand, a Romantic but a royalist and defender of the church, was nonetheless perceptive enough to see the evolution from democratic revolution to an imperialistic despotism under Bonaparte.[175] As Chateaubriand wrote in his memoirs, "From day to day there was taking place the transformation of republicans into imperialists and of the tyranny of all into the despotism of a single man."[176] In the French Revolution, Babbitt said, "[t]he doctrine of popular sovereignty as developed from the *Social Contract* had been found to encourage a sort of chronic anarchy. Inasmuch as society cannot go on without discipline of some kind, men were constrained, in the absence of any other form of discipline, to turn to the discipline of the military type."[177]

Ancient Rome had undergone a similar process: the weakening of religious traditions caused a weakening of the constitutional republic and the rise of an egalitarian democracy. What followed was a period of class warfare and then democratic imperialism. Babbitt quoted Mirabeau's warning to the French revolutionaries about war and democracies: "Free peoples are more eager for war, and the democracies more slaves of their passions than the most absolute autocracies."[178]

Babbitt even pointed to ancient China, where an "unbridled individualism" caused the end of the feudal system, resulting in the "era of the Fighting States."[179] Ancient China exhibited "a mingling of utilitarian and sentimental elements which is closer, perhaps, to our contemporary humanitarianism than anything to be found in Greece or Rome."[180] Even the ancient Chinese did not recognize the deeper causes of war and therefore adopted many of the contemporary schemes to establish peace. "Toward the end, when everything had been tried, including the balance of power, universal brotherhood, and a 'league of nations,' and after the perpetuation of horrors unspeakable, no one apparently had more illusions: the only question was which imperialistic leader should first succeed in imposing his will upon all the others."[181]

Babbitt also dismissed the modern notion that commerce and trade drive peace and amity among nations. The "expansion of the commercialist," he said, is "imperialistic."[182] Military power tends to follow trade because "the flag tends to follow trade," and at this point in history, "it is hardly necessary at this day to refute the notion held by so many liberals of the eighteenth and nineteenth centuries that trade is in itself a pacific agency. Commercial interests lead to clashes and dangerous rivalries between European nations, not merely in Europe itself, but in other parts of the world."[183] In a remark that demonstrates Babbitt's relevance to modern times, he noted that one of the chief causes of twentieth-century imperialism was the "scramble for oil."[184] He also presciently predicted World War II when he pointed out that trade between East and West is more likely to cause war than peace: "The chief problem raised by all this imperialistic expansion is that of the relations between Asia and the Occident. There are possibilities in the present situation that may lead to the real world war, that between East and West, a war to which the recent European struggle is like to seem in retrospect but a faint prelude."[185]

Even more presciently and more specifically, he said the real danger was a US-Japanese conflict:

> There is also the problem of the United States in its relations with the Far East, with the possibility in the offing of a gigantic struggle for the empire of the Pacific. One encounters here the portent of Japan, an Asiatic power that is learning to play the imperialistic game along the most approved Occidental lines, that is even learning to adapt to its own uses the humanitarian-imperialistic cant of the "white man's burden," and is beginning to speak of China as "Japan's burden."[186]

Babbitt continued with his predictions, which are amazingly accurate in light of the fact that the book was published in 1924 and that much of it was written years earlier. Turning to German and Russian ambitions, he declared, "Russia is likely to remain for some time to come a fertile field of imperialistic intrigue, not only on the part of the Russians, but also of Germans and Japanese, and perhaps of Turks, with the whole Moslem world in the background.... [S]o Germany in her desire to get even might be tempted to join with these extra-European forces, even though such action on her part would amount to a betrayal of the vital interests of the cultural group to which she herself belongs."[187] Babbitt's skill in predicting future developments in European politics leading to World War II indicates a genuine realism and sagacity on his part regarding international politics.

In making these predictions in *Democracy and Leadership*, Babbitt pointed out that the scientific progress of the West had provided crusading humanitarianism with unmatched military power. Babbitt quoted a contemporary Indian poet, Rabindranath Tagore, who regularly wrote about relations between the East and West: "The man of the West, he says, has specialized in power and mechanical efficiency and so has been enabled to make himself the bully of the planet; but it is established in the nature of things that bullies shall come to grief."[188] Tagore's solution to this problem of East and West is for the West to adopt "the principle of love," a solution that, Babbitt said, allied Tagore with other "Rousseauistic dreamers."[189]

What was missing in the contemporary leaders of the West, Babbitt believed, was a moral realism. The West had surrendered to the flaccid humanitarianism of Rousseau when what was required was the Buddha's realistic assessment of human nature, with its understanding that life is a personal moral challenge. Philosophies that ignored the human moral dilemma, even so-called realist schools of international relations, were ignoring a fundamental aspect of human nature that is the deepest root of war. Babbitt, for example, scoffed at the arguments of some supporters of science that powerful weaponry would have a deterrent effect and prevent war. "We are told that our means of destruction are growing so terrible that no one will venture to use them—the same argument that was heard before the War. But at the same time that we are heaping up these means of destruction, the breakdown of the traditional controls combined with the failure thus far to supply any adequate substitute, is creating fools and madmen who will not hesitate to use them."[190]

Conflict between human beings, Babbitt asserted, is an inevitable result of the potentialities in the human soul; democratic leaders and the popular will are not exempted from this moral problem. Rather than face this fundamental ethical problem, the West had explicitly denied the "civil war in the cave" and had proffered humanitarianism as the solution to human conflict. Not only had this failed to produce the desired results, it had offered no principled opposition to the imperialistic personality. When conflict developed, leaders misdiagnosed the causes and implemented solutions that might even exacerbate the strife. Only the development of some kind of religious or humanistic understanding that would cause political leaders to engage in personal introspection and ethical work could stem the chaos, disorder, and war that humanitarianism had caused. Human beings who performed this spiritual and ethical work would come together in communion, and that communion would be peaceful. Leaders who had done this ethical work might finally be in a position to display a genuine cosmopolitanism in their relations with other nations.

CHAPTER 6

True and False Cosmopolitanism

The moral man, by living a life of simple truth and earnestness, alone can bring peace and order in the world.
—Confucius

The special danger of the present time would seem to be an increasing material contact between national and racial groups that remain spiritually alien.
—Irving Babbitt, "Buddha and the Occident"

For Irving Babbitt, peace was found in a disposition of character. This disposition, not easily acquired, was not a feeling or emotion and would not be acquired because of an institutional arrangement. Leaders who assumed the mantle of this disposition would display certain recognizable characteristics, among them urbanity and a courteous attitude toward competitors and opponents and a detachment displaying itself as an unwillingness to allow personal or policy decisions to be driven by raw emotion. Such leaders would possess a firm belief in the truth of the most elevated principles of their own culture but would also be respectful of the symbols of other cultures; these leaders would have an inchoate awareness that the symbols of others may represent principles that parallel the leaders' own. In this regard, leaders with peaceful dispositions, while defending their own culture, would not be aggressively dogmatic and would look for what is common and most elevated across cultures. These leaders would not celebrate the eccentricities of diversity but would recognize that diversity may indeed represent different paths to something that unites human beings, not what superficially divides them. The different and highest roads of various cultures might indeed lead to the same place.

Babbitt called this disposition cosmopolitanism. Cosmopolitanism, in his view, was not simply a breezy and sentimental affinity for other cultures, as contemporary advocates of "multiculturalism" sometimes portray it. Genuine cosmopolitanism was, for Babbitt, a recognition that human beings can truly unite only on a higher plane of religious or humanistic understanding, even though different cultures offer different symbolic representations of that higher plane. The prerequisite for national leaders to achieve this cosmopolitanism was, first and foremost, a spiritual or ethical concentration, a mastery of their own passions and impulses. While leaders need not achieve saintliness, they must have done enough ethical work to form a conscience in which they are pulled toward virtue. Cosmopolitan leaders contrasted with temperamental leaders, who would be driven by their egos and would seek to dominate others.

For Babbitt, self-mastery on an ethical level was an admonition found in the great philosophies of East and West.

> If man as a natural phenomenon grows by expanding, man as man grows by concentrating. He proves that he is set above nature, not so much by his power to act, as by his power to refrain from acting. According to Emerson, God himself is defined by the Orientals as the "inner check." I do not happen to know of any oriental book in which this precise phrase occurs, but the idea is found in every truly religious book that was ever written in either the East or the West.[1]

Even for the best leaders, finding common ground could be difficult, not only because of cultural diversity and dogmatic competition but also because this common ground represented something more profound than an emotional sympathy for humanity or a recognition of self-interest. As Babbitt framed the challenge, "[T]rue spirituality insists that men cannot come together in a common sympathy, but only in a common discipline. For example, St. Paul (*doctor gentium*), perhaps the most successful of all cosmopolitans, proclaims that men cannot meet directly and on the level of their ordinary selves. They can come together only by allegiance to a law set above their ordinary selves or to a personality taken as a symbol of this law."[2]

Romantic literature, Babbitt said, shared Rousseau's assumption that "the prime mark of genius is refusal to imitate."[3] Because it centered on personal feelings, originality, and a rejection of standards, Romanticism "appears far more cosmopolitan than it really was."[4] Romantic artists had tired of the narrow smugness and conformity of neoclassical imitation and sought, particularly in the early Renaissance, to create art that was "in a high degree favorable to originality," and this originality "was closely bound up with what is rather vaguely known as individualism."[5] Babbitt believed that the social results of Romantic sensibility and the elevation of originality above all other standards would be more distance, not more unity, between individuals and nations: "In the name of originality art is becoming more and more centrifugal and eccentric."[6]

Babbitt pointed out that in his contemporary world, the quest for originality had gone so far that "many a man passes for original who is in reality only freakish."[7] Babbitt pointed to Aristotle: "The final test of art is not its originality, but its truth to the universal." Aristotle "goes on to say that the superiority of poetry over history lies in the fact that it has more of this universality, that it is more concerned with the essentials and less with the accidents of human nature."[8]

However, Babbitt did not view the proper rejoinder to Romanticism to be a search for universal standards that are not anchored in reality. Human beings are trapped in a present reality from which there is no escape. Therefore, they must deploy their imagination not to fly off into unreality but to find a center amid the wealth of diversity. Those with a sound imagination will "not evade the actual . . . but select from it and seek to impose upon it something of the proportion and symmetry of the model to which it is looking up to and which it is imitating."[9] Babbitt insisted that the "classicist" who possesses this superior quality of imagination must always keep in mind that "he perceives reality only through a veil of illusion. The creator of this type achieves work in which illusion and reality are inseparably blended, work which gives the 'illusion of a higher reality.'"[10]

Literature and the American College was where Babbitt first explored in some detail the philosophical problem that Romantic aesthetics created for the political order. The book was devoted to a theory of education, and one of Babbitt's central arguments was that the true purpose of education is to make human beings cosmopolitan. With an overemphasis on originality, education was not elevating future leaders with the qualities that would unite people; instead, education was breeding a worship of differences. "As a result of our loss of standards, the classicist would complain, we are inbreeding personal and national peculiarities and getting farther and farther away from what is universally human."[11] Babbitt's complaint was not with originality per se but with an originality that refused to recognize commonalities in the human spirit.

According to Babbitt, "Since Rousseau the world has become increasingly familiar with the man who poses and attitudinizes before it and is not satisfied until he can draw its attention to the traits that establish his own uniqueness. The eccentric individualist not only rejoiced in his own singularity, but was usually eager to thrust it on other people. His aim was to startle, or, as the French would say, to *épater le bourgeois*, to make the plain citizen 'stare and gasp.'"[12] In its extreme form, the Romantic becomes, like Rousseau, the "arch-egoist."[13]

Babbitt admitted that what gave life to the Romantic movement was the artificiality of neoclassical art and literature that had "an excessive respect for the past."[14] The solution was not, however, to swing the pendulum wildly in the opposite direction and to focus solely on the quality of originality. In fact, finding the universal expressed in a new way was at the very heart of all great art and literature. "Genuine originality is so immensely difficult because it imposes the task of achieving work that is of general human truth and at the same time intensely individual."[15]

In *The New Laokoon*, Babbitt also hinted at the implications of Romantic aesthetics for politics. He again emphasized that there was much that was "artificial and superficial in the French tradition,—its conventions, and etiquette, and gallantries."[16] However, the danger with throwing out all tradition was "the risk of losing a real virtue, viz., the exquisite urbanity that the French had at their best really succeeded in attaining."[17] Because some conventions were artificial, one could not, Babbitt asserted, dismiss all convention, as some form of decorum is necessary to prevent the triumph of temperamental individuality.

In *The Masters of Modern French Criticism*, Babbitt took this argument one step further by linking Romantic originality with national self-assertion and the roots of conflict in this self-assertion: "When individual or national differences are pushed beyond a certain point what comes into play is not sympathy but antipathy."[18] The worship of national differences would prevent an urbane cosmopolitanism. In his portrait of Madame de Staël, for example, Babbitt connected her perceptive observations about the uniqueness of national cultures to Rousseau's theory of nationalism and argued that her views represented a false and modern conception of cosmopolitanism.

> Her conception of the relation of nationalities to one another simply reproduces on a larger scale the Rousseauistic conception of the proper relation of

the individuals. Each nationality is to be spontaneous and original and self-assertive, and at the same time infinitely open and hospitable to other national originalities. Nationalism in short is to be tempered by cosmopolitanism, and both are to be but diverse aspects of Rousseauistic enthusiasm. The first law for nationalities as for individuals is not to imitate but to be themselves.[19]

Madame de Staël was important intellectually because she had taken the idea of Rousseau's spontaneous individual and applied it to nations, claiming that nations driven by temperamental self-assertion would exhibit peaceful natures. This is a parallel with Rousseau's belief that temperamental individuals would unite in the general will. Babbitt believed that it was utopian to believe that impulsive and temperamental nation-states would live in harmony with one another.

Madame de Staël's false cosmopolitanism, Babbitt said, offered a moral justification for temperamental national expansion based on a belief that one's nation possessed unique and inherently virtuous national traits. "The modern cosmopolitan is to be blamed not for developing on a magnificent scale the virtues of expansion but for setting up these virtues as a substitute for the virtues of concentration. He would have us believe that everyman can fly off on his own tangent, and then in some mysterious manner, known only to romantic psychology, become every man's brother; and that the same process can be repeated on a national scale."[20]

False cosmopolitanism was, Babbitt remarked, "something of romantic sophistry" because it suppressed genuine spiritual experience and obscured the ethical challenges that must be overcome if people were to get along with one another.[21] The Romantic sentimentalist sought to be unique, eccentric, and solitary yet also wished to find communion through sentimentality. But the false cosmopolitan's attempt at unity through emotion, Babbitt said, was an attempt to find communion through the lowest common denominator of human existence and was a sign more of decadence than of peaceful order:

> Few moments are more perilous for a country than when it escapes from its narrow traditional disciplines and becomes cosmopolitan. Unless some new discipline intervenes to temper the expansion, cosmopolitanism may be only another name for moral disintegration. Nations no less than individuals, as history tells us all too plainly, may descend to meet. Their contact with one another may result not in that ideal exchange of virtues of which Madame de Staël dreamed, but in an exchange of vices.[22]

For Babbitt, this false cosmopolitanism represented a historically unique threat to peace because it assumed that the worship of national ego would naturally lead to common ground with other nations similarly oriented. Babbitt argued that recent history more likely pointed to the conclusion that well-armed nations, all with the firm conviction that their national soul was unique and inherently beautiful, would more likely be warlike than peaceful. Babbitt employed a reference from Romantic literature to explain the problem:

> The clashes between states and coalitions of states have, under existing conditions, become clashes between Frankenstein monsters. One should recollect that the Frankenstein monster was not, as is commonly supposed, a soulless monster. On the contrary, as depicted by Mrs. Shelley, he is, in the Rousseauistic sense, a beautiful soul—possibly as a result of having learned to read from works like the *Sorrows of Werther*. He becomes ruthless only when the beauty of his soul and his yearnings for sympathy are underappreciated by others and he is forced back into psychic solitude.[23]

Romanticism tended to create a literature of nationalism that could be understood only through a subrational spirit accessible only by those native to that particular country. Babbitt cited detractors of this type of national literature such as the nineteenth-century French literary critic Désiré Nisard, who objected to the "chimera of a purely national literature" and instead asserted that "what is precious in literature must not be purely national, but universal and human."[24] One could not become cosmopolitan, Nisard complained, and look for common ground across cultures by asserting that literature is comprehended only through a unique national outlook. Nisard "looked on the new cosmopolitanism of comprehension and sympathy as a menace to some of the finest qualities in French literature.[25]

Long before Babbitt began writing extensively about politics, he had developed his concept of true cosmopolitanism in opposition to the false cosmopolitanism of the Romantic movement. In a very early essay, written in 1898, when he was in his early thirties, Babbitt was critical of an unsound cosmopolitanism that naively assumed that nations would come together based on their differences: "In that ideal cosmopolitanism of which Goethe dreamed, each country was to broaden itself by a wise assimilation of the excellencies of other nationalities. The actual cosmopolitanism which has arisen during the present century has perhaps resulted in an interchange of vices rather than of virtues."[26] In his 1915 *Nation* essay, Babbitt contrasted the same ideas as "true" and "false" internationalism.[27]

Throughout his writings, Babbitt preferred to bring his concept of genuine cosmopolitanism into clearer focus by contrasting the genuine cosmopolitanism of Christianity with the false cosmopolitanism of an expansionistic nationalism. Because of its religiosity, the culture of the Middle Ages was, in contrast to modernity, highly cosmopolitan. "This literature that expressed the mind of the Middle Ages was in the highest degree cosmopolitan, but cosmopolitan in the older and what may turn out to be the only genuine sense,—that is, it rested primarily on a common discipline and not on a common sympathy."[28] On this ethical level, people "cease to be, first of all, Jew or Greek, bond or free, male or female, for they have become 'one in Christ.'"[29]

He pointed out that Rousseau had rejected "both institutional Christianity and true Christianity, on the ground that they are antinational" and that the Enlightenment-Romantic rejection of a religious and humanistic view of human nature meant that individuals and nations would not find common ground.[30] "Even etymology tells us that if men wish to move toward a common centre they must not expand and fly off, each on a tangent of his own temperament and impulses, but concentrate. For those who admit that men must move towards some such centre set above their ordinary selves, if civilized society is to endure at all, it follows that the 'civil war in the cave,' instead of being artificial, is a tremendous fact."[31]

Babbitt's political writings therefore did not offer simply a negative critique of modern naturalism; he offered a positive path forward in his concept of true cosmopolitanism. All great cultures, East and West, had deep humanistic or religious traditions that could unite people on the basis of "moderation and good sense and decency."[32] Babbitt's version of true cosmopolitanism emphasized not national differences but a genuinely religious or humanistic outlook that might unite individuals and even national leaders by emphasizing common spiritual experiences. What could draw people together, or what created a genuine cosmopolitan outlook, was religious or ethical discipline. "If we are to unite on the higher levels with other men we must look in another direction than the expansive outward striving of temperament: we must in either the humanistic or religious sense undergo conversion."[33]

Babbitt also believed that a genuinely cosmopolitan person could not be aggressively dogmatic about religious doctrine. Even some genuinely religious personalities in history had mistakenly neglected to find commonalities among different religious traditions, focusing on contrasting dogmas rather than common religious experiences. Traditions and dogmas might, as Burke argued, provide the decent drapery of life and would buttress those who were struggling to perform their duties, but truth was found not in the dogma but in the activity of the soul itself. As Babbitt stated the problem of dogma, "The final reply to all the doubts that torment the human heart is not some theory of conduct, however perfect, but the man of character."[34] Babbitt liked to point to the common spiritual experiences found in Christianity and in Buddhism: "Persons of positive and critical temper who yet perceive the importance of meditation may incline here as elsewhere to put less emphasis upon the doctrinal divergence of Christianity and Buddhism than on their psychological agreement."[35] Leaders from different nations and cultures would not, of course, share the same doctrines and conventions, but if they were engaged in true ethical work, they would find common ground with other leaders of similar orientation.

What struck Babbitt about human history was not, as the Romantic would point out, the sheer variety of human cultures but the central unity that threads through all of the diversity. "A student of the past cannot help being struck by the fact that men are found scattered through different times and countries and living under very different conventions who are nevertheless in virtue of their insight plainly moving towards a common centre."[36] The problem of the one and the many, Babbitt thought, could be solved in actual experience: "Men tend to come together in proportion to their intuitions of the One; in other words the true unifying principle of mankind is found in the insight of its sages. We *ascend* to meet."[37]

Claes G. Ryn devoted an entire book to the idea that international order must ultimately be rooted in a sound cosmopolitanism in which diverse cultures recognize their common humanity.[38] Diverse religious and humanistic traditions may exhibit unique and particular conventions and traditions, yet when examined with some care, this diversity at the highest level is found to be "*a manifestation of universality itself.*"[39] That is, universal human values manifest themselves in a perpetual stream of diversity that displays "richness, strength and adaptability."[40] For Ryn, a leader with a cosmopolitan temperament will recognize that each culture can attain a higher plane of existence by cultivating and developing the richness of its unique historical experience. This particularity is not an obstacle to be overcome but a potentiality for enhancement to be celebrated.

Ryn is enlarging an idea that is implicit to Babbitt's thought but is not always precisely articulated. Even on this higher plane of existence, what is universal will, by the very nature of reality, manifest itself in diverse ways. True cosmopolitanism as extended in this fashion would welcome diversity and see it as strength as long as the diversity was grounded in a sound ethical outlook. In short, Romanticism's celebration of diversity and differences might deserve a partial acceptance that is not often given by Babbitt. Babbitt's emphasis, however, was not on doing justice to possibly valid elements in Romanticism but on the requirement that human beings need to engage in ethical work to avoid a false picture of reality and on the fact that Romanticism went off track when an unchecked imagination asserted utopian visions for the political order.

Seeking to demonstrate the possibility of a genuine cosmopolitanism, Babbitt devoted an entire chapter of *Democracy and Leadership*, "Europe and Asia," to the commonalities of the philosophical traditions of East and West. To analyze what united humanity, Babbitt said, we should notice what East and West have in common, the things that affirm, as Cardinal Newman argued, "that the whole world is sound in its judgments (*Securus judicat orbis terrarium*)."[41]

To perform this task, the analysis cannot be impeded by "theological blinders" or "dogmatic preoccupations" or even by trying to recover, as Burke recommended, "old prejudices and unreasoned habits."[42] While the modern world would no longer accept these traditional symbols, Babbitt was sanguine that the cause was not lost because the unity of mankind could be recovered by pointing to "a purely psychological definition of the vital factor that has plainly tended to drop out in the passage from medieval to modern Europe."[43]

While Asian periods and regions, like Western history, could be characterized as highly civilized or less so, at its height, Asian civilization possessed traits that were highly similar to Christianity. After citing all of the Pauline virtues, including "Love, joy, peace, long-suffering, kindness, goodness, faith, mildness, self-control," Babbitt remarked that "about the middle of the third century before Christ, the Buddhist ruler of India, Asoka, had a very similar list of virtues carved in stone at various points throughout the vast empire: 'Compassion, liberality, truth, purity, gentleness, peace, joyousness, saintliness, self-control.' Thus Buddhism and Christianity, which often seemed hopelessly at variance when approached from the point of view of dogma, confirm one another when studied experimentally and in their fruits."[44] The pathway to peace would be found only in these spiritual and ethical commonalities.

At the center of these commonalities, Babbitt again emphasized, was a certain quality of will:

> I have been trying to show that at the center of the great religious faiths of Asiatic origin is that idea of a higher will that is felt in its relation to man's ordinary will or expansive desires as a power of vital control. The recognition of this higher will, however conceived—whether one say with Christ, "Thy will be done," or with Buddha, "Self is the lord of self; who else can be the lord?—is the source of awe and humility. The submission to this higher will is in its consummation peace.[45]

A focus on the foremost obligation to master oneself and to improve one's own character also tended to mitigate the desire to meddle or even bully in the affairs of others whether on a personal, political, or even international level. "[W]ith the present trend toward 'social justice,' the time is rapidly approaching when everybody will be minding everybody else's business."[46] Babbitt affirmed his agreement with the Platonic notion that the best definition of justice is minding one's own business: "The Platonic definition of justice as doing one's own work or minding one's own business has perhaps never been surpassed."[47]

Unsound cosmopolitanism emphasized activity outside the soul rather than activity internal to it: "Genuine justice seems to demand that men should be judged, not by their intentions or endeavors, but by their actual performance."[48] What the individual owed society was "conscience that is felt as a still small voice that is the basis of real justice."[49] The concept of social justice, Babbitt believed, distracted attention from the ethical work that would be required to bring together humans in a genuine way. Injustices that existed in society, he believed, were the accumulated injustices, writ large, of individual unjust acts committed by individual people.

Modern progressives and altruists would label such an outlook selfish, but Babbitt's retort was that a focus on one's own character was the truest social policy: "There may be something after all in the Confucian idea that if a man only sets himself right, the rightness will extend to his family first of all, and finally in widening circles to the whole community."[50] This passage, more than any other, summarized Babbitt's concept of sound cosmopolitanism. Human beings would be peaceful together when they were united in a common ethical discipline.

Babbitt was a critic of the prevalent belief that virtue involved a commitment to a social cause on the grounds that this activism frequently simply masks a will to power. There were many financial titans, Babbitt pointed out, who through imperialistic personalities had accumulated spectacular wealth and only then espoused the view that their imperialism could be mitigated and cosmopolitanism could be spread by philanthropy. But, as Babbitt said, "A man who amasses a billion dollars is scarcely exemplary, in the Aristotelian sense, even though he proceeds to lay out half a billion upon philanthropy. The remedy for such a failure of the man at the top to curb his desires does not lie, as the agitator would believe, in inflaming the desires of the man at the bottom."[51]

Babbitt's distinction between humanitarianism that characterized virtue as support for social justice and humanism that defined virtue as personal moderation and self-restraint was important in the context of cosmopolitanism, since this distinction was the key to understanding the difference between a sound cosmopolitanism and an unsound cosmopolitanism. Nations that were genuinely cosmopolitan would worry first and foremost about their own probity and the example they were setting before they began meddling in the affairs of others or telling them how to act or govern themselves.

For the humanitarian, Babbitt said, "[m]en are to be brought together, one finds on analyzing this idea of service, by means that are rationalistic and mechanical or else emotional. In either case, the humanitarian assumes that men can meet expansively and on the level of their ordinary selves. But if this notion of union should prove illusory, if men can really only come together only in humble obeisance to something set above their ordinary selves, it follows that the great temple to humanity that has been in the process of erection for several generations is the modern equivalent of the Tower of Babel."[52]

Babbitt recognized the unique problem of achieving a genuine cosmopolitan attitude in the leaders of a democracy. A Rousseauistic view of democracy denied the need for leaders who looked to anything higher than the general will of the people: simply set up the mechanisms for popular rule, and heed the voice of the people. But, as Babbitt pointed out, the will of the people could be quite imperialistic. When not properly led, the people of a democracy could be materialistic and superficial, embodying "a huge mass of standardized mediocrity."[53]

The only method of avoiding egalitarian decline in a democracy would be to elevate the type of aristocratic leader who would be "so loyal to sound standards that he inspires right conduct in others by the sheer rightness of his example."[54] The leader who followed public opinion rather than shaping it through example would stand "for nothing higher than the law of cunning and the law of force, and so is, in the sense I have sought to define, imperialistic."[55]

The French revolutionaries argued that the essence of democracy was overturning a corrupt leadership and replacing it with an undifferentiated popular will. But, according to Babbitt, the revolution demonstrated that "a leader who sets out to be only the organ of a 'general will' . . . will actually become imperialistic," and there are profound implications for international relations in leaders who see themselves merely as enforcers of the popular will.[56] The popular will, as history had demonstrated many times from ancient Greece to the French Revolution, tended not to "promote ethical union among men even across national frontiers." When a democratic population has been "emancipated from traditional standards," popular opinion is often inflamed by "an irresponsible quest for thrills." Democratic regimes of this type tended "in international affairs" to "involve transitions, often disconcertingly sudden, from pacifism to jingoism."[57] As Babbitt regularly pointed out, the yellow journalism of a William Randolph Hearst was an accelerator to inflame public opinion toward war, not a cooling force that counseled deliberation.

When imperialistic leaders appeared, they would, of course, represent themselves to the people not as militarists but as humanitarians. One cannot but reflect on recent headlines in the United States about our wars in the Middle East when considering Babbitt's remark that "A democracy, the realistic observer is forced to conclude, is likely to be idealistic in its feelings about itself, but imperialistic in its practice. The idealism and the imperialism, indeed, are in pretty direct ratio to one another."[58] For example, Babbitt pointed to the failure of Wilsonian idealism, which was based not on a sound moral realism but on a dreamy humanitarianism and had so plainly failed to meet "the test of fruits that they are taking refuge more and more, especially since the war, in their good intentions."[59]

Only those leaders who had "quelled the unruly impulses of their lower nature" would embody this humanistic understanding and bring peace both to their own nation and with other states.[60] This type of cosmopolitan leader "will find that he is moving toward a common center with others who have been carrying through a similar task of self-conquest."[61] Only states with this type of leader would tend toward a peaceful disposition: "A state that is controlled by men who have become just as a result of minding their own business in the Platonic sense will be a just state that will also mind its own business; it will be of service to other states, not by meddling in their affairs on either commercial or 'idealistic' grounds, but by setting them a good example. A state of this kind may hope to find a basis of understanding with any other state that is also ethically controlled."[62] Writ large, the peaceful disposition of a nation's leaders would manifest itself in a peaceful nation.

Genuine cosmopolitanism could be found only in a quality of leadership that was genuinely humanistic or religious. International institutions or legal machinations could not create cosmopolitanism, and, Babbitt insisted, these institutional arrangements were of no use when facing imperialistic leaders. "The hope of cooperation with a state that has an unethical leadership is chimerical. . . . [T]he unit to which all things must finally be referred is not the state or humanity or any other abstraction, but the man of character. Compared with this ultimate human reality every other reality is only a shadow in the mist."[63]

Claes G. Ryn echoes Babbitt in asserting that peace in the contemporary world will be dependent on leaders who can share a cosmopolitanism rooted in ethical character:

> Peace among cultures may be possible in the twenty-first century only if their various elites cultivate the discipline and sensibility of cosmopolitan humanism and are able to impart to their respective peoples some awareness of the shared higher ground of mankind. Each society needs leadership that inspires its people to live up to its own highest moral and cultural standards and that draws attention to how those standards correspond to the aspirations of other peoples.[64]

The implications of Babbitt's outlook for international diplomacy are that world leaders with a truly cosmopolitan outlook will exhibit a healthy respect for the highest traditions of other cultures and not seek to impose the "ideals" of one culture on another. These leaders, Ryn writes, will recognize that "goodness, truth and beauty are in a sense an ever-unfolding discovery."[65] These leaders will get past the dogmatic differences between cultures and recognize that "different traditions may, in spite of their respective weaknesses, serve the same ultimate end in different historical situations."[66]

Ryn also provides an important cautionary note about the potential for modern thinkers to sentimentalize the establishment of a harmonious world community. Ryn's critique of John Dewey, whose "notion of the human community is too affected by sentimental humanitarianism," could be applied to many contemporary notions of world community. In particular, sentimental humanitarianism, Ryn says, creates a "tendency to romanticize human nature, specifically, to discount man's propensity for evil."[67] This sentimental outlook, which saturates modern Western culture, overestimates the ease with which nations may achieve peace based upon, as Ryn says, "fellow feeling."[68]

The United Nations Charter, for example, breezily offers the naive assertion that the organization will assist nations "to practice tolerance and live together in peace with one another as good neighbours."[69] The charter establishes significant rules, processes, and other machinations that are designed to promote world peace but provides no philosophical context about the ethical requirements that could provide a truly common outlook among national leaders. There is no hint about what spiritual glue might be necessary for a peaceful international order. Regarding the futility of international institutions, Babbitt quipped, "Does anyone suppose that when Dante says 'His will is our peace' he means peace of the same quality as that which is to be established (in theory) by a super-committee at Geneva?"[70]

Ryn describes the futility of trying to establish world peace on a sentimental basis: "To minimize the weaknesses of human nature only creates false expectations and increases the likelihood that those weaknesses will be unleashed upon the world. Cross-cultural union is possible, but any progress toward that goal is likely to be limited and to depend most heavily upon the moral self-discipline and responsibility of the parties involved."[71]

The work that tends to bring peace in the soul takes effort. War is common in history because human nature has a strong tendency to want to avoid that ethical work. For Babbitt, modernity had simply refused to recognize that the prerequisite to a peaceful world is sound character on the part of world leaders; the issue had been avoided altogether.

At this point, one may ask whether Babbitt's theory, particularly his concept of cosmopolitanism, had an air of utopianism. Is it realistic to expect world leaders to achieve such a level of self-mastery that they will come together in a kind of religious communion? Is it likely that a Pauline figure would rise to leadership in the West and a Confucian personality would come to lead the East? Is this a realistic hope? If the ascension of saintlike or sage-like figures to positions of leadership is the prerequisite to peace, are not more traditional theories of international relations a more reliable and realistic guide to establishing peace?

In fact, Babbitt seemed quite realistic about attaining this type of ethical leadership. In the closing pages of *Democracy and Leadership*, he simply said that leaders must be found who merely have "some inkling" of the true meaning of culture and civilization.[72] And, in the closing of his famous 1915 *Nation* essay, he did not argue that having superhuman, saintlike leaders provided the only realistic path to peace; he simply said we needed a culture that developed leaders who were "moderate and sensible and decent" and who would set a good example by "practicing the virtues in due proportion."[73] Fifteen years later, he wrote very similar lines in a prominent essay that laid out his definition of humanism: "If the leaders of the various national and cultural groups could bring themselves to display in their dealings with one another moderation, common sense and common decency, that would accomplish a great deal—vastly more than they have been accomplishing of late."[74]

Babbitt's objection to modernity was that naturalism had precluded leaders from even considering that mastering their own temperaments would be an important ingredient in bringing restraint to the international stage. Saints are neither expected nor required, Babbitt would say. Instead, a very good start would be provided by humanistic leaders who are at least aware that there is a human law to which they and their nation may need to conform. At a minimum, national leaders must find something in themselves, something strong enough to "prevail against the powers of individual and national self-assertion."[75]

A cold-eyed assessment of human nature was, for Babbitt, not utopian but moral realism. "A chief task, indeed, of the Socratic critic would be to rescue the noble term 'realist' from its present degradation. A view of reality that overlooks the element in man that moves in an opposite direction from mere temperament, the specifically human factor in short, may prove to be singularly one-sided."[76]

In his actual views on international politics, Babbitt was very much a prescient realist, correctly prognosticating on a host of future challenges that did indeed develop for the United States, many times years after his predictions. He spent a good deal of his writings pointing out how predictions of world peace by utopian idealists had literally been exploded by violent events such as the Great War.

Babbitt had applied his concept of true cosmopolitanism to the tensions and wars of mostly Western European nation-states at the dawn of the twentieth century. While contemporary challenges to world order are different, Babbitt's ideas on moral realism provide a very useful guide to analyzing current affairs.

CHAPTER 7

Babbitt and Contemporary Theories of World Order

> In the post–Cold War world, the most important distinctions among peoples are not ideological, political, or economic. They are cultural.
> —Samuel Huntington, *The Clash of Civilizations and the Remaking of the World Order*

After two world wars and a Cold War, the nations of Western Europe desired to unite themselves around their common culture. The Maastricht Treaty of 1992 united former European enemies into a common economic, political, and cultural community. Nations lacking this common culture, such as Turkey, were deliberately excluded from the European Union despite their NATO membership. Turkey likewise began gravitating away from its Cold War alliances and toward nations with a common culture of Islam. After the Cold War ended, all over the world, political alliances of nations united by a common culture got stronger, while alliances across cultures got weaker. On a worldwide basis, peoples desired to remove themselves from artificial Cold War alliances and to seek refuge in their own cultures, histories, and traditions.

Despite the creation of the EU, leaders of the West were particularly slow to recognize this trend toward common culture, and rather than celebrating and refreshing a common Western culture, they adopted globalist positions and launched global wars to create a "new world order" based on international rules and institutions. One strain of elite culture, particularly in elite universities, felt that its mission, rather than celebrating Western or American civilizational achievements, was to disparage this tradition. In Europe, leaders permitted and even encouraged mass migration from alien cultures, threatening the common European culture.

The result of this dull-witted Western leadership was the rise of nationalism. The Trump phenomenon, the Brexit vote, and the rise of nationalistic political parties across Europe is the popular retort to the Western globalists and their failure to recognize that the world order was realigning itself along civilizational lines. Because elites failed to protect and celebrate Western culture—the original inspiration for the Maastricht Treaty—these populist movements are striving to protect Western culture on a national level. The dangers of populist nationalism have been discussed at length in this book but so has the critical importance of leadership. There should be no doubt that the recent rise of nationalism in the West was a result of highly unimaginative leaders who were incapable of directing popular aspirations in a healthier direction.

Because the politics of nation-states now reflect this cultural and civilizational overlay, the contemporary challenges of world order, of peace, and of war are quite different from the intramural politics of Europe at the turn of the twentieth century that were analyzed by Irving Babbitt. China has emerged as an economic behemoth, casting a long shadow over Asia, the Pacific, and beyond. Russia seems to be returning to its Orthodox and authoritarian roots and asserting itself in areas that share its cultural heritage, presenting significant security challenges by virtue of its enormous nuclear arsenal. A resurgent Islam has inflamed the Middle East and sparked a competition between nations seeking to lead an Islamic civilization. Many regions of the world have suffered violence at the hands of jihadists who have sprung from this Islamic or quasi-Islamic resurgence. The Cold War categories of free, communist, and nonaligned nations are no longer relevant, and the world is generally organizing itself around deeper cultural and historical commonalities.

In addition, the world has undergone an informational and technological revolution that has made it considerably smaller. Jihadists can provoke Western audiences with beheadings shown over the Internet, while the greatest works of political science are also available to world leaders over the Internet.

The West went through a phase of religious wars in the seventeenth century, a post-Enlightenment period of imperialistic nationalism with the French Revolution and Napoleon in the eighteenth century, and a period of nation-state tension and balancing in the nineteenth century. The twentieth century, however, gives one the greatest pause. After the incomprehensibly brutal and nationalistic World War I, the last century witnessed the rise of totalitarian ideology and dictatorship, another world war, and a Cold War confrontation that threatened a nuclear conflagration.

None of these past challenges, however, provides a historical guidepost for analyzing the contemporary strategic situation. Technological change and recent world events have some rough parallels in history, but understanding contemporary trends and problems requires new approaches. Babbitt has much to contribute, but if we are to apply his ideas to the contemporary world, we must develop a framework for explaining and dealing with dominant trends. What are the main challenges in foreign policy and international affairs today, and how are Babbitt's theories relevant to them?

To answer those questions, this chapter examines a representative sampling of three prominent, contemporary, and competing theories of world order and compares those theories to Babbitt's theory of international politics. When, in light of a discussion of these theories, we have settled on a paradigm that seems to encapsulate the current international order and its associated challenges, we turn to Babbitt's view of international relations to see what guidance it may offer in dealing with contemporary events.

Romantic Democratist Ideology and the "End of History"

We turn first to an idealist theory, laid out first at the end of the Cold War by Francis Fukuyama, that argues for the inevitable triumph of Western liberal democracy across the whole world. Leaders who ignore this direction of history, said Fukuyama, will likely be unable to bring "coherence and order to the daily headlines."[1] Fukuyama has revised his theory considerably over the years, but we focus here on his original thesis, which was quite influential among post–Cold War policymakers.

Fukuyama argued in his famous 1989 *National Interest* article that "something very fundamental has happened in world history" and that "there is some larger process at work" to cause "an unabashed victory of economic and political liberalism." "Unmistakable changes" had occurred "in the intellectual climate of the world's two largest communist countries." These changes were reflected in phenomena such as Western consumerism in China, "cooperative restaurants and clothing stores" in Moscow, Beethoven being played in Japanese stores and rock music played in Iran.[2]

These developments, he suspected, were not simply another phase in history "but the end of history as such: that is, the end point of mankind's ideological evolution and the universalization of Western liberal democracy as the final form of human government." For Fukuyama, the "material world" of people actually living in history was lagging behind a human consciousness that had already conceded the victory of Western democracy and liberalism. History itself would eventually catch up *"in the long run."*[3]

Fukuyama expressed regret that Karl Marx had hijacked the dialectical theory of history promulgated by Friedrich Hegel. Fukuyama pointed with sympathy to Alexandre Kojève, a Hegel scholar and Russian émigré to France who argued that Hegel saw the end of history not in a final stage of communism but in the ideals of the French Revolution. "Kojève sought to resurrect the Hegel of the *Phenomenology of the Mind,* the Hegel who proclaimed history to be at an end in 1806. For as early as this Hegel saw in Napoleon's defeat of the Prussian monarchy at the Battle of Jena the victory of the ideals of the French Revolution, and the imminent universalization of the state incorporating the principles of liberty and equality."[4]

The end of history would not mean that world events ceased in 1806. Liberty and equality had not been achieved everywhere—for example, slavery still existed in parts of the world. Nonetheless, from an intellectual perspective, "the *principles* of the liberal democratic state could not be improved upon." "There was no more work for philosophers as well, since Hegel (correctly understood) had already achieved absolute knowledge."[5]

Kojève and other Hegelians would decry economic materialists and superficial political pundits who failed to see the power of ideas in shaping human consciousness and driving the process of history. The ideals of the French revolutionaries and American Framers, once formed in the human consciousness, would shape history forever after.

> For Kojève, as for all good Hegelians, understanding the underlying processes of history requires understanding developments in the realm of consciousness or ideas since consciousness will ultimately remake the material world in its own image. To say that history ended in 1806 meant that mankind's ideological evolution ended in the ideals of the French or American Revolutions: while particular regimes in the real world might not implement these ideas fully, their theoretical truth is absolute and could not be improved upon.[6]

After sympathetically laying out Kojève's analysis of Hegel, Fukuyama turned to the question of the value of Kojève's theory for interpreting contemporary events. In short, he asked, "Have we in fact reached the end of history?" Is liberalism the final word on life and politics that can resolve all the mysteries of human life or at least provide the final intellectual structure for human beings pondering the "contradictions" of their existence?

Fukuyama then argued that the two great challenges to liberal democracy, fascism and communism, had both been defeated on the all-important level of ideas. Even in 1940, the future of fascism was, for Fukuyama, intellectually exhausted, since all it promised was the total war of "expansionist ultranationalism."[7] According to Fukuyama, fascism's material defeat in 1945 meant that it was defeated both materially and intellectually and would not have substantial appeal in the future.

Communism, on the other hand, with its Hegelian core, retained greater intellectual appeal and would not be so easy to defeat. However, over the long run, the material success of the huge middle class in capitalist societies such as the United States had defeated the Marxist intellectual assertion that a clash between capital and labor would destroy capitalism. Fukuyama observed that "[a]s Kojève (among others) noted, the egalitarianism of modern America represents the essential achievement of the classless society envisioned by Marx."[8] With these realizations, communism had lost its appeal, particularly among the young, and the major European communist parties had suffered from political atrophy.

Having described the inherent weaknesses of communism and fascism, Fukuyama turned to his view of how the ideals of Western liberal democracy had invaded the consciousness of Asia and the Middle East. The American occupation after World War II had introduced Western liberal democracy to one of the most important countries in Asia; Japan, Fukuyama argued, then made an important "contribution . . . to world history by following in the footsteps of the United States to create a truly universal consumer culture that has become both a symbol and an underpinning of the universal homogenous state." Other Asian nations such as South Korea also followed this pattern, whereby the consumer culture and material success open the door to political liberalism. Even in Khomeini's Iran, a traveler would notice "the omnipresent signs advertising the products of Sony, Hitachi, and JVC, whose appeal remained virtually irresistible and gave the lie to the regime's pretensions of restoring a state based upon the rule of the *Shariah*."[9]

Fukuyama next turned to China, where, he argued, Marxism-Leninism had largely collapsed as an intellectually credible theory. China's economy had been restructured on principles that belied communism, and a new atmosphere of capitalism, risk, and economic "dynamism" had taken hold. "But anyone familiar with the outlook and behavior of the new technocratic elite now governing China knows that Marxism and ideological principle have become virtually irrelevant as guides to policy, and that bourgeois consumerism has real meaning in that country for the first time since the revolution."[10]

Fukuyama then considered the Soviet Union, where a substantial reformist turn was apparent in 1989, the time of Fukuyama's analysis. Gorbachev was facing serious short-term challenges from conservatives who opposed substantial reform. But, Fukuyama argued, the intellectual die had been cast, and an "astonishing transformation" in the "sphere of ideology and consciousness"[11] would eventually cause the tide of history to bring liberalism to the Soviet Union.

This intellectual transformation in the Soviet Union, according to Fukuyama, was unpredictable. Gorbachev's perestroika was unlikely to fill the intellectual vacuum that the collapse of Marxism has created, but the future shape of Soviet ideology was less important than the fact that it had been slain by liberalism and that no competing political ideology would arise to compete with liberal democracy. "But at the end of history it is not necessary that all societies become successful liberal societies, merely that they end their ideological pretensions of representing different and higher forms of human society."[12]

After he considered specific regimes that might be a challenge to liberalism, Fukuyama considered two other potential challenges: religion and nationalism. He pointed to the rise of religious fundamentalism around the world but in a single paragraph swept away the possibility of religion as a serious competitor to liberalism because "[m]odern liberalism itself was historically a consequence of the weakness of religiously-based societies which, failing to agree on the nature of the good life, could not provide even the minimal preconditions of peace and stability."[13] Although Islam advocates a universal theocratic state to compete with liberalism, Fukuyama was skeptical that this option would hold any universal appeal. Religious sentiments, Fukuyama concluded, could be satisfied as a private activity within the sphere of liberalism.

The last possible challenge to liberalism might be nationalism. Fukuyama admitted that nationalism had been a plague on the Western world since Napoleon and argued that most nationalism was not the virulent sort embodied by

National Socialism. Rather, nationalism generally represented competition among various cultural groups and thus was not a coherent threat to liberalism. He believed that while it might cause conflict, nationalism was not an existential or intellectual threat to liberalism.

Fukuyama finally concluded that liberalism had overcome its major intellectual and political competitors. Although he acknowledged that many nations, particularly in the Third World, were still "very much mired in history," communism, nationalism, and religion had been sufficiently discredited in the consciousness of most major regions of the world. The battle of ideas seemed to have ended, and the end of history meant that we had entered a "de-ideologized world."[14]

Fukuyama argued that many observers of international relations had not caught up to this shifting consciousness and remained trapped in the obsolete paradigm of balance-of-power theory. He took issue with Charles Krauthammer's prediction that when the Soviet Union shed communism, Russia's "behavior [would] revert to that of nineteenth century imperial Russia." Fukuyama argued that to "take 'neo-realist' theory seriously, one would have to believe that 'natural' competitive behavior would reassert itself among OECD states were Russia and China to disappear from the face of the earth."[15]

Fukuyama asserted that "the evolution of human consciousness" had made a return to balance-of-power theory impossible and concluded with a series of predictions and assertions that, with the benefit of hindsight, seem more than slightly off the mark. He predicted that the Soviet Union would probably not revert to nineteenth-century imperial Russia or return to communism, as "from their writings and from my own personal contacts with them, there is no question in my mind that the liberal Soviet intelligentsia rallying around Gorbachev has arrived at the end-of-history view in a remarkably short time, due in no small measure to the contacts they have had . . . with the larger European civilization around them." With the end of history and ideology, Russia would turn its attention to economic concerns and to a view of world affairs in which "the use of military force becomes less legitimate."[16]

Regarding China, the end of history and ideology would follow a similar path. Since Chinese leaders had begun their "liberal" reforms, "Chinese competitiveness and expansionism on the world scene had virtually disappeared," and while China had engaged in some "troublesome" conduct on the international stage, that conduct was related to its commercial strategies—for example, selling missile technology to the Middle East.[17]

This new liberal consciousness would translate into a world in which economic concerns dominated and major war was less likely. "And the death of this ideology means the growing 'Common Marketization' of international relations, and the diminution of the likelihood of large-scale conflict between states." Wars, Fukuyama said, would still happen where regimes had not yet escaped history, but those wars would likely involve smaller countries, since the United States, Russia, China, and other large powers were in the process of exiting history. The end of history, he said, would be boring. Martial virtues would wither, ideological debates would recede, and "there will be neither art nor philosophy, just the perpetual care taking of the museum of history."[18]

Within a dozen or so years of the publication of Fukuyama's article, world events reduced his prognostications to rubble. The United States was involved in three major wars in the Middle East, driven by many of the geostrategic motivations that he predicted would wither: balance-of-power theory (Gulf War 1) and religious fundamentalism (9/11). Russia has developed a nineteenth-century authoritarian government and invaded Crimea, destabilized eastern Ukraine, and launched military operations in Syria. China has launched an unprecedented rearmament and through its military power has become threatening to a number of its neighbors, including Vietnam, Japan, and others, by claiming rights to various islands where in recent history China had no legal claim. Chinese leadership under President Xi Jinping has moved in a decidedly illiberal rather the liberal direction. Religious fundamentalism overwhelmed the Arab Spring in the Middle East, and Fukuyama's assertion that religion would not be a legitimate competitor to democratic liberalism in that region is untenable. Far from adopting a liberal democratic consciousness, the Middle East is in the process of actively repudiating liberal principles and is in fact doing so by utilizing consumer culture techniques such as Twitter and Facebook that Fukuyama argued would promote the success of liberalism. Beheadings published on Facebook and YouTube seem not to embody the "universal consumer culture" that Fukuyama argued would foster liberal values.

Even in the realm of ideas or "consciousness," democratic liberalism is losing its appeal among many peoples of the globe. Ballooning debt, racial and ethnic tensions, cultural decadence, and dysfunctional political institutions have rocked the democratic regimes of the West. Developing nations are more likely to emulate the model of Singapore, South Korea, or China than that of Great Britain, the United States, or France.

Irving Babbitt would likely have scoffed at Fukuyama's paradigm of world order. Fukuyama's view was that history was not shaped by the struggles and choices that happen in the breasts of individual leaders. His paradigm is the Rousseauistic model with a quasi-Hegelian flair. History, he thought, would reshape human nature through a new consciousness, and the historical dialectic has created the final "Idea" of government: liberal democracy and market-based economies. In Fukuyama's paradigm, peace would be the inevitable result of this mysterious historical process and not of the temperament, restraint, and personal sagacity of leaders.

Babbitt would have pointed out that the future success of liberal democracy would not be related to a mysterious Hegelian historical process but would be determined by the quality of the leadership in those democracies. Even if world events seemed to portend a rise of democratic regimes (which seems less and less the case), one should not assume that this trend would lessen the chances of world conflict; rather, it could worsen world order. Liberal democracy presupposes leaders who exhibit moderation, restraint, ethical behavior, and self-control. These qualities were not apparent in the American leaders who launched the invasion of Iraq, demonstrating that liberal democracy provides no relief from the vices of human nature. In diagnosing world order, Babbitt would ask about the characteristics that the world's emerging leaders are likely to exhibit.

Babbitt also would have predicted that the adoption of Fukuyama's outlook by American leaders would breed not cosmopolitanism but imperialism. The assertion that liberal democracy should be the only aspiration of governments around the world would result in war because it would declare all nonliberal governments illegitimate. George W. Bush embodied this spirit of democratic imperialism when he declared an international crusade for democracy in his Second Inaugural Address: "So it is the policy of the United States to seek and support the growth of democratic movements and institutions in every nation and culture, with the ultimate goal of ending tyranny in our world." Bush asserted that this task was not "primarily the task of arms," yet he launched two major wars to create democracies in Iraq and Afghanistan. He also embraced Fukuyama's quasi-Hegelian historicism by asserting, "History also has a visible direction, set by liberty and the Author of Liberty."[19]

A harsher critic might argue that Fukuyama is the kind of grotesque gnostic intellectual who claims secret knowledge about the direction of history and whose historicist theories are then used to justify disastrous political decisions such as the Iraq War. Similar historicist and idealistic theories, it can be argued, were influential in justifying the inhumanity of the twentieth century. For the purposes of this book, it is enough to argue that Fukuyama's model was wrong, did not prove predicative or sagacious, operated in a dream world of idealism rather than reality, and, as Babbitt would argue, suffered from a failure to consider the potentialities of human nature in shaping world events.

Realism without a Moral Center: Kissinger

Henry Kissinger has been one of the most prolific commentators on world affairs and has for years been considered the paradigmatic realist. While Kissinger has analyzed a bewildering set of world events going back to the 1950s, his general theory of world order has remained consistent. For Kissinger, peace depends on "a system of independent states refraining from interference in each other's domestic affairs and checking each other's ambitions through a general equilibrium of power."[20] For Kissinger, the Peace of Westphalia and to some degree the Congress of Vienna embodied such an arrangement, offering the lesson that realism and balance-of-power theory are indispensable outlooks in analyzing world events.

Kissinger seeks to extinguish any hint of idealism. He believes that European statesmen of those eras "reserved judgment on the absolute in favor of the practical and the ecumenical," creating order "from multiplicity and restraint."[21]

At the time, non-European nations or empires, such as China and the Ottoman Empire, did not accept these Westphalian principles. Yet as European influence spread, the Westphalian principles spread, too, despite the competing worldviews in other regions: "Westphalian principles are . . . the sole generally recognized basis of what exists of a world order."[22] The modern system of nation-states, which now "encompasses every culture and region," is a creation of Westphalia, and the rules of engagement among nation-states are still guided by Westphalia. Out of Westphalian principles grew the contemporary network of international institutions, trade treaties, international financial systems, and other "accepted principles of resolving international disputes" that "set limits on the conduct of wars when they do occur."[23]

However, Kissinger expresses deep concern that the Westphalian system has begun to fray. Religious fundamentalists in the Middle East pine for a regional or even worldwide caliphate. Some large Asian nations look back to a time when they were regional hegemons and nation-states were less important than imperial warrants. The United States—the nation that kept world order for decades—has been traumatized by successive wars and has historically been ambivalent about Westphalian balance-of-power principles that contrast with the US propensity for democratic idealism.

Kissinger is concerned that these fissures in the Westphalian system are leading to a crisis in world order. He worries that "all of the major centers of power practice elements of Westphalian order to some degree, but none considers itself the natural defender of the system. All are undergoing significant internal shifts. Can regions with such diverse cultures, histories, ands traditional theories of order vindicate the legitimacy of any common system?"[24]

The problem for Kissinger is that the Westphalian system was easier to implement and maintain in the small geographic area of Western Europe with a common culture and civilization than it is in the modern world: "The smaller the geographic area to which it applies and the more coherent the cultural convictions within it, the easier it is to distill a working consensus. But in the modern world the need is for a global world order. An array of entities unrelated to each other by history or values (except at arm's length), and defining themselves essentially by the limits of their capabilities, is likely to generate conflict, not order." What Kissinger recommends is "a modernization of the Westphalian system informed by contemporary realities."[25]

Kissinger sees the world always precariously balanced and ready to tip into imbalance and conflagration rather than moving, Hegelian-style, toward some mysterious consensus of consciousness. Diverse histories and cultures prevent leaders from a variety of power centers from accepting the same rules. Order can erode as a consequence of swings in relative economic and military power or of religious eruptions and ideological outbursts. The only answer to this volatility is for enlightened leaders in the most important power centers of the world to accept the Westphalian consensus, "a set of commonly accepted rules that define the limits of permissible action and a balance of power that enforces restraint where rules break down, preventing one political unit from subjugating all others."[26]

Such a consensus will not prevent all conflict but will mitigate the possibility of a fundamental breakdown in world order. "A consensus on the legitimacy of existing arrangements does not—now or in the past—foreclose competitions or confrontations, but it helps ensure that they will occur as adjustments within the existing order rather than as fundamental challenges to it."[27]

While Kissinger has always been described as a realist or a balance-of-power theorist, there is a kernel of something deeper in his thought. Kissinger strongly implies that for world order to take hold, leaders must have a certain *temperament*. There is an unmistakable similarity between Kissinger's language and concepts and those of the authors of *The Federalist*, who urged the construction of a system in which the passions and ambitions of the people would be cooled "through the medium of a chosen body of citizens, whose wisdom may best discern the true interest of their country" and who would be "least likely to sacrifice it to temporary or partial considerations."[28] When Kissinger says that the Westphalian system was designed so that nation-states could "check each other's ambitions through a general equilibrium of power," the echo of James Madison in *Federalist 51* is clear: "The provision for defence must in this, as in all other cases, be made commensurate to the danger of the attack. Ambition must be made to counteract ambition."[29]

For Kissinger, the Westphalian leader achieves order not simply through a balance of power but through "restraint," a word he uses several times to describe what is required of leaders. Enlightened diplomats must accept certain "limits of permissible action." Kissinger does not use philosophical language to describe this type of self-control but instead uses the term *consensus legitimacy* or refers to the quest to find leaders and nations who accept certain rules that will lead them to act with "restraint when rules break down" and will not collaborate in "subjugating" other nations. Kissinger states explicitly that a balance of power "does not in itself secure peace." The essential ingredient in Kissinger's thought is enlightened and restrained leaders who recognize the realities of power politics but who can then craft a common consensus of legitimacy. A balance of power must be "thoughtfully assembled and invoked" so that it can "limit" and "curtail" the "fundamental challenges" to an orderly world.[30]

Kissinger's realism contrasts strongly with Fukuyama's idealism. Kissinger, in fact, gives Fukuyama a kind of rhetorical pat on the head in the last paragraph of his 2014 book, *World Order*: "Long ago, in youth, I was brash enough to think myself able to pronounce on 'The Meaning of History.' I now know that meaning is a matter to be discovered, not declared."[31]

Kissinger may eschew any moral dimension to his thought, but he implicitly acknowledges that the clever navigation of power politics will not be enough to ensure world order. His thought is more complex and philosophical than even he may be aware of, for he has an inchoate sense that a "common order" will require leadership by persons of a certain moral temperament and character. Leaders must be willing to refrain, to set limits on their own (and their nation's) ambitions, to find common ground with diverse cultures, and to achieve cosmopolitanism in their approach toward different cultures. "The mystery to be overcome is one all peoples share—how divergent historic experiences and values can be shaped into a common order."[32]

Kissinger does not address this philosophical challenge in his writings. He presents a commonsense, realistic analysis of contemporary world affairs and the obstacles to creating a Westphalian order when contemporary events display a resurgent Islam, a democracy-crusading United States, rising hegemony in parts of Asia, the explosive growth of deadly weaponry, and other impediments to finding a "common order." He seems to avoid taking the next step of exploring deeper sources of the desirable restraint and cosmopolitanism and instead insists on proceeding from a kind of self-contained amoral balance-of-power realism. This is in contrast to Babbitt's moral realism, which argued that the *creation* of Westphalian leaders of moderate temperament is at the heart of solving problems of war and peace. Babbitt argued that the more fundamental challenge is how to shape the culture and the educational system to produce leaders of moderation, character, and self-control. Where does one find, or how does a civilization produce, leaders of a Westphalian temperament? If one ignores the moral challenge of how to actually cultivate the moderation and restraint of the Westphalian statesman, Babbitt pointed out, peace is unlikely. Kissinger maintains a clear realism that Babbitt would have embraced, because idealists have caused so much damage to the world order in recent centuries. Babbitt, however, would have asked Kissinger to focus on how the culture and the educational system shape or fail to shape the temperate Westphalian leaders.

A Clash of Civilizations

While Kissinger's contemporary writings provide a well-informed description of the challenges of modern international affairs, they lack an analytical paradigm for explaining why contemporary challenges have arisen. Why did the first post–Cold War conflagration take place in the former Yugoslavia? Why has a resurgent Russia attacked Crimea and Ukraine? Why did Western European nationalism partially recede and give birth to a common market, currency, and even political order? Why has Greece been the most uncomfortable participant in the EU and turned to Russia for support? Why has travel increased exponentially between mainland China and Taiwan? Why has Turkey become more Islamic and less Western in its culture and politics? Why has the United States not succeeded in bringing Western democracy to the Middle Eastern nations that it invaded?

These developments in world events are neither explained nor anticipated by either Fukuyama or Kissinger. For perhaps the soundest of widely known paradigms for explaining contemporary events, we turn to Harvard historian and political scientist Samuel Huntington, who published a much-discussed article, "The Clash of Civilizations" in *Foreign Affairs* in 1993 and a book-length work, *The Clash of Civilizations and the Remaking of the World Order*, eighteen years later. In these writings, Huntington seeks to explain the world that emerged after the Cold War and then, in the book's conclusion, offers a very specific description of how leaders from different civilizations might create peace in this new world order. Huntington's description of how civilizations might come together in peace is strikingly similar to Babbitt's concept of cosmopolitanism.

Huntington opens his book by describing the ways in which many current theories of world order are unsatisfying. He sees some merit in portions of these theories but ultimately finds them wanting. Liberal democracy has not triumphed, as Fukuyama predicted, and the many theories that split the world into two camps—for example, rich and poor or civilized and barbaric—do not capture the complexity of the current environment. The realist theories that view state actors as the most important units of analysis fail to capture how international alliances are increasingly formed not on the basis of pure national interest but because "publics and statesmen are less likely to see threats emerging from people they feel they understand and can trust because of shared language, religion, values, institutions and culture."[33] Finally, Huntington addresses the "chaos" theories of Zbigniew Brzezinski and Daniel Patrick Moynihan. The world is indeed chaotic, he points out, but the truth is more complex: "The world may be chaos but is not totally without order."[34]

Huntington accepts that some of these theories could help explain pieces of the world scene, but he believes that none could serve as a contemporary paradigm of the current world order. Instead, he argues that the world that emerged after the Cold War features a multiplicity of civilizations organized around common cultures.

In the post–Cold War world, for the first time in history, global politics has become multipolar *and* multicivilizational.

> In the post–Cold War world, the most important distinctions among peoples are not ideological, political, or economic. They are cultural. Peoples and nations are attempting to answer the most basic question humans can face: Who are we? And they are answering that question in the traditional way human beings have answered it, by reference to the things that mean the most to them. People define themselves in terms of ancestry, religion, language, history, values, customs, and institutions. They identify with cultural groups: tribes, ethnic groups, religious communities, nations, and, at the broadest level, civilizations.[35]

Huntington observes that as the free, communist, and nonaligned blocs faded from history, the world has organized itself around "seven or eight" civilizational units: Western, Latin American, African, Islamic, Sinic, Hindu, Orthodox, Buddhist, and Japanese. He explains that "the rivalry of the superpowers is replaced by the clash of civilizations" and that threats to world order were most dangerous when they represented "cultural conflicts" found "along the fault lines between civilizations," such as in the former Yugoslavia and Ukraine.[36]

Before we discuss themes and ideas common to Babbitt and Huntington, we should ask whether Babbitt influenced Huntington. We can say with some confidence that Huntington had read Babbitt, a famous Harvard predecessor. Huntington may have been nudged to do so by reading Russell Kirk. In a 1957 article on conservative thought, "Conservatism as an Ideology," Huntington harshly criticizes Kirk's *Conservative Mind* as an "effort to uncover a conservative intellectual tradition in America" by "resurrecting political and intellectual figures long forgotten." Huntington remarks that "few enterprises could be more futile or irrelevant" and argues that many of the figures resurrected by Kirk are not defenders of "established institutions" but "malcontents" who were severe critics of American culture and society.[37]

Huntington argues that Babbitt was one of these "malcontents" who "fled from America to Buddhism."[38] We can surmise from this statement that Huntington's sole exposure to Babbitt was not through Kirk's summary of Babbitt's thought in *The Conservative Mind*. That book contains twenty-one pages that mention or discuss Babbitt's thought with four mentions of "Buddha" or "Buddhism" as an influence on Babbitt's thought. There are a similar number of mentions of Plato, Socrates, and Aristotle. One could not conclude from Kirk's summary alone that Babbitt had "fled . . . to Buddhism." Huntington might have reached his conclusion on the basis of Babbitt's last written essay, "Buddha and the Occident," a companion to his translation of *The Dhammapada* published posthumously in 1936.

Huntington's characterization of Babbitt's thought as representing a flight to Buddhism has an element of truth. Babbitt certainly felt that the Western tradition of abstract rationalism and sentimental Romanticism contained the seeds of errors that might be corrected by an exposure to the great religious and humanistic thinkers of Asia. The West had been diverted from its classical and Christian traditions and from the perspective of ethics had been diverted into the worship of science and sentimental humanitarianism. The Asian focus on ethical concentration and the higher will was a fitting antidote to these Western trends. The thrust of Babbitt's thought was not an abandonment of the West and a flight into Buddhism, however. It was a project of diagnosis and treatment to strengthen the West through an ecumenical exposure to other humanistic and religious traditions that could balance adverse trends in Western thought.

This leaves open the question of whether Babbitt's thought influenced Huntington. It is clear that Huntington was familiar with Babbitt, and some circumstantial evidence indicates that Babbitt's ideas made their way into Huntington's theories. The conclusions to Huntington's two most important works feature concepts and terminology that contain significant echoes of Babbitt. Huntington's last book, *Who Are We: The Challenges to America's Nationality*, concludes that Americans had three alternative ways to consider their national identity: cosmopolitan, imperialistic, and nationalistic. These are key concepts in Babbitt's theory of internationalism.

Yet these concepts have different meanings for Huntington, which seems to indicate only a partial influence for Babbitt. He saw cosmopolitanism as an outlook that develops between world leaders who have access to a certain understanding of human existence and who can see the opportunity for peace with leaders of similar ethical elevation. For Huntington, cosmopolitanism simply meant globalism: "The ideal would be an open society with open borders, encouraging subnational ethnic, racial, and cultural identities, dual citizenship, diasporas, and led by elites who increasingly identified with global institutions, norms, and rules rather than national ones."[39]

Yet on the subject of imperialism, Babbitt and Huntington shared nearly identical views. For Babbitt, imperialism was driven by humanitarianism, a desire to "serve" fellow human beings that ignored the ethical obligations of individuals. Huntington similarly characterized imperialism as driven by "humanitarian intervention" and "foreign policy as social work."[40] Babbitt's phraseology was similar: "The humanitarian would, of course, have us meddle in foreign affairs as part of his program of world service."[41] At least one sentence from Huntington's book could have been written by Babbitt: "The imperial impulse was thus fueled by beliefs in the supremacy of American power and the universality of American values."[42] American imperialism was a crusade by the nation that felt itself superior. Huntington wrote, "In the cosmopolitan alternative, the world reshapes America. In the imperial alternative, America remakes the world."[43]

Finally, Huntington's concept of nationalism, while different from Babbitt's, clearly contained elements of Babbitt's view of history and culture. Babbitt viewed nationalism as a modern disease, a product of Rousseau's vision of a diversity of nations with separate and distinct democratic national wills that would push up against neighboring states. This form of nationalism would prevent nations from finding common ground and in Babbitt's view led to the Great War.

Huntington's term *nationalism* was not a pejorative but merely descriptive. Nationalism was the sum total of a nation's "culture, values, traditions and institutions."[44] Yet Huntington had a broader definition of nationalism when he asserted that much of the success of America is bound up with "its Anglo-Protestant culture and its religiosity."[45] This view was not very different from Babbitt's assertion that America's greatness derived from a genuine Christian humility found in a character such as Washington: "Our unionist leaders, Washington, Marshall and Lincoln, though not narrowly orthodox, were still religious in the traditional sense."[46]

Yet Babbitt and Huntington probably had different understandings of nationalism because of the historical realities of nationalism that each faced. Babbitt faced the growth of a centrifugal nationalism in Europe that led to the disaster of World War I, a cataclysmic event for the West. The greatest danger for the contemporary world comes from the post–Cold War order, in which, as Huntington pointed out, the world had divided into civilizational blocs with separate and distinct religious and cultural traditions. As the nations of Western Europe in the early twentieth century could not find common ground, so the great civilizational blocs of the twenty-first century—Western, Orthodox, Sinic, and Islamic—either have clashed or seem destined to clash. For Huntington, the two predominant American paradigms for foreign policy were a soft, sentimental globalism based on international institutions and an imperialistic, ideological democracy promotion necessitating American invasions. He believed both to be unsuited to addressing the challenges arising from the clash of civilizational blocs because their premises represented a fundamental refusal to recognize the reordering of the world along civilizational lines since the end of the Cold War.

Huntington argued that after the Cold War "the U.S. government has had extraordinary difficulty adapting to an era in which global politics is shaped by cultural and civilizational tides."[47] The first Bush administration and the Clinton administration continued to operate under the assumption that global and "multicivilizational" mechanisms would be more important than historical and cultural heritage. This oversight led to terrible blunders in US foreign policy decision making. Huntington pointed to several important mistakes of US foreign policy in the immediate post–Cold War world:

> The Bush and Clinton Administrations supported the unity of a multicivilizational Soviet Union, Yugoslavia, Bosnia, and Russia, in vain efforts to halt the powerful ethnic and cultural forces pushing for disunion. They promoted multicivilizational economic integration plans which are either meaningless, as with APEC, or involve major unanticipated economic or political costs, as with NAFTA and Mexico. They attempted to develop close relationships with the core states of other civilizations in the form of a "global partnership" with Russia or "constructive engagement" with China, in the face of the natural conflicts of interest between the United States and those countries. At the same time, the Clinton Administration failed to involve Russia wholeheartedly in the search for peace in Bosnia, despite Russia's major interest in that war as Orthodoxy's core state. Pursuing the chimera of a multicivilizational country, the Clinton Administration denied self-determination to the Serbian and Croatian minorities and helped bring into being a Balkan one-party Islamist partner of Iran. In similar fashion the U.S. government also supported the subjection of Muslims to Orthodox rule, maintaining that "Without question, Chechnya is part of the Russian federation."[48]

This failure to recognize the emergence of civilizational blocs has continued to generate fundamental errors in US diplomacy. Among the endless examples, a few of the most important include probably the greatest US blunder, the belief by many prominent policymakers that the Iraqi people would heartily embrace a model of Western democracy and ignore many generations of sectarian and ethnic connections. More recently, US diplomats in Ukraine severely underestimated Russia's potential reaction to a US-backed 2014 coup that led directly to the Russian invasion of Crimea. In the case of Ukraine, the supposed desirability of democracy promotion blinded Obama administration policymakers to the importance of the cultural and historical desire of Orthodox Russia to preserve its links to Orthodox peoples in Crimea and eastern Ukraine. The drift of Turkey away from NATO and that of Greece from the EU as well as the partial accommodation of Taiwan toward China were all largely unanticipated by US policymakers, who continue to stress international organizations and norms.

Huntington believed that the failure to recognize the civilizational model had been driven by two separate and distinct US foreign policy approaches. First, there were the soft globalists, such as Barack Obama, who argued that international law, institutions, and norms should underlie US foreign policy decision making. The approach of the soft globalists is marked by summitry and international conferences designed to address human rights, environmentalism, nuclear proliferation, and other multicivilizational issues.

Huntington made clear that the far greater danger to the international order would be the democracy crusading promoted by neoconservative foreign policy elite who populated the Bush administration. "In the emerging world of ethnic conflict and civilizational clash, Western belief in the universality of Western culture suffers from three problems: it is false; it is immoral; and it is dangerous." It is false, Huntington said, because the Fukuyama thesis is false: the world's cultural diversity is not eroding and giving way to Western values. It is immoral, Huntington said, because "of what would be necessary to bring it about." As in Iraq, the resistance to the imposition of Western values is significant, and only brutal imperialistic tactics have any hope of success in the imposition of those values. On a worldwide scale, the attempt to impose these values would be catastrophic. Finally, "Western universalism is dangerous to the world because it could lead to a major intercivilizational war between core states, and it is dangerous to the West because it could lead to the defeat of the West."[49] The failure to recognize the historical and cultural claims of China in the Sinic region or of Russia in the Orthodox region could generate a world war of unimaginable proportions. The obliviousness of US policymakers in backing a coup in Ukraine, for example, was the kind of reckless interventionism that could initiate a chain of events leading to a nuclear conflict.

Huntington, like Babbitt, urged moderation and restraint: "The prudent course for the West is not to attempt to stop the shift in power but to learn to navigate the shallows, endure the miseries, moderate its ventures, and safeguard its culture." Much like Babbitt, Huntington argued that Western values are rooted in unique historical and cultural traditions such as "Christianity, pluralism, individualism, and the rule of law."[50] These values had made the West great, but they were unique to the West; while they might be admired by other civilizations, their adoption would not result from Western leaders simply proclaiming them to be universal. And their forced imposition at gunpoint would generate enormous cultural resistance. Huntington argued that Western leaders should prioritize renewal at home, not evangelization abroad: "The principal responsibility of Western leaders, consequently, is not to attempt to reshape other civilizations in the image of the West, which is beyond their declining power, but to preserve, protect and renew the unique qualities of Western civilization."[51]

Historically, while Babbitt faced a clash of European nation-states and Huntington saw a clash of civilization blocs, their situations were analogous, and Babbitt's ideas still apply to a conflict between civilizations. When faced with a volatile international order both at the turn of the twentieth century and in the post–Cold War environment, US policymakers responded with two similarly feckless foreign policy approaches. The first was a sentimental internationalism that placed inordinate faith in international institutions and that soft-pedaled deep historical and culture differences rooted in religion and history. The second was a democratic imperialism that sought to impose "universal" Western values under the false belief that the spread of those values would lead to peace and that soft-pedaled the deep historical and cultural differences between societies.

While Babbitt and Huntington agreed on the folly of certain foreign policy approaches rooted in a misplaced idealism, they were applying their principles to different aspects of the international order. Babbitt foresaw the danger of tensions between civilizations but wrote about foreign policy and international affairs largely in the context of the Great War and the potential coming clash of European nation-states. In Huntington's case, the world had become what contemporary theorists characterize as smaller. Huntington warned of clashes between blocs of civilizations that, as a consequence of technology, were more easily coming into contact and that in many important respects lack common outlooks, values, and institutions.

Both Babbitt and Huntington diagnosed and then rejected the two modern forms of idealism in foreign policy, and they arrived at very similar conclusions concerning the solution to the challenges that idealism posed for the international order. At the very end of *The Clash of Civilizations*, Huntington paralleled Babbitt in arguing that while cultural and historical diversity is a fact of existence and cannot be ignored, human beings can and at times do unite on a higher religious or humanistic level. Huntington said that "whatever the degree to which they divided humankind, the world's major religions—Western Christianity, Orthodoxy, Hinduism, Buddhism, Islam, Confucianism, Taoism, Judaism—also share key values in common."[52]

Huntington then argued that "commonalities" between culturally diverse civilizations could unite humankind on a higher level, a level that he characterized as "Civilization."[53] Babbitt, too, termed the higher striving of humanity as a quest for "civilization." Unlike Babbitt, Huntington did not try in any depth to explain what "commonalities" might have the desired effect. He did, however, ask precisely the question that Babbitt had asked—whether the religious and dogmatic differences between societies could be overcome by a common humanism that would cultivate the *higher* commonalities that can be drawn out of the cultural diversity. When Babbitt argued for his New Humanism, he asked and addressed the same questions that Huntington later asked: "Is there a general, secular trend, transcending individual civilizations, towards higher levels of Civilization?"[54] Since this is a topic that Babbitt explored in considerable depth, a deeper familiarity with Babbitt might have filled a gap in Huntington's work on international relations.

Huntington seemed as one with Babbitt in arguing that the only true answer to the challenges of the international order would be found when world leaders united on a higher plane while respecting cultural diversity: "The futures of both peace and Civilization depend upon understanding and cooperation among the political, spiritual, and intellectual leaders of the world's major civilizations."[55]

While Huntington's more philosophical musings never went as deep as Babbitt's and Huntington never defined his terms as clearly as Babbitt, Huntington embraced in his own way Babbitt's ultimate conclusion that questions of war and peace revolve around the ability of leaders to attain a higher plane of existence. If leaders meet on a lower plane, disastrous conflict may result. Huntington wrote: "In the greater clash, the global 'real' clash, between Civilization and barbarism, the world's great civilizations, with their rich accomplishments in religion, art, literature, philosophy, science, technology, morality, and compassion, will also hang together or hang separately."[56]

Huntington provided a valuable paradigm for understanding the contemporary international order. He also offered a conclusion very similar to Babbitt's when he declared that leaders must respect and to some extent absorb the great human achievements across civilizations, achievements that would of necessity also bear the distinctive marks of the world's diverse cultures and civilizations. Babbitt and Huntington serve as reminders to US policymakers that a strong dose of humility and a healthy respect for other cultures and civilizations, made possible by a proper familiarity with their own, represent the path to peace. Going considerably beyond Huntington, Babbitt provided a major and indispensable supplement to the best of international relations theory.

Conclusion

> Societies are not made of sticks and stones, but of men whose individual characters, by turning the scale one way or the other, determine the direction of the whole.
>
> —Plato, *The Republic*

Since the Spanish-American War of 1898 and particularly since the end of the Cold War, America has regularly gone abroad in search of monsters to destroy. For more than a century, American democracy's most distinguishing feature arguably has been a penchant for international warfare. In recent decades, American adventurism has accelerated to far-flung regions of the world that share little cultural or historical commonality with the United States, and long wars have been engaged that are little related to American national interests.

For example, just as the specter of nuclear war was lifting at the end of the Cold War and America had an historic opportunity to shore up the republic at home, President George H. W. Bush was assembling a Western army of a half million to intervene in an intramural dispute within the Arab world, and that army was inserted into an Arab world that was witnessing an Islamic resurgence and growing cultural distance from the West.

That growing Islamic revulsion to the West then manifested itself in the terrible attacks of 9/11, instigating two long and failed Western military interventions in the Middle East predicated on the assumption that what the Islamic world lacks is liberal Western values and American-style liberty. With the Iraq War of 2003, the parallels between the rhetoric of the imperial Jacobins and that of George W. Bush were on full display, and such rhetoric continues in a bipartisan foreign policy establishment that, like the Jacobins' antipathy toward European monarchs, views the primary goal of American foreign policy as that of cashiering foreign dictators and unleashing the popular will around the world under the false assumption that democracy is peace and peace is democracy. The foreign policy establishment's calls for US engagement in numerous global conflicts is justified by what Irving Babbitt would describe as humanitarianism, a noblesse oblige that asserts that American elites know what is best for other cultures and nations. As former Secretary of State Madeline Albright famously said: "But if we have to use force, it is because we are America; we are the indispensable nation. We stand tall and we see further than other countries into the future."[1] From Bill Clinton's wars of choice in the Balkans to George Bush's preemptive war in Iraq to Barack Obama's decapitation of the Libyan regime, the policy of the United States has been to use force wherever and whenever it chooses, even when such interventions have a tenuous connection to the US national interest.[2]

The US Constitution, once a bulwark against such military adventurism, no longer serves as a significant limiting factor in these decisions about war and peace. That great document, which warns the republic to pay heed to restraint, has been cast aside. This lack of constitutional restraint, Babbitt would say, is not a policy error but a manifestation of the lack of ethical restraint in America's leadership. None of the US military interventions since the Iraq War have secured the congressional approval of a declaration of war, and neither the executive nor the legislative branch apparently feels any urgency to embrace their traditional constitutional roles. Congress seems to have abdicated one of its primary Article I powers, and the executive, the benefactor of the congressional abdication, seems happy to embrace its new extraconstitutional powers. Likewise, other Article I powers of the Congress to appropriate funds (or not) for these military operations have not served as a restraining force against interventionism. For example, a recent study released by the Watson Institute at Brown University estimates that the costs of war since 2001 are a staggering $4.7 trillion.[3] Despite the country's huge deficits and national debt, these wars have been lavishly funded (often with off-budget "emergency funds").

Thoughtful Americans may want to step back and consider whether our American democracy is beginning to exhibit the imperial ambitions of the late Athenian democracy and the Roman republic. Given the number of innocents killed, the staggering level of American dead and wounded, religious and ethnic diasporas caused, deep resentments generated, and chaos unleashed, Americans may want to reflect on the degree to which our military interventions may have been prideful and imperialistic wars of aggression rather than selfless humanitarian missions. Americans may also want to reflect on the historical fact that great republics tend not to survive endless warfare.

With his theory of imperialism, Babbitt pointed squarely at deep cultural currents that shape the temperament of the leaders who ultimately determine war and peace. The fact that the current foreign policy establishment exudes an imperialistic outlook does not derive from mere policy errors that can simply and easily be corrected by a new president and a new policy paper. The American posture of endless wars, Babbitt would say, has been shaped by far deeper cultural, moral, and intellectual currents that have developed over three hundred years, currents that were stoutly resisted by the American Framers. These moral and cultural forces are now so dominant that they promote foreign policy imperialism even for presidents elected on a platform of restraint.

In the world of ideas, a reconsideration of the very concept of an idealistic and humanitarian foreign policy seems warranted. The two most prominent schools of idealism in US foreign policy, a soft globalism of international institutions and a crusading spirit of democracy promotion, have often undermined international peace and stability. The failures of these two types of humanitarianism derive not primarily from an inability to find the proper tactics to implement their ideas but from the unsound philosophical and imaginative premises underlying idealism itself.

Claes G. Ryn has pointed out that Babbitt's characterization of idealism as deriving from an "idyllic imagination" does not completely capture the pernicious nature of idealism. "Ideals" imply good intentions that could be realized if only the proper strategies could be employed, be it through international institutions or military tactics and solutions. But as Ryn points out, "The problem is not with poorly chosen means but with the impossible dream itself. The dream ignores the basic facts of life, specifically the need for moral character."[4] If "idealism" were instead to gain a reputation as an intellectual pejorative, it might signal that the West is gaining a more rational perspective on foreign policy. Rather than a foreign policy consensus that stresses "noble ideals," US policymakers may wish to consider a more realistic emphasis on our national interests combined with humility and a respect for other nations.

Babbitt always believed that the foreign policy failures that he witnessed did not involve strictly intellectual errors but sprang from a decaying culture in need of a kind of spiritual awakening, a moral conversion among the nation's leaders and in the culture that would restore restraint and humility. Just as a dissolute and boastful person will not get along with others without a sincere change of heart, a well-armed nation puffed up on self-congratulatory conceits will also not bring order or peace to the world without undergoing what Plato called the *periagoge*, a turning-around of the whole soul.[5]

If the central axiom of classical political philosophy—that is, the city is the soul written in large letters—is correct, then Babbitt's theory of imperialism has a compelling internal logic: the aggressive soul will give birth to the aggressive nation. By his assertion of this anthropological principle, Babbitt therefore locates himself squarely in the tradition of classical and Christian political philosophy. Plato, Aristotle, Augustine, Aquinas, and a number of other traditional Western political philosophers have all emphasized the foundational assumption that the tendencies of good and evil found in human heart will exhibit themselves on a larger scale in the regime.[6]

Yet Babbitt makes a unique philosophical contribution by extending this city-soul parallel to the field of international affairs. In his analyses of Napoleon and World War I, for example, he applies the city-soul parallel to the interactions *between* nation-states. Therefore, one might postulate that there is a "Babbitt Corollary" to the city-soul principle that may be described as the world-city-soul principle. The international order, no less than the domestic order, will reflect the soul type of world leaders and the cultures that those leaders represent.

When the Western world exploded in mass warfare in 1914, Babbitt analyzed events through this extended world-city-soul paradigm, and in 1917 he wrote,

> Christianity, before its present humanitarian perversion, showed the force of a right example in solving the problem that now concerns us, in promoting peace. "My peace I give unto you." Humanism is at one with religion in asserting that a doctrine that professes peace must show its efficacy, first of all, by establishing peace in the breast of the individual. To suppose that men who are filled individually with every manner of restlessness, maddened by the lust for power and speed, votaries of the god Whirl, will live in peace either with themselves or with others, is the vainest of chimeras. Whatever degree of peace is ever achieved in international relations in particular will be due to the fact that the

responsible leaders in the countries concerned are not mere imperialistic expansionists, but, whether as a result of religious or humanistic discipline, have submitted a vital impulse to a no less vital control; there will then be hope that they may get within hailing distance of one another, even hope that they may subordinate to some extent the private interests of their respective states to the larger interests of civilization.[7]

At the turn of the twentieth century, Babbitt believed that Rousseauistic propaganda about the natural goodness of the human heart had, 150 years later, given birth to a rabid nationalism in the West. With the elimination of traditional responsibility of individuals to rein in their passions, Romanticism and utilitarianism brought an intellectual, moral, and political disaster for the West as growing military power and prowess were unrestrained by any countervailing moral force. Aided by utilitarianism, Western leaders now had vast powers for mass killing at their disposal yet lived in an intellectual milieu in which spontaneous outbursts of nationalism by agitated populations were thought to be a form of democratic virtue. Appeals for peace on the basis of higher, transnational moral aspirations went unheeded. "Europe," Babbitt lamented in 1915, "is to-day less cosmopolitan in any genuine sense of the word than it was at almost any period in the Middle Ages."[8]

Babbitt can teach Americans today that US national security challenges are substantially more complex than is presently understood. They require a long-term solution that would involve a substantial cultural renovation rather than simply improved policy analysis. For the United States to find common ground with other nations, a kind of cultural conversion seems required, yet politicians and policy analysts who are far downstream from moral and spiritual matters seem neither inclined nor equipped to consider or understand the need for such a cultural renewal. A more fruitful alternative may be to turn to those in society who move and shape the spirit: artists, poets, authors, filmmakers, educators, clergy, and others who influence the imagination.

Babbitt would wholeheartedly agree that politicians' outlooks are the products of deeper cultural currents and that a healthy culture is more likely to produce healthy politicians. Yet with respect to the contemporary United States, the prudential question is whether there is enough time and enough cultural raw materials to conduct such a renovation. While small pockets of cultural resistance and renewal exist, the prospect for wholesale cultural renovation seems dim. In academia, for example, there is increasing hostility to and sometimes deliberate suppression of Western traditions rather than attempts to breathe new life into them.

The present condition of the United States is one in which the possibility of a broad and profound cultural renewal may be remote. The cultural degeneration is so acute that political problems might portend a gradual or even catastrophic decline. Yet Babbitt deplored historical determinism, and he believed that human beings and nations make their own fate through deliberate moral exertions. The only possible remedy for the current conditions would, for Babbitt, be the emergence of leaders who are sensible, moderate, and decent so that the body politic can undergo a period of political stabilization. As James Madison said about ancient Athens, "In these critical moments, how salutary will be the interference of some temperate and respectable body of citizens. . . . What bitter anguish would not the people of Athens have often escaped, if their government had contained so provident a safeguard against the tyranny of their own passions?"[9]

Notes

Introduction

1. A more contemporary example may be found in the rise of the Nazi Party and Hitler's appointment as German chancellor. While neither Hitler nor the Nazis achieved popular majorities in the presidential or Reichstag elections, their substantial success at the polls did put them in a position to abolish the constitution and assume dictatorial powers.
2. Huntington, *Who Are We?* 363.
3. Babbitt, *Rousseau and Romanticism*, 298.
4. Huntington, *Who Are We?* 363–64.
5. Bush, "Selected Speeches."
6. Babbitt, *Democracy and Leadership*, 156.
7. Babbitt, *Rousseau and Romanticism*, 376.
8. Babbitt, *Rousseau and Romanticism*, 329.
9. Babbitt, *Democracy and Leadership*, 226.
10. Bush, "Freedom Agenda."
11. Irving Babbitt, lecture notes, 1923, trans. Martine Berliet and William S. Smith, 1, Papers of Irving Babbitt, Box 19, Folder "Paris Lecture, 1923," Harvard University Archives, Pusey Library, Cambridge, MA.
12. Babbitt, *On Being Creative*, 232.
13. Babbitt, lecture notes, 1923, 1.
14. Babbitt, *Democracy and Leadership*, 141.
15. Burke, *Reflections*, 152.
16. Voegelin, *Order and History*, 109.
17. Babbitt, lecture notes, 1923, 13.
18. Babbitt, *Rousseau and Romanticism*, 176.
19. Babbitt, *Rousseau and Romanticism*, 177.
20. For concise biographical sketches of Babbitt, see Ryn, introduction to *Character*

and Culture, ix–l; Kirk, introduction, 1–68. One might surmise that Babbitt held on to life for an extra day to avoid passing on July 14, Bastille Day.

21. See Nevin, *Irving Babbitt,* 100–124.

Chapter 1

1. Muller, *Great Learning*; also quoted in Ryn, *America the Virtuous,* 208.
2. See Babbitt, *On Being Creative,* 76; Babbitt, *New Laokoon,* 200; Babbitt, *Literature and the American College,* 86; Babbitt, *Democracy and Leadership,* 25.
3. Babbitt, *On Being Creative,* xiv–xv.
4. Babbitt, *Rousseau and Romanticism,* 16.
5. Babbitt, "Pascal," 467.
6. Babbitt, *On Being Creative,* xv.
7. Babbitt, *Masters of Modern French Criticism,* 114.
8. Babbitt, *Democracy and Leadership,* 28.
9. Babbitt, "Humanism," 41.
10. Babbitt, *On Being Creative,* xvi–xvii.
11. Babbitt, *On Being Creative,* xxxv–xxxvi.
12. Babbitt, *On Being Creative,* xxii.
13. Babbitt, *Rousseau and Romanticism,* 255.
14. Babbitt, *Democracy and Leadership,* 27.
15. Babbitt, *Rousseau and Romanticism,* 390–91.
16. Babbitt, *Rousseau and Romanticism,* 150.
17. Babbitt, *Rousseau and Romanticism,* 151.
18. Babbitt, *Rousseau and Romanticism,* 148.
19. Babbitt, *Rousseau and Romanticism,* 150.
20. Babbitt, *Rousseau and Romanticism,* 147–48.
21. Babbitt, "Humanism," 40–41.
22. Babbitt, *On Being Creative,* 123.
23. Babbitt, *On Being Creative,* 122–23.
24. Babbitt, *Democracy and Leadership,* 130.
25. Ryn, *Will, Imagination, and Reason,* 42.
26. Babbitt, *Masters of Modern French Criticism,* 347–48.
27. Babbitt, *Rousseau and Romanticism,* 128.
28. Babbitt, *Democracy and Leadership,* 184.
29. Babbitt, *Democracy and Leadership,* 186.
30. Babbitt, *Masters of Modern French Criticism,* 26.
31. Babbitt, *Masters of Modern French Criticism,* 274.
32. Babbitt, *On Being Creative,* 121.
33. Babbitt, *Masters of Modern French Criticism,* 271.
34. Babbitt, *Masters of Modern French Criticism,* 273.

35. Babbitt, *Rousseau and Romanticism*, 115.
36. Babbitt, *Democracy and Leadership*, 184.
37. Babbitt, "Humanism," 47.
38. Ryn, introduction to *Rousseau and Romanticism*, xxxviii.
39. See Nevin, *Irving Babbitt*, 125–43.
40. Babbitt, *Democracy and Leadership*, 204.
41. Babbitt, *Democracy and Leadership*, 213.
42. Babbitt, *Masters of Modern French Criticism*, 370.
43. Babbitt, *Masters of Modern French Criticism*, 370n.
44. Babbitt, *Rousseau and Romanticism*, 117.
45. Nevin, *Irving Babbitt*, 143.
46. For a critique of Babbitt's view of religion, see Eliot, "Religion without Humanism," 105–12.
47. Babbitt to More, June 12, 1932, quoted in Nevin, *Irving Babbitt*, 142.
48. Babbitt, "Pascal," 468.

Chapter 2

1. Babbitt, *Literature and the American College*, 207.
2. Babbitt, *Rousseau and Romanticism*, 1xx.
3. Babbitt, *Literature and the American College*, 89.
4. Babbitt, "Humanism," 39.
5. Babbitt, "Humanism," 30.
6. Babbitt, "Humanism," 30.
7. Babbitt, "Humanism," 26.
8. Babbitt, *Literature and the American College*, 74.
9. Nevin, *Irving Babbitt*, 20.
10. Babbitt, "Humanism," 31.
11. Babbitt, "Humanism," 31–32.
12. Babbitt, *Democracy and Leadership*, 222.
13. Babbitt, *Masters of Modern French Criticism*, 203.
14. Babbitt, *Democracy and Leadership*, 162.
15. Babbitt, "Humanism," 32.
16. Babbitt, *Character and Culture*, 229.
17. Babbitt, *Literature and the American College*, 90.
18. Babbitt, *Literature and the American College*, 92.
19. Babbitt, *Democracy and Leadership*, 25.
20. Babbitt, *Democracy and Leadership*, 59.
21. Babbitt, *Democracy and Leadership*, 45.
22. Babbitt, *Rousseau and Romanticism*, 358.
23. Babbitt, *Rousseau and Romanticism*, 359.

24. Babbitt, *Rousseau and Romanticism*, 117.
25. Babbitt, *Rousseau and Romanticism*, 116.
26. Babbitt, review of *La Religion de J. J. Rousseau*, 445.
27. Babbitt, *Rousseau and Romanticism*, 117.
28. Babbitt, *Rousseau and Romanticism*, 119.
29. Babbitt, *Rousseau and Romanticism*, 118–19.
30. Babbitt, *Rousseau and Romanticism*, 119.
31. Babbitt, *Rousseau and Romanticism*, 120.
32. Babbitt, *Rousseau and Romanticism*, 121.
33. Babbitt, *Masters of Modern French Criticism*, 237.
34. Babbitt, *Masters of Modern French Criticism*, 238–39.
35. Babbitt, *Masters of Modern French Criticism*, 239.
36. Babbitt, *Masters of Modern French Criticism*, 151.
37. Babbitt, *Masters of Modern French Criticism*, 231.
38. Babbitt, "Humanists and Humanitarians," 288.
39. Babbitt, *Rousseau and Romanticism*, 346.
40. Babbitt, *Democracy and Leadership*, 25.
41. Babbitt, *Rousseau and Romanticism*, 331.
42. Babbitt, *Rousseau and Romanticism*, 363.
43. Babbitt, *Democracy and Leadership*, 158.
44. Babbitt, "Bicentenary of Diderot," 332.
45. Babbitt, *Democracy and Leadership*, 167.
46. Babbitt, *Democracy and Leadership*, 159.
47. Babbitt, review of *La Religion de J. J. Rousseau*, 442.
48. Babbitt, *Democracy and Leadership*, 90.
49. Babbitt, *Rousseau and Romanticism*, 122.
50. Babbitt, *Masters of Modern French Criticism*, 239.
51. Babbitt, *Rousseau and Romanticism*, 255.
52. Babbitt, *Democracy and Leadership*, 95.
53. Babbitt, *Literature and the American College*, 97.
54. Babbitt, *Democracy and Leadership*, 96.
55. Babbitt, *Democracy and Leadership*, 95.
56. Babbitt, "Political Influence of Rousseau," 69.
57. Babbitt, "Political Influence of Rousseau," 69.
58. Babbitt, *Democracy and Leadership*, 99.
59. Babbitt, review of *La Religion de J. J. Rousseau*, 442.
60. Babbitt, *Democracy and Leadership*, 100.
61. Babbitt, *Rousseau and Romanticism*, 154.
62. Babbitt, *Rousseau and Romanticism*, 155.
63. Babbitt, *Rousseau and Romanticism*, 157.
64. Babbitt, *Literature and the American College*, 97.

65. Babbitt, *Rousseau and Romanticism*, 328–29.
66. Babbitt, *Rousseau and Romanticism*, 155.
67. Babbitt, *Rousseau and Romanticism*, 143. Laurence Sterne, a novelist and contemporary of Rousseau, had developed a lavish affection for a donkey. This caused Babbitt to remark, "The ass does not really come into its own until a later stage in the movement. Nietzsche has depicted the leaders of the nineteenth century as engaged in a veritable onolatry or ass-worship" (*Rousseau and Romanticism*, 144).
68. Babbitt, *Rousseau and Romanticism*, 146.
69. Babbitt, *Rousseau and Romanticism*, 145.
70. Babbitt, *Rousseau and Romanticism*, 140.
71. Babbitt, *Rousseau and Romanticism*, 140–41.
72. Babbitt, *Rousseau and Romanticism*, 141–42.
73. Babbitt, "Humanists and Humanitarians," 288.
74. Stanlis, "Babbitt, Burke, and Rousseau," 148.
75. For the revolutionary nature of sentimental humanitarianism, see chapter 4.
76. Babbitt, *Literature and the American College*, 90.
77. Babbitt, *Democracy and Leadership*, 23–24.
78. Babbitt, *Rousseau and Romanticism*, 130.
79. Babbitt, "Bicentenary of Diderot," 330.
80. Babbitt, review of *La Religion de J. J. Rousseau*, 446.
81. Babbitt, *Rousseau and Romanticism*, 129–30.
82. Babbitt, *Rousseau and Romanticism*, 147.
83. Babbitt, *Rousseau and Romanticism*, 128.
84. Babbitt, *Democracy and Leadership*, 96.
85. Babbitt, *Rousseau and Romanticism*, 123.
86. Babbitt, *Democracy and Leadership*, 148.
87. Babbitt, *Rousseau and Romanticism*, 154.
88. Babbitt, *Rousseau and Romanticism*, 154.
89. Babbitt, *Rousseau and Romanticism*, 79.
90. Babbitt, *Rousseau and Romanticism*, 136–37.
91. Babbitt, *Rousseau and Romanticism*, 137.
92. Babbitt, *Democracy and Leadership*, 155.
93. Babbitt, *Democracy and Leadership*, 152.

Chapter 3

1. Ryn, *America the Virtuous*, 50.
2. Mencken, review of *Democracy and Leadership*, 123.
3. Aristotle, *Basic Works*, 1305–6.
4. Babbitt, "Political Influence of Rousseau," 67. Babbitt was more critical of Vaughan in *Democracy and Leadership*: "Professor Vaughan, again, the editor of a recent

edition of Rousseau's political writings, remarked in his introduction, apparently without awakening any special contradiction or surprise, that in the essentials of political wisdom Burke is 'immeasurably inferior to the man of whom he never speaks but with scorn and loathing; to the despised theorist, the metaphysical madman of Geneva'" (140).

5. Babbitt, "Political Influence of Rousseau," 67.
6. Babbitt, *Rousseau and Romanticism*, 387.
7. Rousseau, *Emile*, book 1, "La seule habitude qu'on doit laisser pendre à l'enfant est de n'en contracter aucune," quoted in in Babbitt, *Rousseau and Romanticism*, 387.
8. Babbitt, *Rousseau and Romanticism*, 386.
9. Babbitt, *Rousseau and Romanticism*, 385–86.
10. Babbitt, *Rousseau and Romanticism*, 387.
11. Babbitt, *Rousseau and Romanticism*, 387.
12. Babbitt, "Political Influence of Rousseau," 70.
13. Babbitt, "Political Influence of Rousseau," 70.
14. Babbitt, "Political Influence of Rousseau," 70.
15. Nevin, *Irving Babbitt*, 100.
16. Nevin, *Irving Babbitt*, 21.
17. Babbitt, however, did not view Eliot's personal moral character as inspired by either Bacon or Rousseau. Babbitt believed Eliot to be a Puritan. See Babbitt, *Literature and the American College*, 96.
18. Babbitt, *Literature and the American College*, 97, quoting Eliot's 1900 address to the National Education Association.
19. See Panichas and Ryn, *Irving Babbitt in Our Time*, 229-30.
20. Babbitt, *Literature and the American College*, 96.
21. Babbitt, *Rousseau and Romanticism*, 388–89.
22. Babbitt, *Literature and the American College*, 110.
23. Babbitt, *Masters of Modern French Criticism*, 338.
24. Babbitt, *Literature and the American College*, 114-15.
25. Babbitt, *Literature and the American College*, 114.
26. Babbitt, *Literature and the American College*, 113.
27. Babbitt, *Literature and the American College*, 115.
28. Babbitt, *Character and Culture*, 227.
29. Rousseau, *Confessions*, 327–28.
30. Babbitt, *Character and Culture*, 227.
31. Babbitt, *Character and Culture*, 228.
32. Babbitt, *Character and Culture*, 227–28.
33. Babbitt, *Rousseau and Romanticism*, 78–79.
34. Babbitt, "Political Influence of Rousseau," 67.
35. Babbitt, *Character and Culture*, 228.
36. Babbitt, *Democracy and Leadership*, 109.

37. Babbitt, *Democracy and Leadership*, 109.
38. Babbitt, *Democracy and Leadership*, 110.
39. Babbitt, *Democracy and Leadership*, 111.
40. Babbitt, *Democracy and Leadership*, 144.
41. Babbitt, "Political Influence of Rousseau," 68.
42. Babbitt, *Democracy and Leadership*, 141.
43. Babbitt, *Literature and the American College*, 115.
44. Babbitt, "Political Influence of Rousseau," 68.
45. Babbitt, "Political Influence of Rousseau," 69.
46. Babbitt, *Rousseau and Romanticism*, 347. (Babbitt also footnotes this paragraph with a reference to Fichte's writings: "Reden an die deutsche Nation, XII.")
47. Babbitt, "Political Influence of Rousseau," 71.
48. Irving Babbitt, lecture notes, 1923, trans. Martine Berliet and William S. Smith, 3, Papers of Irving Babbitt, Box 19, Folder "Paris Lecture, 1923," Harvard University Archives, Pusey Library, Cambridge, MA.
49. Babbitt, "Political Influence of Rousseau," 71.
50. Babbitt, *Rousseau and Romanticism*, 347.
51. Babbitt, *Rousseau and Romanticism*, 136.
52. Schama, *Citizens*, 591.
53. Schama, *Citizens*, 592.
54. Babbitt, *Democracy and Leadership*, 272–73.
55. Babbitt, *Democracy and Leadership*, 273.
56. Babbitt, *Democracy and Leadership*, 320–21.
57. Burke, *Reflections*, 118.
58. Burke, *Reflections*, 151.
59. Babbitt, *Democracy and Leadership*, 322.
60. Babbitt, *Democracy and Leadership*, 323.
61. Babbitt, *Democracy and Leadership*, 323.
62. Babbitt, *Character and Culture*, 245.
63. Babbitt, "Political Influence of Rousseau," 69.
64. Babbitt, *Democracy and Leadership*, 272.
65. Babbitt, *Democracy and Leadership*, 273.
66. Babbitt, *Democracy and Leadership*, 271–72.
67. Babbitt, *Rousseau and Romanticism*, 379.
68. Hamilton, Jay, and Madison, *Federalist*, 371.
69. Babbitt, *Democracy and Leadership*, 273.
70. Babbitt, *Democracy and Leadership*, 299.
71. Hamilton, Jay, and Madison, *Federalist*, 327.
72. Babbitt, *Literature and the American College*, 115n.
73. Babbitt, *Democracy and Leadership*, 331.
74. Babbitt, *Democracy and Leadership*, 333.

75. Babbitt, *Democracy and Leadership*, 27, 28.
76. Babbitt, *Democracy and Leadership*, 272–73.
77. Babbitt, *Democracy and Leadership*, 274.
78. Babbitt, *Democracy and Leadership*, 289.
79. Babbitt, *Democracy and Leadership*, 290.
80. Hein, "George Washington," 36.
81. Babbitt, *Democracy and Leadership*, 298.
82. Babbitt, *Democracy and Leadership*, 298.
83. Babbitt, *Democracy and Leadership*, 299.
84. Babbitt, *Democracy and Leadership*, 232.
85. Babbitt, *Democracy and Leadership*, 229.
86. Babbitt, *Democracy and Leadership*, 299.
87. Babbitt, *Democracy and Leadership*, 229.
88. Babbitt, *Democracy and Leadership*, 290–91.

Chapter 4

1. Ryn, *America the Virtuous*, 51.
2. Thomas Jefferson to James Madison, Paris, January 30, 1787, https://www.monticello.org/site/jefferson/little-rebellionquotation
3. Babbitt, "Pascal," 466.
4. Babbitt, anonymous review of *Annales de la Société Jean-Jacques Rousseau*, 191.
5. Quoted in Babbitt, *New Laokoon*, 97.
6. Babbitt, *Rousseau and Romanticism*, 110–11.
7. Babbitt, *Rousseau and Romanticism*, 111.
8. Babbitt, "Political Influence of Rousseau," 68.
9. Babbitt, *Democracy and Leadership*, 99–100.
10. Quoted in Babbitt, *Rousseau and Romanticism*, 140.
11. Babbitt, *On Being Creative*, xv.
12. Babbitt, "New History of the French Revolution," 653.
13. Babbitt, *Rousseau and Romanticism*, 135.
14. Babbitt, review of *L'Etat de Guerre*, 238.
15. Babbitt, *Rousseau and Romanticism*, 193–94.
16. Ryn, "Power without Limits," 19.
17. Ryn, "Power Without Limits," 22.
18. Schama, *Citizens*, 792.
19. Babbitt, *Literature and the American College*, 139.
20. Schama, *Citizens*, 792.
21. Babbitt, *Masters of Modern French Criticism*, 42.
22. Babbitt, *Masters of Modern French Criticism*, 39.
23. Babbitt, *Character and Culture*, 228–29.

24. Ryn, *America the Virtuous*, 19.
25. Babbitt, *Rousseau and Romanticism*, 135.
26. Babbitt, *Rousseau and Romanticism*, 136.
27. Babbitt, *Democracy and Leadership*, 149–50.
28. Babbitt, *Rousseau and Romanticism*, 136.
29. Babbitt, *Rousseau and Romanticism*, 4.
30. Babbitt, *New Laokoon*, 79.
31. Babbitt, *Rousseau and Romanticism*, 73.
32. Babbitt, *Rousseau and Romanticism*, 73–74. In 1730 Rousseau tried to set himself up as a music instructor in Lausanne, offering to conduct an orchestra and perform a piece that he had written. Rousseau had little musical training, and the result was a terrible cacophony that brought howls of laughter from the audience. Rousseau refers to the incident in book 4 of his *Confessions*, although his autobiographical account may downplay the truly ridiculous nature of the incident. See Rousseau, *Confessions*, 144–47.
33. Babbitt, *Rousseau and Romanticism*, 74.
34. Babbitt, *Rousseau and Romanticism*, 79.
35. Babbitt, *Democracy and Leadership*, 150.
36. Schama, *Citizens*, 770.
37. Babbitt, *Democracy and Leadership*, 150.
38. Babbitt, *Democracy and Leadership*, 150.
39. Babbitt, *Democracy and Leadership*, 151.
40. Schama, *Citizens*, 783.
41. Irving Babbitt, lecture notes, 1923, trans. Martine Berliet and William S. Smith, 15, Papers of Irving Babbitt, Box 19, Folder "Paris Lecture, 1923," Harvard University Archives, Pusey Library, Cambridge, MA.
42. Babbitt, *Democracy and Leadership*, 151.
43. Babbitt, "Political Influence of Rousseau," 69.
44. Babbitt, review of *La Religion de J. J. Rousseau*, 443.
45. Babbitt, review of *La Religion de J. J. Rousseau*, 443.
46. Burke, *Reflections*, 173.
47. Babbitt, review of *La Religion de J. J. Rousseau*, 443.
48. Babbitt, anonymous review of *Annales de la Société Jean-Jacques Rousseau*, 192.
49. Babbitt, *Democracy and Leadership*, 100–101.
50. Babbitt, *Democracy and Leadership*, 98.
51. Babbitt, *Democracy and Leadership*, 99.
52. Babbitt, *Democracy and Leadership*, 106.
53. Babbitt, *Rousseau and Romanticism*, 329.
54. Babbitt, *Democracy and Leadership*, 122.
55. Babbitt, *Democracy and Leadership*, 122.
56. Babbitt, *Democracy and Leadership*, 122–23.
57. Babbitt, *Democracy and Leadership*, 123.

58. Babbitt, *Democracy and Leadership*, 124.
59. Burke, *Reflections*, 172–73.
60. Babbitt, *Democracy and Leadership*, 125.
61. Babbitt, *Democracy and Leadership*, 125.
62. Babbitt, *New Laokoon*, 195.
63. Burke, *Reflections*, 91.
64. Babbitt, *Rousseau and Romanticism*, 378.
65. Babbitt, "Humanism," 35.
66. Babbitt, *New Laokoon*, 196.
67. Babbitt, *New Laokoon*, 196.
68. Babbitt, *New Laokoon*, 197.
69. Babbitt, *Rousseau and Romanticism*, 193.
70. Babbitt, *Democracy and Leadership*, 127.
71. Burke, *Reflections*, 89–90.
72. Babbitt, "Political Influence of Rousseau," 67.
73. Babbitt, *Democracy and Leadership*, 127–28.
74. Babbitt, *Democracy and Leadership*, 129.
75. Babbitt, *Rousseau and Romanticism*, 124.
76. Babbitt, *Rousseau and Romanticism*, 124–25.
77. Babbitt, *Rousseau and Romanticism*, 125–26.
78. Babbitt, *Rousseau and Romanticism*, 125.
79. Babbitt, "Racine and the Anti-Romantic Reaction," 481.
80. Babbitt, *Democracy and Leadership*, 129.
81. Babbitt, *Democracy and Leadership*, 132.
82. Babbitt, *Democracy and Leadership*, 131.
83. Babbitt, *Rousseau and Romanticism*, 49.
84. Babbitt, *Rousseau and Romanticism*, 51.
85. Babbitt, *Democracy and Leadership*, 131.
86. Babbitt, *Rousseau and Romanticism*, 49.
87. Rousseau, *Social Contract*, 49.

Chapter 5

1. Schama, *Citizens*, 591. The Declaration of Pillnitz was a joint statement of support for Louis XVI and opposition to the French revolutionaries by Austria and Prussia.
2. Schama, *Citizens*, 592–93.
3. Quoted in Schama, *Citizens*, 592.
4. Quoted in Schama, *Citizens*, 594.
5. Schama, *Citizens*, 595.
6. Schama, *Citizens*, 597.

7. Roberts, *Napoleon*, 13.
8. Quoted in Roberts, *Napoleon*, 355.
9. Schama, *Citizens*, 858.
10. Schama, *Citizens*, 706.
11. Babbitt, *Literature and the American College*, 101.
12. Babbitt, *Literature and the American College*, 101.
13. Babbitt, *Literature and the American College*, 171.
14. Babbitt, *Literature and the American College*, 171.
15. Babbitt, *Literature and the American College*, 210.
16. Babbitt, *Democracy and Leadership*, 31–32.
17. Babbitt, *New Laokoon*, 230. Babbitt's commentary on music was somewhat controversial as he was not a musical expert.
18. Babbitt, *New Laokoon*, 64.
19. Babbitt, *New Laokoon*, 241.
20. Babbitt, *New Laokoon*, 241–42.
21. Babbitt, *New Laokoon*, 242n.
22. In *Democracy and Leadership*, Babbitt summarized the themes of his previous books in what appears to be chronological order (30–32), beginning with *Literature and the American College*. Curiously, he discusses *The Masters* out of order, prior to *The New Laokoon*. This is likely because many of the discrete chapters on French writers in *Masters* or large parts of it were written well prior to *The New Laokoon*. Babbitt published essays, for example, on Brunetière in 1897, on Taine in 1898, on Renan in 1902, and on Saint-Beuve in 1909—prior to the publication of *The New Laokoon*.
23. Babbitt, *Democracy and Leadership*, 31.
24. Babbitt, *Democracy and Leadership*, 31.
25. Babbitt, *Democracy and Leadership*, 31.
26. Babbitt, *Masters of Modern French Criticism*, 55.
27. Babbitt, *Masters of Modern French Criticism*, 55.
28. Babbitt, *Masters of Modern French Criticism*, 129.
29. Babbitt, *Masters of Modern French Criticism*, 129.
30. Babbitt, *Masters of Modern French Criticism*, 386.
31. Babbitt, *Masters of Modern French Criticism*, 387.
32. Babbitt, *Masters of Modern French Criticism*, 387–88.
33. See Babbitt, anonymous Review of *Jean Jacques Rousseau*, 313; Babbitt, anonymous review of *Annales de la Société Jean-Jacques Rousseau*, 191–92; Babbitt, "Bicentenary of Diderot," 329–32; Babbitt, review of *The Drift of Romanticism*, 386–89.
34. Gamble, "'Fatal Flaw' of Internationalism," 5.
35. More to Babbitt, February 15, 1915, Papers of Irving Babbitt, Box 8, Folder "More to Babbitt Correspondence, 1896–1915," Harvard University Archives, Pusey Library, Cambridge, MA.

36. Babbitt to More, March 14, 1915.
37. Babbitt to More, April 27, 1915, Papers of Irving Babbitt, Box 9, Folder "Babbitt to More Correspondence, January 1922–January 1934."
38. Babbitt to More, June 23, 1915, Papers of Irving Babbitt, Box 9, Folder "Babbitt to More Correspondence, January 1922–January 1934."
39. Irving Babbitt, "The Breakdown of Internationalism [1915]" (manuscript), Papers of Irving Babbitt, Box 16.
40. Babbitt, "The Breakdown of Internationalism [1915]" (manuscript), 19.
41. Babbitt, "The Breakdown of Internationalism [1915]" (manuscript), 19.
42. Babbitt, "The Breakdown of Internationalism [1915]" (manuscript), 19.
43. P. 678 of the *Nation* article alone contains passages that are repeated in *Rousseau and Romanticism* on pp. 346 (Napoleon), 192 (Stendhal), 130 (Diderot), 143 (Burke), 347 (Fichte), and 362 and 147 (Goethe).
44. Curiously, Babbitt's *Nation* essay cites several thinkers from French Romanticism and the Enlightenment but never mentions Rousseau by name. Further, when he reused material from the essay in *Rousseau and Romanticism*, he did so precisely in the context of Rousseau's thought. For example, Babbitt introduces a Diderot quotation in *Rousseau and Romanticism* by saying, "Diderot put the underlying thesis of the new morality almost more clearly than Rousseau," but in the *Nation* piece, Babbitt does not mention Rousseau. Babbitt's original manuscript makes no mention of Rousseau, and the omission is not discussed in Babbitt and More's correspondence regarding the essay.
45. Babbitt, "Breakdown of Internationalism," June 17, 1915, 677.
46. Babbitt, "Breakdown of Internationalism," June 17, 1915, 677.
47. Babbitt, "Breakdown of Internationalism," June 17, 1915, 677.
48. Babbitt, "Breakdown of Internationalism," June 17, 1915, 678. The reference to the Champ de Mars likely invokes a rally attended by thousands of people in Paris on July 14, 1790. Even Parisians who could not attend the rally raised their hands in the direction of the Champ de Mars, and all took an oath of loyalty to the nation, the king, and the new constitution. Many revolutionaries viewed the rally as a visible expression of Rousseau's general will and a sign of the emerging Utopia in France.
49. Babbitt, "Breakdown of Internationalism," June 17, 1915, 677.
50. Babbitt, "Breakdown of Internationalism," June 17, 1915, 678.
51. See Babbitt, "Breakdown of Internationalism," June 17, 1915, 677n.
52. Babbitt, "Breakdown of Internationalism," June 17, 1915, 678.
53. Babbitt, "Breakdown of Internationalism," June 17, 1915, 678.
54. Babbitt, "Breakdown of Internationalism," June 17, 1915, 678.
55. Babbitt, "Breakdown of Internationalism," June 17, 1915, 679.
56. Babbitt, "Breakdown of Internationalism," June 17, 1915, 679.
57. Babbitt, "Breakdown of Internationalism," June 17, 1915, 679.
58. Babbitt, "Breakdown of Internationalism," June 17, 1915, 679.
59. Babbitt, "Buddha and the Occident," 117.

60. This is a theme even more fully developed in *Democracy and Leadership*.
61. Babbitt, "Breakdown of Internationalism," June 17, 1915, 679. It took courage for Babbitt to argue that Germany was being partially scapegoated for its role in the Great War. Babbitt's *Nation* essay was published shortly after Germany had used poison gas in Belgium, inflicting fifty-eight thousand Allied casualties.
62. Babbitt, "Breakdown of Internationalism," June 17, 1915, 679.
63. Babbitt, *Rousseau and Romanticism*, 349.
64. Babbitt, *Rousseau and Romanticism*, 350.
65. Babbitt, "Breakdown of Internationalism," June 17, 1915, 679.
66. Babbitt, "Breakdown of Internationalism," June 17, 1915, 679.
67. Babbitt, "Breakdown of Internationalism," June 17, 1915, 680.
68. Babbitt, "Breakdown of Internationalism," June 24, 1915, 704.
69. Babbitt, "Breakdown of Internationalism," June 24, 1915, 704.
70. Babbitt, "Breakdown of Internationalism," June 24, 1915, 704.
71. Babbitt, "Breakdown of Internationalism," June 24, 1915, 704.
72. Babbitt, "Breakdown of Internationalism," June 24, 1915, 704.
73. Babbitt, "Breakdown of Internationalism," June 24, 1915, 704.
74. Babbitt, "Breakdown of Internationalism," June 24, 1915, 704.
75. Babbitt, "Breakdown of Internationalism," June 24, 1915, 705.
76. Babbitt, "Breakdown of Internationalism," June 24, 1915, 705.
77. Babbitt, "Breakdown of Internationalism," June 24, 1915, 705.
78. Babbitt, "Breakdown of Internationalism," June 24, 1915, 705.
79. Babbitt, "Breakdown of Internationalism," June 24, 1915, 705.
80. Babbitt, "Breakdown of Internationalism," June 24, 1915, 705.
81. Babbitt, "Breakdown of Internationalism," June 24, 1915, 705.
82. Babbitt, "Breakdown of Internationalism," June 24, 1915, 705.
83. Babbitt, "Breakdown of Internationalism," June 24, 1915, 705.
84. Babbitt, "Breakdown of Internationalism," June 24, 1915, 705.
85. Babbitt, "Breakdown of Internationalism," June 24, 1915, 705.
86. Babbitt, "Breakdown of Internationalism," June 24, 1915, 705.
87. Babbitt, *Rousseau and Romanticism*, 128.
88. Babbitt, "Breakdown of Internationalism," June 24, 1915, 705.
89. Babbitt, *Rousseau and Romanticism*, 128.
90. Babbitt, "Breakdown of Internationalism," June 24, 1915, 705.
91. Babbitt, "Breakdown of Internationalism," June 24, 1915, 705–6.
92. Babbitt, "Breakdown of Internationalism," June 24, 1915, 706.
93. Babbitt, "Breakdown of Internationalism," June 24, 1915, 706.
94. Babbitt, *On Being Creative*, 210.
95. Babbitt, "Breakdown of Internationalism," June 24, 1915, 706.
96. Babbitt, "Breakdown of Internationalism," June 24, 1915, 706.
97. Babbitt, "Breakdown of Internationalism," June 24, 1915, 706.

98. Babbitt, "Breakdown of Internationalism," June 24, 1915, 706.
99. Babbitt, "Political Influence of Rousseau," 72.
100. Babbitt, "Political Influence of Rousseau," 68.
101. Babbitt, "Political Influence of Rousseau," 70n.
102. Babbitt, "Political Influence of Rousseau," 70.
103. Babbitt, *Rousseau and Romanticism*, 194n, 409n.
104. See Babbitt, *Democracy and Leadership*, 43.
105. Babbitt, *Democracy and Leadership*, 43.
106. Babbitt, *Democracy and Leadership*, 43.
107. Babbitt, *Democracy and Leadership*, 43.
108. Babbitt, *On Being Creative*, 187.
109. Babbitt, *Literature and the American College*, 171.
110. Babbitt, *Literature and the American College*, 172.
111. Babbitt, *Democracy and Leadership*, 32.
112. More to Babbitt, July 10, 1919, Papers of Irving Babbitt, Box 8, Folder "More to Babbitt Correspondence, 1896–1915."
113. Babbitt to More, November 5, 1923.
114. Babbitt to More, September 17, 1923, Papers of Irving Babbitt, Box 9, Folder "Babbitt-More Correspondence, January 1922–January 1934."
115. Irving Babbitt, lecture notes, 1923, trans. Martine Berliet and William S. Smith, 22, Papers of Irving Babbitt, Box 19, Folder "Paris Lecture, 1923," Harvard University Archives, Pusey Library, Cambridge, MA.
116. See Babbitt, "Breakdown of Internationalism," June 17, 1915; Babbitt, "Breakdown of Internationalism," June 24, 1915; Babbitt, "Political Influence of Rousseau."
117. More to Babbitt, April 16, 1923, Papers of Irving Babbitt, Box 9, Folder "Babbitt-More Correspondence, January 1922–January 1934."
118. Babbitt to More, September 17, 1923.
119. More to Babbitt, April 16, 1923.
120. Babbitt, *Democracy and Leadership*, 27–28.
121. Babbitt, *Democracy and Leadership*, 31.
122. Babbitt, *Democracy and Leadership*, 31.
123. Babbitt, *Democracy and Leadership*, 31.
124. Babbitt, *Democracy and Leadership*, 32.
125. Babbitt, *Democracy and Leadership*, 32.
126. Babbitt, *Democracy and Leadership*, 35.
127. Babbitt, *Democracy and Leadership*, 171.
128. Babbitt, *Democracy and Leadership*, 171.
129. Babbitt, *Democracy and Leadership*, 170.
130. Babbitt, *Democracy and Leadership*, 32.
131. Babbitt, *Democracy and Leadership*, 37.
132. Babbitt, *Democracy and Leadership*, 37–38.

133. Babbitt, *Democracy and Leadership*, 38–39.
134. Babbitt, *Democracy and Leadership*, 40.
135. Babbitt, *Democracy and Leadership*, 41.
136. Babbitt, *Democracy and Leadership*, 29.
137. Babbitt, *Democracy and Leadership*, 30.
138. Babbitt, *Democracy and Leadership*, 47.
139. Babbitt, *Democracy and Leadership*, 47–48.
140. Babbitt, *Democracy and Leadership*, 49–50.
141. Babbitt, *Democracy and Leadership*, 56.
142. Babbitt, *Democracy and Leadership*, 59.
143. Babbitt, *Democracy and Leadership*, 161.
144. Babbitt, *Democracy and Leadership*, 166.
145. Babbitt, *Democracy and Leadership*, 59.
146. Babbitt, *Democracy and Leadership*, 117.
147. Babbitt, *Democracy and Leadership*, 61.
148. Babbitt, *Democracy and Leadership*, 62.
149. Babbitt, *Democracy and Leadership*, 60, 63.
150. Babbitt, *Democracy and Leadership*, 65.
151. Babbitt, *Democracy and Leadership*, 68.
152. Babbitt, *Democracy and Leadership*, 75.
153. Babbitt, *Democracy and Leadership*, 144.
154. Babbitt, *Democracy and Leadership*, 144.
155. Babbitt, *Democracy and Leadership*, 83
156. Babbitt, *Democracy and Leadership*, 83.
157. Babbitt, *Democracy and Leadership*, 68.
158. Babbitt, *Democracy and Leadership*, 74–75.
159. Babbitt, *Democracy and Leadership*, 363.
160. Babbitt, *Democracy and Leadership*, 366.
161. Babbitt, *Democracy and Leadership*, 84.
162. Babbitt, "New History."
163. Babbitt, "New History," 653.
164. Babbitt, *Democracy and Leadership*, 147.
165. Babbitt, *Democracy and Leadership*, 91, 128.
166. Babbitt, *Democracy and Leadership*, 140.
167. Babbitt, *Democracy and Leadership*, 143, 141.
168. Babbitt, *Democracy and Leadership*, 153.
169. Babbitt, *Democracy and Leadership*, 153–54.
170. Babbitt, *Democracy and Leadership*, 154; see also Babbitt, "Breakdown of Internationalism," June 17, 1915, 677.
171. Babbitt, *Democracy and Leadership*, 155.
172. Babbitt, *Democracy and Leadership*, 221.

173. Babbitt, *Democracy and Leadership*, 156.
174. Babbitt, *Democracy and Leadership*, 152.
175. Chateaubriand's *The Genius of Christianity* earned him an appointment by Napoleon as the French ambassador to the Holy See, but Chateaubriand's later criticisms of Napoleon as a dangerous dictator resulted in his banishment from Paris.
176. Quoted in Babbitt, *Democracy and Leadership*, 152–53.
177. Babbitt, *Democracy and Leadership*, 152.
178. Babbitt, *Democracy and Leadership*, 176.
179. Babbitt, *Democracy and Leadership*, 175.
180. Babbitt, *Democracy and Leadership*, 175.
181. Babbitt, *Democracy and Leadership*, 175.
182. Babbitt, *Democracy and Leadership*, 176.
183. Babbitt, *Democracy and Leadership*, 177.
184. Babbitt, *Democracy and Leadership*, 177.
185. Babbitt, *Democracy and Leadership*, 177–78.
186. Babbitt, *Democracy and Leadership*, 178–79.
187. Babbitt, *Democracy and Leadership*, 179.
188. Babbitt, *Democracy and Leadership*, 187.
189. Babbitt, *Democracy and Leadership*, 188.
190. Babbitt, *Democracy and Leadership*, 167–68.

Chapter 6

1. Babbitt, *New Laokoon*, 201.
2. Babbitt, "Breakdown of Internationalism," June 17, 1915, 679–80.
3. Babbitt, *Rousseau and Romanticism*, 34.
4. Babbitt, *Masters of Modern French Criticism*, 81.
5. Babbitt, *Literature and the American College*, 187.
6. Babbitt, *Literature and the American College*, 188.
7. Babbitt, *Literature and the American College*, 186.
8. Babbitt, *Literature and the American College*, 189.
9. Babbitt, *Rousseau and Romanticism*, 102.
10. Babbitt, *Rousseau and Romanticism*, 102.
11. Babbitt, *Literature and the American College*, 188.
12. Babbitt, *Literature and the American College*, 191–92.
13. Babbitt, *Literature and the American College*, 193.
14. Babbitt, *Literature and the American College*, 194.
15. Babbitt, *Literature and the American College*, 195.
16. Babbitt, *New Laokoon*, 42.
17. Babbitt, *New Laokoon*, 42–43.
18. Babbitt, *Masters of Modern French Criticism*, 20.

19. Babbitt, *Masters of Modern French Criticism*, 18–19.
20. Babbitt, *Masters of Modern French Criticism*, 27, 28.
21. Babbitt, *Masters of Modern French Criticism*, 27, 28.
22. Babbitt, *Masters of Modern French Criticism*, 29.
23. Babbitt, *Democracy and Leadership*, 157–58.
24. Babbitt, *Masters of Modern French Criticism*, 87.
25. Babbitt, *Masters of Modern French Criticism*, 87, 88.
26. Irving Babbitt, "Light and Shades of Spanish Character," in *Character and Culture*, 14 (originally published in *Atlantic Monthly*, August 1898, 190–97).
27. Babbitt, "Breakdown of Internationalism," June 17, 1915, 677.
28. Babbitt, *Masters of Modern French Criticism*, 26.
29. Babbitt, "Breakdown of Internationalism," June 17, 1915, 680.
30. Babbitt, *Democracy and Leadership*, 118.
31. Babbitt, "Breakdown of Internationalism," June 17, 1915, 680.
32. Babbitt, *Rousseau and Romanticism*, 388.
33. Babbitt, *Rousseau and Romanticism*, 329.
34. Babbitt, *Democracy and Leadership*, 197.
35. Babbitt, "Buddha and the Occident," 121.
36. Babbitt, *Rousseau and Romanticism*, 175–76.
37. Babbitt, *Masters of Modern French Criticism*, 55.
38. See Ryn, *Common Human Ground*.
39. Ryn, *Common Human Ground*, 1.
40. Ryn, *Common Human Ground*, 1.
41. Babbitt, *Democracy and Leadership*, 180.
42. Babbitt, *Democracy and Leadership*, 181.
43. Babbitt, *Democracy and Leadership*, 181.
44. Babbitt, *Democracy and Leadership*, 184–85.
45. Babbitt, *Democracy and Leadership*, 188.
46. Babbitt, *Democracy and Leadership*, 225.
47. Babbitt, *Democracy and Leadership*, 223.
48. Babbitt, *Democracy and Leadership*, 228.
49. Babbitt, *Democracy and Leadership*, 225.
50. Babbitt, *Democracy and Leadership*, 226.
51. Babbitt, *Democracy and Leadership*, 229–30.
52. Babbitt, *Democracy and Leadership*, 260–61.
53. Babbitt, *Democracy and Leadership*, 269.
54. Babbitt, *Democracy and Leadership*, 271.
55. Babbitt, *Democracy and Leadership*, 271.
56. Babbitt, *Democracy and Leadership*, 292.
57. Babbitt, *Democracy and Leadership*, 293.
58. Babbitt, *Democracy and Leadership*, 293–94.

59. Babbitt, *Democracy and Leadership*, 315.
60. Babbitt, *Democracy and Leadership*, 335.
61. Babbitt, *Democracy and Leadership*, 335.
62. Babbitt, *Democracy and Leadership*, 335.
63. Babbitt, *Democracy and Leadership*, 335–36.
64. Ryn, *Common Human Ground*, 36.
65. Ryn, *Common Human Ground*, 92.
66. Ryn, *Common Human Ground*, 93.
67. Ryn, *Common Human Ground*, 96.
68. Ryn, *Common Human Ground*, 96.
69. "Preamble to the United Nations Charter," http://www.un.org/en/sections/un-charter/preamble/index.html
70. Babbitt, *On Being Creative*, xli.
71. Ryn, *Common Human Ground*, 96.
72. Babbitt, *Democracy and Leadership*, 339.
73. Babbitt, "Breakdown of Internationalism," June 24, 1915, 706.
74. Babbitt, "Humanism," 49.
75. Babbitt, *Masters of Modern French Criticism*, 30.
76. Babbitt, *On Being Creative*, 213.

Chapter 7

1. Fukuyama, "End of History?" 3.
2. Fukuyama, "End of History?" 3.
3. Fukuyama, "End of History?" 4, emphasis in original.
4. Fukuyama, "End of History?" 4–5.
5. Fukuyama, "End of History?" 5.
6. Fukuyama, "End of History?" 8.
7. Fukuyama, "End of History?" 9.
8. Fukuyama, "End of History?" 9.
9. Fukuyama, "End of History?" 10.
10. Fukuyama, "End of History?" 11.
11. Fukuyama, "End of History?" 12.
12. Fukuyama, "End of History?" 13.
13. Fukuyama, "End of History?" 14.
14. Fukuyama, "End of History?" 15.
15. Fukuyama, "End of History?" 15, 16.
16. Fukuyama, "End of History?" 17.
17. Fukuyama, "End of History?" 17.
18. Fukuyama, "End of History?" 18.
19. Bush, "Selected Speeches," 274, 278.
20. Kissinger, *World Order*, 3.

21. Kissinger, *World Order*, 4.
22. Kissinger, *World Order*, 6.
23. Kissinger, *World Order*, 7.
24. Kissinger, *World Order*, 8.
25. Kissinger, *World Order*, 9-10, 373.
26. Kissinger, *World Order*, 9.
27. Kissinger, *World Order*, 9.
28. Hamilton, Jay, and Madison, *Federalist*, 46.
29. Hamilton, Jay, and Madison, *Federalist*, 268.
30. Kissinger, *World Order*, 9.
31. Kissinger, *World Order*, 374.
32. Kissinger, *World Order*, 10.
33. Huntington, *Clash of Civilizations*, 34.
34. Huntington, *Clash of Civilizations*, 35.
35. Huntington, *Clash of Civilizations*, 21.
36. Huntington, *Clash of Civilizations*, 28.
37. Huntington, "Conservatism as an Ideology," 471-72.
38. Huntington, "Conservatism as an Ideology," 472.
39. Huntington, *Who Are We?* 363.
40. Huntington, *Who Are We?* 363.
41. Babbitt, *Democracy and Leadership*, 296.
42. Huntington, *Who Are We?* 364.
43. Huntington, *Who Are We?* 363.
44. Babbitt, *Democracy and Leadership*, 364.
45. Huntington, *Who Are We?* 365.
46. Babbitt, *Democracy and Leadership*, 277.
47. Huntington, *Clash of Civilizations*, 309.
48. Huntington, *Clash of Civilizations*, 308-9.
49. Huntington, *Clash of Civilizations*, 311.
50. Huntington, *Clash of Civilizations*, 311.
51. Huntington, *Clash of Civilizations*, 311.
52. Huntington, *Clash of Civilizations*, 320.
53. Huntington, *Clash of Civilizations*, 320.
54. Huntington, *Clash of Civilizations*, 320.
55. Huntington, *Clash of Civilizations*, 321.
56. Huntington, *Clash of Civilizations*, 321.

Conclusion

1. https://1997-2001.state.gov/statements/1998/980219a.html
2. For a recent history of US interventions in the Balkans as wars of choice, see Gibbs, *First Do No Harm*.

3. See Crawford, "US Budgetary Costs of Wars."

4. Ryn, "Power without Limits," 19–20.

5. For a discussion of the Greek term *periagoge*, see Voegelin, *Order and History*, 67–68.

6. Maybe the most famous exposition of this concept is found in the *Republic*, where, in Book IX, Plato describes the different parts of the soul before laying out the regime types that correspond to those tendencies.

7. Babbitt, "Breakdown of Internationalism," June 24, 1915, 706.

8. Babbitt, "Breakdown of Internationalism," June 24, 1915, 677.

9. Hamilton, Jay, and Madison, *Federalist*, 327.

Bibliography

A. Writings of Irving Babbitt

Papers of Irving Babbitt. Harvard University Archives, Pusey Library, Cambridge, MA.
Anonymous review of *Annales de la Société Jean-Jacques Rousseau*, vol. 8. *Nation*, August 28, 1913, 191–92.
Anonymous review of *Jean-Jacques Rousseau*, by Gerhard Gran. *Nation*, March 27, 1913, 313.
"Bergson and Rousseau." *Nation*, November 14, 1912, 452–55.
"The Bicentenary of Diderot." *Nation*, October 9, 1913, 329–32.
"The Breakdown of Internationalism." *Nation*, June 17, 1915, 677–80.
"The Breakdown of Internationalism." *Nation*, June 24, 1915, 704–6.
"Buddha and the Occident." In *The Dhammapada*. 1936. New York: New Directions, 1965.
Character and Culture. 1940. New Brunswick, NJ: Transaction, 1995.
Democracy and Leadership. 1924. Indianapolis: Liberty Classics, 1979.
"Humanism: An Essay in Definition." In *Humanism and America*, ed. Norman Foerster. New York: Farrar and Rinehart, 1930.
"Humanists and Humanitarians" (letter to the editor). *Nation*, September 2, 1915.
Irving Babbitt: Representative Writings. Ed. George Panichas. Lincoln: University of Nebraska Press, 1981.
"Light and Shades of Spanish Character." *Atlantic Monthly*, August 1898, 190–97.
Literature and the American College. Washington, DC: National Humanities Institute, 1986.
The Masters of Modern French Criticism. Boston: Houghton Mifflin, 1912.
"A New History of the French Revolution" (anonymous review of *The French Revolution: A Study in Democracy*, by Nesta H. Webster). *Weekly Review*, June 23, 1920, 653.
The New Laokoon: An Essay in the Confusion of the Arts. 1910. London: Forgotten, 2012.

On Being Creative, and Other Essays. Cambridge, MA: Riverside, 1932.
On Literature, Culture, and Religion. Ed. George A. Panichas. New Brunswick, NJ: Transaction, 2005.
"Pascal" (review of *Pascal*, by Viscount St. Cyres). *Nation*, November 17, 1910, 466–69.
"The Political Influence of Rousseau." *Nation*, January 18, 1917, 67–72.
"Racine and the Anti-Romantic Reaction" (review of *Le Romantisme Français*, by Pierre Lassere, and of *Jean Racine*, by Jules Lemaître). *Nation*, November 18, 1909, 480–82.
Review of *La Religion de J. J. Rousseau*, by Pierre Maurice Masson. *Modern Philology* 15 (November 1917): 441–46.
Review of *L'Etat de Guerre et Projet de Paix Perpétuelle: Essays by Jean-Jacques Rousseau*, ed. Shirley G. Patterson. *Weekly Review*, September 10, 1921, 237–39.
Review of *The Drift of Romanticism*, by P. E. More. *Yale Review* 3 (January 1914): 386–89.
Rousseau and Romanticism. New Brunswick, NJ: Transaction, 1991.
"Saint-Beuve" (review of *Charles Augustin Sainte-Beuve*, by C. M. Harper). *Nation*, June 24, 1909, 622–24.

B. Secondary Literature

Aristotle. *The Basic Works of Aristotle.* Ed. and intro. Richard McKeon. New York: Random House, 1941.
Aristotle. *The Ethics of Aristotle.* Trans. J. A. K. Thomson. Baltimore: Penguin, 1958.
Aristotle. *The Politics.* Trans T. A. Sinclair. New York: Penguin, 1980.
Arnold, Matthew. *Culture and Anarchy.* Middletown, DE: Feather Trail, 2009.
Bacevich, Andrew J. *The New American Militarism.* Oxford: Oxford University Press, 2005.
Brzezinski, Zbigniew. *Out of Control: Global Turmoil on the Eve of the Twenty-First Century.* New York: Scribner, 1993.
Burke, Edmund. *The Best of Burke: Selected Writings and Speeches of Edmund Burke.* Ed. Peter J. Stanlis. Washington, DC: Regnery, 1963.
Burke, Edmund. *On Taste; On the Sublime and Beautiful; Reflections on the French Revolution; A Letter to a Noble Lord.* New York: Collier, 1937.
Burke, Edmund. *Reflections on the Revolution in France.* Ed. Conor Cruise O'Brien. London: Penguin, 1982.
Bush, George W. *Decision Points.* New York: Crown, 2010.
Bush, George W. "Freedom Agenda." https://georgewbush-whitehouse.archives.gov/in focus/freedomagenda/
Bush, George W. "Inaugural Address, January 20, 2005." In *Papers of George W. Bush.* Washington, DC: US Government Printing Office, 2005.
Bush, George W. "Selected Speeches of President George W. Bush: 2001–2008." https://georgewbush-whitehouse.archives.gov/infocus/bushrecord/documents/Selected_Speeches_George_W_Bush.pdf

Cicero. *The Basic Works of Cicero*. Ed. Moses Hadas. New York: Modern Library, 1951.
Confucius. *The Analects*. Oxford: Oxford University Press, 1993.
Crawford, Neta C. "US Budgetary Costs of Wars through 2016: $4.79 Trillion and Counting: Summary of Costs of the US Wars in Iraq, Syria, Afghanistan and Pakistan and Homeland Security." Watson Institute for International and Public Affairs, Brown University, September 2016. http://watson.brown.edu/costsofwar/files/cow/imce/papers/2016/Costs%20of%20War%20through%202016%20FINAL%20final%20v2.pdf
Eliot, T. S. "Religion without Humanism." In *Humanism and America*, ed. Norman Foerster. New York: Farrar and Rinehart, 1930.
Elsea, Jennifer K., and Matthew C. Weed. "Declarations of War and Authorizations for the Use of Military Force: Historical Background and Legal Implications." *Congressional Research Service*, April 18, 2014. https://www.fas.org/sgp/crs/natsec/RL31133.pdf
Emerson, Ralph Waldo. *Basic Selections from Emerson*. Ed. Eduard C. Lindeman. New York: Mentor, 1954.
Foerster, Norman, ed. *Humanism and America: Essays on the Outlook of Modern Civilisation*. New York: Farrar and Rinehart, 1930.
Fukuyama, Francis. "The End of History?" *National Interest*, Summer 1989, 3–18.
Gamble, Richard M. "The 'Fatal Flaw' of Internationalism: Babbitt on Humanitarianism." *Humanitas* 2, no. 1 (1996): 4–18.
Gamble, Richard M. *The War for Righteousness: Progressive Christianity, the Great War, and the Rise of the Messianic Nation*. Wilmington, DE: ISI, 2003.
Gibbs, David N. *First Do No Harm: Humanitarian Intervention and the Destruction of Yugoslavia*. Nashville: Vanderbilt University Press, 2009.
Hamilton, Alexander, John Jay, and James Madison. *The Federalist*. Ed. George W. Carey and James McClellan. Indianapolis: Liberty Fund.
Hein, David. "George Washington and the Patience of Power." *Modern Age* 57 (Fall 2015): 35–43.
Hindus, Milton. *Irving Babbitt, Literature, and the Democratic Culture*. New Brunswick, NJ: Transaction, 1994.
Hobbes, Thomas. *Leviathan*. New York: Penguin, 1968.
Hoeveler, J. David. *The New Humanism*. Charlottesville: University of Virginia Press, 1977.
Huntington, Samuel P. "The Clash of Civilizations." *Foreign Affairs* 72 (1993): 22–49.
Huntington, Samuel P. *The Clash of Civilizations and the Remaking of the World Order*. New York, Simon and Schuster, 2011.
Huntington, Samuel P. "Conservatism as an Ideology." *American Political Science Review* 51 (1957): 454–73.
Huntington, Samuel P. *Who Are We? The Challenges to America's National Identity*. New York: Simon and Schuster, 2004.

Kagan, Robert. *Dangerous Nation*. New York: Random House, 2006.
Kirk, Russell. *The Conservative Mind: From Burke to Eliot*. Washington, DC: Regnery, 2001.
Kirk, Russell. *Edmund Burke: A Genius Reconsidered*. Wilmington, DE: Intercollegiate Studies Institute, 1997.
Kirk, Russell. Introduction to *Literature and the American College*, by Irving Babbitt. Washington, DC: National Humanities Institute, 1986.
Kissinger, Henry. *World Order*. New York: Penguin, 2014.
Leander, Folke. *Humanism and Naturalism: A Comparative Study of Ernest Seillière, Irving Babbitt, and Paul Elmer More*. Göteborg: Elanders Boktryckeri, 1937.
Leander, Folke. *The Inner Check*. London: Wright, 1974.
Ledeen, Michael. "The War on Terror Won't End in Baghdad." *Wall Street Journal*, September 4, 2002. http://www.wsj.com/articles/SB1031093975917263555
Lehman, David, ed. *Oxford Book of American Poetry*. Oxford: Oxford University Press, 2006.
Litke, Justin B. *Twilight of the Republic: Empire and Exceptionalism in the American Political Tradition*. Lexington: University Press of Kentucky, 2013.
Locke, John. *Two Treatises of Government*. New York: Cambridge University Press, 1965.
Manchester, Frederick, and Odell Shepard, eds. *Irving Babbitt, Man and Teacher*. New York: Greenwood, 1969.
May, Larry, ed. *War: Essays in Political Philosophy*. Cambridge: Cambridge University Press, 2008.
McMahon, F. E. *The Humanism of Irving Babbitt*. Washington, DC: Catholic University of America Press, 1931.
Mencken, H. L. Review of *Democracy and Leadership*, by Irving Babbitt. *American Mercury*, September 1924, 123–27.
Muller, Charles, trans. *The Great Learning*. http://courseweb.stthomas.edu/sjlaumakis/GreatLearning2.PDFAs
Nevin, Thomas R. *Irving Babbitt: An Intellectual Study*. Chapel Hill: University of North Carolina Press, 1984.
Nisbet, Robert. *The Present Age: Progress and Anarchy in Modern America*. Indianapolis: Liberty Fund, 1988.
Obama, Barack. "Full Transcript: President Barack Obama's Inaugural Address." http://abcnews.go.com/Politics/Inauguration/president-obama-inauguration-speech-transcript/story?id=6689022
Panichas, George A. *The Critical Legacy of Irving Babbitt: An Appreciation*. Wilmington, DE: ISI Books, 1999.
Panichas, George A., and Claes G. Ryn, eds. *Irving Babbitt in Our Time*. Washington, DC: Catholic University of America Press, 1986.
Plato. *The Republic*. Trans. Desmond Lee. London: Penguin Classics, 1955.

Roberts, Andrew. *Napoleon: A Life*. New York: Viking, 2014.
Rousseau, Jean-Jacques. *The Confessions*. Trans J. M. Cohen. New York: Penguin, 1953.
Rousseau, Jean-Jacques. *Emile*. Trans Barbara Foxley. London: Everyman's Library, 1974.
Rousseau, Jean-Jacques. *The Political Writings of Jean-Jacques Rousseau*. Ed. C. E. Vaughan. 2 vols. New York: Putnam's, 1915.
Rousseau, Jean-Jacques. *The Social Contract*. Trans Maurice Cranston. Middlesex: Penguin, 1968.
Rousseau, Jean-Jacques. *The Social Contract; and, The First and Second Discourses*. Ed. and intro. Susan Dunn. New Haven: Yale University Press, 2002.
Ryn, Claes G. *America the Virtuous: The Crisis of Democracy and the Quest for Empire*. New Brunswick, NJ: Transaction, 2003.
Ryn, Claes G. *A Common Human Ground: Universality and Particularity in a Multicultural World*. Columbia: University of Missouri Press, 2003.
Ryn, Claes G. *Democracy and the Ethical Life*. Washington, DC: The Catholic University of America Press, 1990.
Ryn, Claes G. "The Ideology of American Empire." *Orbis*, Summer 2003, 383–97.
Ryn, Claes G. Introduction to *Character and Culture: Essays on East and West*, by Irving Babbitt. New Brunswick, NJ: Transaction, 1995.
Ryn, Claes G. Introduction to *Democracy and Leadership*, by Irving Babbitt. 1924. Indianapolis: Liberty Classics, 1979.
Ryn, Claes G. Introduction to *Rousseau and Romanticism*, by Irving Babbitt. 1919. New Brunswick, NJ: Transaction, 1991.
Ryn, Claes G. "A Jacobin in Chief." *American Conservative*, April 11, 2005. https://www.theamericanconservative.com/articles/a-jacobin-in-chief/
Ryn, Claes G. "The Moral Path to Peace." *American Conservative*, December 2, 2014. https://www.theamericanconservative.com/articles/the-moral-path-to-peace/
Ryn, Claes G. *The New Jacobinism: America as Revolutionary State*. Bowie, MD: National Humanities Institute, 1991.
Ryn, Claes G. "Power without Limits: The Allure of Political Idealism and the Crumbling of American Constitutionalism." *Humanitas* 26 (2013): 5–27.
Ryn, Claes G. *Will, Imagination, and Reason: Babbitt, Croce, and the Problem of Reality*. New Brunswick, NJ: Transaction, 1997.
Schama, Simon. *Citizens: A Chronicle of the French Revolution*. New York: Random House, 1989.
Stanlis, Peter. "Babbitt, Burke and Rousseau: The Moral Nature of Man." In *Irving Babbitt in Our Time*, ed. George A. Panichas and Claes G. Ryn. Washington, DC: Catholic University of America Press, 1986.
Tocqueville, Alexis de. *Democracy in America*. New York: Random House, 1990.
Voegelin, Eric. *The Collected Works of Eric Voegelin*. Vol. 5, *Modernity without Restraint*. Ed. Manfred Henningsen. Columbia: University of Missouri Press, 1999.

Voegelin, Eric. *From Enlightenment to Revolution*. Durham, NC: Duke University Press, 1975.
Voegelin, Eric. *Order and History*. Vol. 3, *Plato and Aristotle*. Baton Rouge: Louisiana State University Press, 1957.
Yarbrough, Steven R. *Irving Babbitt*. Boston: Twayne, 1987.

Index

aesthetics: Babbitt's early writings on human nature and, 24; *Democracy and Leadership* on, 116, 123; *The New Laokoon* on, 104–5, 142; and political order, *Literature and the American College* on, 141
Afghanistan, 163
African civilization, in post–Cold War order, 169
Albright, Madeline, 178
altruism, as Western elite virtue, 39
American Anti-Imperialist League, 109
American education, Babbitt on Rousseau's influence on, 57
America the Virtuous (Ryn), 14–15
amoral realism: of Kissinger, 9, 164–67. *See also* moral realism
anarchy: Babbitt on unleashing popular passions and, 75; chronic, popular sovereignty and, 134–35; of the imagination, Babbitt on, 104–5, 125; in Jacobin France and Rousseauistic democracy, 73–74; social, Burke on Rousseau's liberty and, 93–94
animals, elevation of, in Romantic ethics, 44–45, 187n67
anti-intellectualism, of Rousseau vs. Burke, Babbitt on, 97
APEC (Asia-Pacific Economic Cooperation), 172
Aquinas, Thomas, 27, 180
Arab Spring, religious fundamentalism and, 162
aristocratic leadership: Babbitt contrasting Rousseau and Burke on, 132; Babbitt on democratic societies and, 131; Babbitt on Rousseau's hostility to, 87–88, 132; Burke and Babbitt on innovations in, 95; in Geneva, Rousseau decrying, 80; Jacobins' blame for universal fraternity failure on, 113; shaping public opinion through example of, 149–50
aristocratic temperament, Babbitt on class warfare and, 74–75
Aristophanes, 29, 114
Aristotle: Babbitt on Christianity and, 25; Babbitt's theory of human nature and, 17–18; Babbitt's writings on education and, 54–56; on city-soul principle, 180; on democracy as death of liberty, 7; on man as creature of two laws, 19; on power of reason vs. power of will, 20; on remedy for economic inequality, 74; Romanticism as defined by, 85; similarities between Confucius and, 128; on superiority of poetry over history, universality of, 141
armaments industry, Babbitt on end of war and, 113
art, neoclassical critiques of Romantic revolt in, 96
Article I powers of Constitution, 178
Asia and Asian civilization: Babbitt's study of Western Christianity and, 10, 147; Westphalian principles and, 164–65. *See also* East Asian philosophers, Babbitt's theory of human nature and, 17–18, 20–21

Asoka, Buddhist ruler of India, 147
Atlantic Monthly, 108
atom bomb, cult of science and, 39
Augustine, Saint, 180
Augustinian Christians, Babbitt's inference of Buddha on, 27
Austria, Declaration of Pillnitz and, 192n1

Babbitt, Irving: biographical information, 11–12, 184n20; Fukuyama's world order and, 162–63; Huntington on, 169–70; relevance to contemporary world, 157; on special danger of the present time, 139. *See also* "The Breakdown of Internationalism"; *Democracy and Leadership*; *Literature and the American College*; *The Masters of Modern French Criticism*; *The New Laokoon*; *Rousseau and Romanticism*
Babson, Roger W., 112
Bacon, Francis: Babbitt's humanitarianism and, 31; as father of scientific naturalism and subsequent moral breakdown, 33–34; Harvard's Eliot influenced by, 58–59; Rousseau's sentimental naturalism as next step after, 40; substitution of kingdom of man for Kingdom of God by, 33; as superficial in definition of work, 32; worship of science and, 29
balance-of-power theory, 162, 164. *See also* Westphalian system
Balkans, wars of choice in, 178, 201n2
behavior, human: Babbitt on American legislatures micromanaging every aspect of, 118; as choice, 124
Bergson, Henri, 48, 114
Berlioz, Hector, 49
"Bicentenary of Diderot" (Babbitt), 107
Bismarck, Otto von, 111
Blake, William, 41
Boutroux, Émile, 4
"The Breakdown of Internationalism" (Babbitt, 1915): on attaining ethical leadership, 153; contrasting true and false internationalism, 145; on democracy without disciplinary virtues as international menace, 117; on democratic imperialism and American society, 117–18; on futility of humanitarian peace-making schemes, 112–13; Gamble article on, 14; on historical example of losing moral bearings and becoming imperialistic, 114–15; on humanitarian crusading rather than self-reform by, 118–19; on intellectual line from French Revolution to Great War, 110; linking Romantic ethics and imperialism, 115–16; on naive idealism and utilitarian efficiency, 113–14; on peace and world leaders capable of self-control, 118–19; published in the *Nation*, 109; quoting Diderot on the new morality but not Rousseau, 194n44; on restoring sound understanding of human nature, 116–17; on Romantic assumptions about human nature and Terror, 110–11; *Rousseau and Romanticism* themes similar to, 110

Brexit vote, 156
Brown University, Watson Institute at, 178
Brzezinski, Zbigniew, 168
Buddha: Babbitt on Augustinian Christians and, 27; on dualism of human nature, 34; on human nature as personal moral challenge, 136–37; on self-mastery vs. conqueror in battle, 103; on submitting ordinary self to divine will, 25
"Buddha and the Occident" (Babbitt), 169–70
Buddhism: Babbitt's human nature theory and, 20–21; common spiritual experiences in Christianity and, 146, 147–48; Huntington on Babbitt and, 169–70; religious outlook on politics and, 128
Burke, Edmund: American Constitution representing views of, 69; on aristocratic leadership, Babbitt contrasting Rousseau with, 132; Babbitt on anti-intellectualism of, 97; Babbitt's criticism of Vaughan on, 187–88n4; Babbitt's view of liberty and, 67–68; on course of French Revolution, 102; French revolutionaries' hostility to religion and, 89; on French Revolution homicides, 77; on imagination, 23, 94–95; on judging by social groupings vs. personal merits, 86; on old prejudices and unreasoned habits, 147; opposition to Rousseauistic Jacobinism by, Babbitt on, 91–93; on prudential endeavors, 7; on traditions and dogmas, 146; on "wisdom of the ages," 59
Bush, George H. W. and administration, 172, 177
Bush, George W. and administration, 1, 4, 163, 177–78

Calvinists, 48
Cargill, Oscar, 12
Carlyle, Thomas, 51
Catholic Church: outer authority over humans' souls and, 36; Rousseau's and French Jacobins' hostility to, 88. *See also* Christianity; church; clergy
The Catholic University of America, two-day conference on Babbitt (1983), 13
Champ de Mars rally, loyalty oath during, 111, 194n48
Channing, W. H., 17
chaos theories, Huntington on, 168
character: German *Kultur* and, 65; one's own, Babbitt on social policy as focus on, 148; peace as disposition of, 139; of world leaders, as prerequisite to peaceful world, 152. *See also* moral character
Charles I, King of England, Scotland, and Ireland, 67
Chateaubriand, François-René de, 134, 198n173
Chechnya (Muslim state), Orthodox rule of Russia and, 172
checks: and balances, Babbitt comparing Rousseau's popular sovereignty with, 64–65; on human desire for dominion, 128; Kissinger on world order and, 166; on the relativism of popular sovereignty, 131; on temperamental selves, Rousseau's ethical philosophy and, 91. *See also* inner check; institutional checks
China: ancient, end of feudal system and era of the Fighting States in, 135; emergence as economic behemoth, 156; Fukuyama on collapse of Marxism-Leninism in, 160, 161; rearmament and military threats by, 162; US failure to recognize Sinic civilization and, 173; Western consumerism in, 157; Westphalian principles and, 164. *See also* Sinic civilization
Christ, spirit of, Babbitt on peaceful world and recovering, 114
Christianity: Babbitt on Asian elements of, 25; Babbitt on fanaticism and intolerance of, 28; Babbitt on higher will over imagination of, 24; Babbitt's humanism vs. religiously inclined intellectuals on, 26–27; as check on lust for power, 128–29; common spiritual experiences in Buddhism and, 146, 147–48; decline of, nation-state rise and, 130; institutional, naturalism eroding authority of, 31; medieval, as religious political form, 128; medieval, dualistic view of human nature embraced by, 35; Napoleon's opposition to, 101; outer authority over humans' souls and, 36; Rousseau's hostility to, 89; sentimental humanitarianism compared with, 43–44; submission to will of God and, 129; true cosmopolitanism of, expansionistic nationalism compared with, 145; Western ethical standards and conventions and, 124; Western values and, Babbitt and Huntington on, 174. *See also* church; clergy; religion
Christian scholars, on divine quality in human beings with intellect, 20
church: Rousseau as inspiration for attacks on, 43. *See also* Catholic Church; clergy; religion
Cicero, 19
Citizens (Schama), 83
city-soul principle, Babbitt Corollary to, 180–81
civilization(s): Babbitt on Rousseau's rebellious hatred of, 79–80; Babbitt's ideas applicable to conflict between, 174; breaking down individuals' attachments to, 64; Burke on benefits of, 92–93; as enemy of democracy, Rousseau on, 80–81; Huntington on clashes among multiple units of, 168–76; institutions of, French revolutionaries and, 92–93, 99; as orderly transmission of right habits, 56–57; as source of corruption of human souls, Rousseau on, 62–63
civil war in the cave, 47, 73, 111, 137, 145
"The Clash of Civilizations" (Huntington), 168
The Clash of Civilizations and the Remaking of the World Order (Huntington), 168
classical formalism, Romantic, Babbitt's critique of, 24
class warfare, 74, 75, 89–91, 135
clergy, 50, 88–89, 99, 101, 113. *See also* Catholic Church; Christianity; religion
Clinton, Bill and administration, 172, 178
Cold War, 1, 155–56, 169
collective general will, Rousseau on social order and, 63–64

commerce, international, as imperialistic, 135
Committee on Public Safety, Reign of Terror and, 102
common culture: European Union formation and, 155–56; Westphalian principles and, 165. *See also* culture
communes, sentimental humanitarianism and, 46
communism, Fukuyama on defeat of, egalitarian modern America and, 159, 161
community, humanitarian naturalism and. *See* Rousseau, Jean-Jacques
concentration: virtues of, decadent imperialism and, 115. *See also* ethical concentration
Confessions (Rousseau), 60, 61, 116
Confucius: Babbitt on higher will over imagination of, 24; Babbitt's theory of human nature and, 18, 20–21; on moral man, 139; on setting oneself right which extends to whole community, 148; similarities between Greek philosophers and, 128
Congress, US, declarations of war and, 178
Congress of Vienna, 164
conscience: Asian philosophers on primacy of will and, 20; Babbitt's human law and, 18–19; Christian notion of, Rousseau on discarding of, 47, 65; as cosmopolitanism prerequisite, 140. *See also* higher will
consensus legitimacy, Kissinger on world order and, 166
"Conservatism as an Ideology" (Huntington), 169
The Conservative Mind (Kirk), 13, 14, 169
Considerations on the Government of Poland (Rousseau), 54, 63–64
conspiracies, losses in French Revolutionary Wars and, 102
Constitution, US: as anti-imperialistic, 2; as bulwark against military adventurism, 178; as bulwark against popular impulse, 71–72; dualism of human nature and, 53; popular reverence for, 78–79; Washington's Farewell Address expressing spirit of, 5
constitutionalism: British tradition of, *The Federalist* and, 77; popular sovereignty and radical democracy compared with, 69, 70; Washingtonian, Babbitt on inner veto of, 72–73
contemporary challenges: Babbitt's ideas on moral realism and, 153; politics of nation-states and, 156; review of, 15, 167–68. *See also* civilization(s)
cosmopolitanism: Babbitt on sharing an ethical center and, 11; Babbitt's theory of, compared with utopianism, 152–53; Babbitt's vs. Huntington's meaning for, 170; as common understanding uniting leaders and nations, 9–10; of de Staël, Babbitt on false and modern conception of, 142–43; education's purpose and, 141–42; Huntington's peace in new world order and, 168; as peaceful disposition, 139–40; personal introspection and ethical work by political leaders and, 137; Rousseau's sympathy as foundation of ethics and, 104; Ryn on international order in, 146–47. *See also* false cosmopolitanism; true cosmopolitanism
The Critique of Humanism (Grattan, ed.), 12
cult of noble savage, 41. *See also* noble savage
cult of ruthless power, Napoleon and, 134
cult of science, 39, 65–66
cultural diversity, neoconservative belief in universality of western culture and, 173
culture: Burke on human nature and tradition and, 92–93; diverse, Babbitt on common ground and, 10; of Promethean individualism, 114. *See also* civilization(s); common culture; Greece, ancient; Rome, ancient

Dante, 24–25, 27, 34, 152
Danton, Georges, 87
decadent imperialism, 115, 126–28. *See also* democratic imperialism; imperialism
decaying democracy, Babbitt on class warfare as sign of, 74
Declaration of Pillnitz, 99–100, 192n1
Declaration of the Rights of Man and Citizen, 67, 100
Deism, rise of scientific authority and, 36–37
democracy: assumption that peace is, 178; Babbitt on hollow formalism of French aristocracy and, 95–96; Babbitt on Rousseau's ethical mindset and, 91–92; Babbitt on Rousseau's Romanticism and, 85–86; Babbitt on using moral imagination to renew society for, 96–98; Babbitt's types of, 53, 69–70, 73–74; Burke on institutions and traditions of civilization and, 92–93; Burke on moral imagination and, 94–95; college education and high standards for, 59–60; constitutional

vs. direct type of, 69–70, 77–79; dearth of scholarship on Babbitt's views of imperialism and, 14–15; healthy, Babbitt on characteristics of, 71–72; as imperialism, 99–137; Jacobin rejection of aristocracy and, 87–88; Jacobin rejection of religion and, 88–89; liberal, failure of Fukuyama's theories on, 162–63; liberal, Fukuyama on obstacles to, 159–61; as revolution, 77–98; Robespierre on corruption of nation's virtue and, 86–87; Rousseau on civilization's institutions and, 80–82; Rousseau on leadership in, 79–81; Rousseau on wealthy class and, 89–91; Rousseau's form of liberty and, 93–94; Rousseau's idealism contrasted with Terror of, 82–85. *See also* democratic imperialism; democratic regimes; Rousseauistic democracy

Democracy and Leadership (Babbitt): on attaining ethical leadership, 152–53; Babbitt clarifying theme of, 123–24; Babbitt invites More's thoughts on, 123; on checks on human desire for dominion, 128–29; comparisons of Eastern and Western religions in, 13, 147; on controlling decadent imperialism, 127–28; on democratic imperialism and ethics, 132–33; explication of imperialism in, 103; as humanism discussion, 108–9; on humanitarianism and pacifism, 134; on human nature as personal moral challenge, 136–37; on imperialism of twentieth-century, 135–36; on imperialism types and phases, 126–27; on leadership against capricious popular opinion, 131–32; on moral character of democratic leaders, 69–70; on philosophy of naturalism thwarting peace, 129–30; on popular sovereignty and chronic anarchy, 134–35; research and writing of, 121–22; on sound education and sound constitutionalism, 72; summarizing themes of previous books, 193*n*22; on uncontrolled and undisciplined imagination, 125–26; on unity across national boundaries, 130–31

"Democracy Limited: Irving Babbitt's Classicism" (Kariel), 14

democratic imperialism: in ancient Rome, 135; Babbitt on ethics and, 132–33; Babbitt on naturalism and, 30; Babbitt's argument about American society and, 117–18; Babbitt's theory of, 17; post–Cold War US foreign policy based on, 174; Seillière's theory of, 119–20. *See also* decadent imperialism; imperialism

democratic liberalism: failure of Fukuyama's theories on, 162–63; Fukuyama on obstacles to, 159–61

democratic regimes: Babbitt on intellectual and moral errors underlying, 4–5; imperial ambitions of, 2; moral character of leaders of, 4; without disciplinary virtues as international menace, 117

de Staël, Madame, 77, 142–43

Dewey, John, 151–52

The Dhammapada (Babbitt translation and essay), 13, 22, 169–70

dialectical materialism, Rousseau and theory of, 90

Diderot, Denis, 39, 47, 60, 194*n*44

Dijon Academy, essay contest and prize of, 60–61

direct democracy, 69–70, 77–79

disciplinary virtues: common, cosmopolitan leaders and, 140; imaginative recovery of, decadent imperialism and, 115

Discourse on the Arts and Sciences (Rousseau), 60–61. *See also* First Discourse

Discourse on the Origins of Inequality (Rousseau). *See Second Discourse*

diversity: leaders with peaceful dispositions on, 139–40. *See also* civilization(s)

divine right theory of kings, 130

dogma, religious, Babbitt on true cosmopolitanism and, 145–46

dualism of humans: American Constitution reflecting, 53, 73; Babbitt on scientific naturalism and sentimental naturalism and, 30; Babbitt's humanism as affirmation of, 19; denial of, repudiating religious and humanistic ethics, 34; between man naturally good and his institutions, Rousseau on, 61; naturalism of Renaissance obscuring, 35–36; Romanticism acceptance of Baconian rationalism on lack of, 41. *See also* human soul

East: Babbitt on commonalities of Western philosophical traditions with, 147; humanistic or religious traditions uniting people in, 145; religions of, as antidote to Romantic societal anarchy, 106. *See also* Asia and Asian civilization education: Babbitt on Rousseau's theories of habits and, 55–57; Babbitt's writings on, 54–55, 118; Rousseau's theories of, 54, 61–63. *See also* Eliot, Charles W.; *Emile*; Harvard; *Literature and the American College*

Edwards, Jonathan, 48

egalitarian democracy, in ancient Rome, 135

Eighteenth Amendment (prohibition), 68

eleutheromania (revolutionary disease born of Rousseau), 94

Eliot, Charles W., 12, 13, 57–59, 188*nn*17–18

Eliot, T. S., 26, 28

elite class, Babbitt on class warfare and, 74–75

Emerson, Ralph Waldo: Babbitt quoting poetry of, 18; on human experience, 10; on human nature and New England town meeting, 79–80; on law for man and law for thing, 17, 32; on neglecting human law in favor of natural law, 34; on self-mastery on an ethical level, 140

Emile (Rousseau): breaking down individuals' attachments to civilization, 64; Eliot's adoption of advice for Harvard of, 58; as guide to understanding his political thought, 55; on how to educate a child, 54, 56; superstructure of Rousseau's political theory and, 62. *See also* education

emotional humanitarianism, Rousseau's, 31

emotional naturalism, 29–30, 33

Encyclopedists, 40

English Revolution of 1688, 110

Enlightenment: rejecting religious and humanistic human nature, 145; worship of science and, 29. *See also* Rousseau, Jean-Jacques

epistemology: Burke on imagination by democratic leaders and, 132; *Democracy and Leadership* (Babbitt) as contribution to, 122

ethical concentration: Asian focus on, Babbitt and, 170; Babbitt on Rousseau's emotional naturalism and, 40; cosmopolitan leadership and, 140; French Romanticism influence on German thought and, 111; human beings subject to human law and, 5; of individuals, progressives' focus on institutional reform vs., 127; as key to ordering reality and to social peace, Babbitt on, 28; military and imperialistic leaders without, 115; overemphasis on grace and neglect of, 27; sentimental humanitarianism on true virtue as rejection of, 44

ethics: Babbitt on democratic imperialism and, 132–33; Babbitt on restoring proper role of will and imagination and, 116; Burke on Rousseauistic Jacobinism and, Babbitt on, 91; modern, Babbitt on scientific naturalism and sentimental naturalism and, 30; Romantic, Babbitt on imperialism and, 115–16; Romantic, Babbitt's critique of, 105; Rousseau's, as attempt to justify moral laxity, 44; Rousseau's, as parody of ethics, 45; of US leaders, military adventurism and, 178; weakening of outer standards of conduct and, 106–7

Europe: Babbitt on commonalities of philosophical traditions of Asia and, 147; Burke on revolutionary mind-set and social order in, 91–92; Central, post–French Revolution wars in, 100–102; migration from alien cultures and common culture of, 156; rise of nationalistic political parties across, 156

European Union, 155, 165

evil: of civilization and its representatives, Rousseau on, 81; failure to exercise vital control and, 22; Keats's "Prometheus Unbound" as solution to, 34; potential for, 10; Renaissance obscuring potential for, 35–36; Rousseau and Diderot on struggle between good and, 47; Rousseau's transfer from individual to society of, 42–43; source of, Rousseau's repudiation of self-mastery and, 43

Facebook, 162

false cosmopolitanism, 142–43, 144, 148. *See also* cosmopolitanism

fascism, 159. *See also* Hitler, Adolf

"The 'Fatal Flaw' of Internationalism: Babbitt on Humanitarianism" (Gamble), 14

The Federalist: constitutionalism of, as Babbitt democratic theory, 77; constitutionalism of, popular sovereignty as opposite of, 69, 70–71; on human nature and democratic theory, 51; Kissinger on Westphalian principles and, 166; Rousseauistic admiration for rebellion in the US vs. constitutional tradition of, 78–79; skepticism of 'pure democracy' in, 78. *See also* Framers of the American Constitution

Fichte, Johann Gottlieb, 65, 111
Fielding, Henry, 42
First Discourse (Rousseau), 40. *See also Discourse on the Arts and Sciences*
Foerster, Norman, 12
force. *See* wars
Foreign Affairs, 168
foreign policy: Babbitt on morality shaping, 9–10; Huntington on morality shaping, 173–74; neoconservative, 173; soft globalist, 173, 179; study of Babbitt's theories and, 7–8; US moral and cultural forces and imperialistic, 179; US post–Cold War mistakes in, 172–73. *See also* imperialism; international relations
Framers of the American Constitution, 2, 158, 179. *See also The Federalist*
France: invasion of, by other revolutionary governments, 133; Jacobin, as democracy with imperial ambitions, 2, 3; Jacobin, as unsound democracy and threat to personal liberty, 73–74; Parliament abolished (1848), 107. *See also* French Jacobins; French Revolution
Frankenstein monster, common suppositions about, 144
Frederick the Great, wars of, 112
Freedom Agenda, 6. *See also* Bush, George W. and administration
frein vital (vital brake), 105
French Jacobins: blaming priests and nobles for failure of universal fraternity, 113; as brotherhood of Cains, 51; de-Christianization of France by, 88–89; Declaration of Pillnitz as opposition to, 192n1; murderous hatred of traditional elites by, 84–85; rhetorical parallels of GW Bush with, 177–78; Rousseau as inspiration for, 43, 66; wars of late eighteenth and early nineteenth centuries and, 101–2; Washington eschewing alliance with, 73. *See also* Jacobin Clubs; Robespierre, Maximilien
French Revolution: American constitutionalism compared with, 69; atrocities of, 77; Babbitt on intellectual line to Great War from, 110, 133; Babbitt's interest in origins of, 14; book review on French people as victims during, 131–32; democratic outlook of revolutionaries in, 133; justification for Terror and, 87; Kant's "Perpetual Peace" essay and, 112–13; Napoleon on his rule and, 134; Napoleon's patriotic militarism as culmination of, 101; as representative of Rousseau's philosophical Romanticism, 82–84; Rousseau's sentimental humanitarianism and, 49–51; Utopias of, Louis Napoleon Bonaparte's dictatorship and, 107
Fukuyama, Francis: Hegelian idealism of, 9, 157–64; Kissinger on, 166

Gamble, Richard, 14, 108
Gandhi, teaching of, 113
Geneva's Petit Conseil, Rousseau on revolution against, 80
The Genius of Christianity (Chateaubriand), 198n173
Germany: Babbitt on twentieth-century imperialism and, 136; Hitler and Nazi Party in, 183n1; *Kultur* (intellectual tradition) and nationalism in, 65–66, 111; as scapegoated for Great War role of, Babbitt on, 195n61; as traitor nation, 113; vital expansion of, lead-up to World War I and, 105. *See also* fascism
Giotto, 27
globalism, Huntington on international law and, 4
Goethe, Johann Wolfgang von, 110, 111, 133, 144
Gorbachev, Mikhail, 160, 161
grace: Babbitt on self-mastery and overemphasis on, 27; Rousseau's reaction against, 48
Grattan, C. Hartley, 12
Great War: Babbitt comparing Peloponnesian War to, 114; Babbitt on Germany's scapegoating for role in, 195n61; Babbitt on intellectual line from French Revolution to, 110, 133; Babbitt's draft essay on West's moral crisis and, 108; Babbitt's interest in origins of, 14; failure of pacifist advocacy to stop, 112–13, 134; German *Kultur* and nationalism and, 66; new nationalism and, 130; scientific humanitarianism obscuring danger of, 38; vital expansion of Germany and lead-up to, 105

Greece, ancient: as democracy with imperial ambitions, 2, 3; epochs of decadence in, 115; imagination and higher and lower nature of man in, 125; late military ambitions of, American democracy compared with, 178–79; on man as creature of two laws, 19; Peloponnesian War as crime against, 114; popular governments of, Framers' knowledge of, 78

Greek philosophers, classical: Babbitt's theory of human nature and, 17–18; on children's good habits as basis of their virtue, 56; curriculum for a formative education and, 59–60; on divine quality in human beings with intellect, 20; on individual as unit of analysis of societal decadence or health, 127; similarities between Confucius and, 128

Greenslet, Ferris, 122

Guadet, Elie, 100

habits: Babbitt on education and transmission of, 59–60, 118; Babbitt on Rousseau's theories of education and, 55–56; good, Babbitt on democratic leaders' acquisition of, 75

Hamilton, Alexander, 70–71

hard-power humanitarianism, 4, 6

Harvard, 12, 13, 55, 57–58

Hawkins, John, 42

Hearst, William Randolph, 150

Hegel, Friedrich, dialectical theory of history of, 158, 163

Hérault de Séchelles, Marie-Jean, 100

Herder, Johann Gottfried, 103

higher will: Asian focus on, Babbitt and, 170; Babbitt on humanists and, 26; Babbitt's view of, 22; Christian submission to will of God and, 129; internal struggle between lower self and, 37

Hindu civilization, in post–Cold War order, 169

Hinduism, in India, *Laws of Manu* and, 128

Hindu texts, ancient, inner check concept in, 21–22

history: Aristotle on superiority of poetry over, 141; Babbitt on central unity of diversity in, 146; end of, Fukuyama on, 157–64

Hitler, Adolf, 183*m*

Hobbes, Thomas, 129, 131

Houghton Mifflin, on *Democracy and Leadership* title, 122

Hugo, Victor, 45

humanism: Babbitt contrasting scientific and sentimental humanitarianism with, 30–31; Babbitt examining human nature and, 10; Babbitt on attaining ethical leadership and, 153; Babbitt on great religious traditions vs., 26; Babbitt on true cosmopolitanism drawing people together and, 145; Babbitt's world-city-soul principle and, 180–81; common, Babbitt and Huntington on cultural diversity and, 175–76; critical, Babbitt's defense of, 105–6; imaginative recovery of disciplinary virtues through, 115; true cosmopolitanism of leadership based on, 151; on virtue as personal moderation and social restraint, 149

Humanism and Naturalism: A Comparative Study of Ernest Seilliere, Irving Babbitt, and Paul Elmer More (Leander), 13

Humanism in America (Foerster, ed.), 12

humanistic political forms, 128

"Humanitarian and Humanistic ideals: Charles W. Eliot, Irving Babbitt, and the American Curriculum at the Turn of the 20th Century" (Smilie), 13

humanitarian crusaders: Babbitt on pacifists as, 134; Great War and, 133; international, Robespierre and France as, 100; societal reforms of, as threats to individual liberties, 68; US democracy promotion and, 167, 177–78, 179. *See also* humanitarians

humanitarianism: Babbitt on erroneous understanding of, 5; Babbitt on imperialism and, 170–71; corrupting education's primary goal of transmitting right habits, 59–60; Rousseauistic, American education and, 57; as solution to human conflict, West on, 137; US foreign policy and, 4, 178; on virtue as support for social justice, 149. *See also* scientific humanitarianism; sentimental humanitarianism

humanitarian naturalism, people in community and, 114

humanitarian peace-making schemes, Babbitt on futility of, 112–13, 134

humanitarians: Babbitt on crusading rather than self-reform by, 118–19; imperialistic leaders representing to the people as, 150. *See also* humanitarian crusaders

Humanitas (journal), 13, 14
human law: as distinct from laws of nature, 18–19; Eastern and Western religious and humanistic traditions united in affirmation of, 128; Rousseau's and scientific humanitarianism's repudiation of, 31. *See also* law for man
human nature: Babbitt on restoring realistic view of, 5; Babbitt on Romantic assumptions about, 110–11; Babbitt's theory of, 17–18; Babbitt's understanding of, 54–55; Burke on culture and tradition and, 92–93; Burke's critique of, Babbitt on, 91; Framers of the Constitution on, 69; humanitarian, as naive and shallow, 112; Rousseau linking democratic theory to his theories on, 63
human soul: anthropological principle that political order is reflection of leaders, 17–18; anthropological principle that society is man and, 8–9; Aristotle on society mediating law of measure within, 19; Babbitt on imagination shaping, 22–23; Babbitt on scientific humanitarianism and, 32; Babbitt's quest to locate divine or deeply human aspect of, 10; conflict between human beings and, 137; energy of, Aristotle on power of will and, 20; inner check and strengthening of, 21; naturalism obscuring dual nature of, 35–36; naturalists refusing to recognize ethical and spiritual struggle within, 34; political disorders and disorders of, 11; recognizing richness and nobility of other great civilizations and, 9–10; requirements of human law as inner check on, 28; scientific method applied to, 37; as source for understanding political disorders, 5; standards of taste and, 24. *See also* higher will
humility: respect for other cultures and civilizations and, 176, 179–80. *See also* self-mastery
Huntington, Samuel: on Babbitt, 169–70; Babbitt's understanding of morality shaping foreign policy and, 9–10; on civilizational blocs and US diplomatic errors, 172–73; on cultural distinctions after the Cold War, 155; on cultural diversity and common humanism, Babbitt and, 175–76; on globalism and international law, 4; on multipolar politics, 168–69; on US foreign policy paradigms, 171–72; on US moderation and restraint, Babbitt and, 173–74

idealism: Fukuyama's democratic liberalism theories and, 157–64; naturalism in ethics and, 106–7; Ryn on Babbitt's characterization of, 179
idealists, political: Babbitt on humanitarian activists exempting selves from decency and decorum as, 116–17; immunity against condemnation despite links with brutality by, 83
illusion: disciplined imagination in contrast to, 125; of higher reality, finding a center in, 141
imagination: Babbitt on restoring proper role of, 116; Babbitt on shaping of, 22–23; Burke on reality of human existence and, 94–95; definition of, 125; as essential to democratic leadership, Burke on, 132; influencers of, US cultural conversion and, 181; Rousseau on political action based on, 95; uncontrolled and undisciplined, 125–26. *See also* moral imagination
imperialism: Babbitt and Huntington on, 170–71; Babbitt linking Romantic ethics and, 115–16; Babbitt's books on his theory of, 103–5; Babbitt's emerging theory of, 105; dearth of scholarship on Babbitt's views of democracy and, 14–15; foreign policy aggression and, 11; French Jacobins on, 100–102; genuine, Babbitt's guide to diagnosing, 3; idealistic, as danger in American popular culture, 6; intemperate leadership and, 3–4, 6; irrational, 114–15, 120; modern, Babbitt on Rousseau's cult of emotionalism and, 107; pejorative connotations of, 1; Seillière's influence on Babbitt connecting Romanticism and, 120–21. *See also* decadent imperialism; democratic imperialism
income inequality, Babbitt on class warfare and, 74–75
individualism: Babbitt on decline of elite class and, 74–75; Babbitt on leaders with standards set above their ordinary selves and, 70; Babbitt on revolutionary mind-set and, 91–92; Burke on respect for the past and, 93; in China, era of the Fighting States and, 135; Promethean, culture of, 114; religious leaders on danger of, 36; self-confidence in the Renaissance and, 35; Western values and, Babbitt and Huntington on, 174. *See also* anarchy; checks; ethics

individuality: inner resources for high standards in inner life and, 124; Rousseau on civilization and, 81–82; Rousseau on genius as refusal to imitate and, 140–41; Rousseau on social order and, 63–64; social contract theory on consent to participate and, 94; temperamental, Babbitt on decorum and, 142. *See also* human nature
inner check: Babbitt's theory of human nature and, 28; Babbitt's use of, 21–22; God defined by Orientals as, Emerson on, 140; Hindu concept of, Rousseau on discarding of, 47; Taine's unwillingness to recognize, 37. *See also* checks; institutional checks
inner life. *See* higher will
instinct: Rousseau on virtue and, 41–42; Rousseau's glorification of, 42–44, 48
institutional checks: Babbitt comparing Rousseau's popular sovereignty with, 71; Babbitt on Senate, Constitution, and Supreme Court as, 72. *See also* checks; inner check
intellect, Babbitt on moral choices and, 21
Intellectual America: Ideas on the March (Cargill), 12
intemperate leadership: cosmopolitan leadership compared with, 140; imperialism and, 3–4, 6, 18
international institutions: genuine cosmopolitanism and, 151; soft globalist US foreign policy and, 173, 179; Westphalian principles and, 164
internationalism: Babbitt on Rousseauistic nationalism and, 104; Rousseauistic nationalism and, 103
international order. *See* world order
international peace. *See* peace
international relations: Babbitt on order in, 8–10; examining Babbitt's ideas on, 10; realist schools of, human moral dilemma and, 137; Rousseau's redefining of education and, 57; Ryn on cosmopolitan leaders' outlook and, 151; study of Babbitt's theories and, 7–8; theoretical analysis of macro trends, 17. *See also* foreign policy
Internet, 156, 162
Iran, 157, 159
Iraq, 4, 163, 173, 177–78
Irving Babbitt: An Intellectual Study (Nevin), 14

Irving Babbitt in Our Time (Ryn and Panichas, eds.), 14
Islam, 25, 156, 160, 167
Islamic civilization, 169, 171
Isnard, Maximin, 100

Jacksonian democracy, 69, 77
Jacobin Clubs, 100, 101. *See also* French Jacobins
Jansenists, 48
Japan, 136, 157, 159, 169
Jefferson, Thomas, 78
Jeffersonian democracy, 67, 69, 72–73, 77, 78
Jesuits, outer authority over humans' souls and, 36
Jesus, Babbitt on Renan's portrayal of, 25
Joubert, Joseph, 23, 47, 84
Journal of Thought, 13
Juvenal, 126

Kant, Immanuel, 22, 111, 112–13
Kariel, Henry, 14
Keats, John, 34
Kirk, Russell, 13, 14, 169
Kissinger, Henry, 9, 164–67
Kojève, Alexandre, 158, 159
Krauthammer, Charles, 161
Kropotkin, Pyotr Alexeevich, 43
Kultur (German intellectual tradition), 65

Lanson, Gustave, 84
Lasserre, Pierre, 81
Latin American civilization, 169
law for man: Eliot's educational standards and, 58; Emerson on law for thing and, 17, 32; naturalism's denial of, 34. *See also* human law
law for thing: Emerson on law for man and, 17, 32
law of cunning: leader following public opinion and, 149–50; as marker of epoch of decadence, 115
law of force: leader following public opinion and, 149–50; as marker of epoch of decadence, 115; Rousseau's theory of education and, 57
law of measure: Aristotelian goal of education and discovery of, 56; in Confucianists and Aristotelians, 128; mediating, Aristotle on

society's assisting individuals with, 19; scientific enquiry replacing, 31
laws of decency and decorum, Babbitt on humanitarian activists exempting selves from, 116
Laws of Manu (India), 128
laws of nature, human law as distinct from, 18–19
leaders: democratic, achieving true cosmopolitan attitude in, 149; modern, Babbitt on moral realism and, 153; with peaceful dispositions, 139–40; Rousseau on abstract equality without reverence for, 96–97; Westphalian, Kissinger on world order and restraint by, 166. *See also* political leaders
leadership: democratic, Babbitt contrasting Rousseau vs. classical philosophers on, 88; egalitarian, aristocratic leadership compared with, 131, 132; intemperate, cosmopolitan leadership compared with, 140; intemperate, imperialism and, 3–4, 6, 18; Swiss peasants' need for, Rousseau's observations of, 79; unimaginative, rise of nationalism in the West and, 156. *See also* aristocratic leadership
Leander, Folke, 13
"Lettres la Montagne" (Rousseau), 80
liberal democracy: failure of Fukuyama's theories on, 162–63; Fukuyama on obstacles to, 159–61
liberty: Aristotle on democracy as death of, 7; Babbitt on collective general will as end of, 64; Burke vs. Rousseau on anarchy and, 93–94; Rousseau compared with Babbitt and Burke on, 67–68
Lippmann, Walter, 30
literature: of nationalism, Romanticism and, 144; neoclassical critiques of Romantic revolt in, 96
Literature and the American College (Babbitt): as analysis of scientific and sentimental humanitarianism, 46; lacking direct use of 'imperialism' in, 120–21; on loss of standards, 141–42; opposing democratization of curriculum under elective system, 12, 58–59; on Rousseau and American higher education, 57; summarizing theme of, 193n22; on war and peace and education, 103–4

Locke, John, 94, 130
Louis Napoleon Bonaparte, 107
Louis XIV, 81–82, 100, 192n1; court of, 49, 95–96
Lovejoy, Arthur, 13
love of country, Rousseau on love of fellow humans vs., 63–64
Lyon, France, revolutionary purging in, 87

Maastricht Treaty (1992), 155, 156
MacGregor, Rob Roy, 57
Machiavelli, Niccolò, 129, 131
Machiavellian revolutionaries, Rousseau's theory of education and, 57
Madison, James, 71, 166, 182
Marshall, John, 72, 171
Marx, Karl, 43, 90, 158
Marxism-Leninism, in China, Fukuyama on collapse of, 160
The Masters of Modern French Criticism (Babbitt), 25, 105–7, 142–43, 193n22
measure. *See* law of measure
Mencken, H. L., 54
Mercure de France, 60
Middle Ages, as cosmopolitan, 145
Middle East: competition among nations to lead Islamic civilization in, 156; US involvement in major wars in, 162, 172, 177–78; Westphalian principles and, 164–65. *See also* Islamic civilization
migration, into Europe from alien cultures, common culture and, 156
military dictatorship, French populist revolution transformed into, 102
military power, 6, 135, 136
minority, dictating political order of radical democracy, 75
Mirabeau, count of, 135
Les Miserables (Hugo), 45
mob tyranny, 131. *See also* Terror, Reign of
Modern Age (journal), 13
Modern Language, 13
monarchy, 43, 100, 101
moral authority, Rousseauistic democracy not subject to, 54
moral character: of democratic leaders, Babbitt on, 3, 69–70; of leaders, Kissinger on, 166–67; Ryn on Babbitt's characterization of idealism and, 179–80. *See also* character

moral choices: Babbitt on U.S. cultural conversion and, 181–82; obligation to act when facing, 21–22

moral disintegration, false cosmopolitanism as, 143

moral imagination: exercising and cultivating higher will and, 23, 94–95; leaders' role to renew society using, 96. *See also* imagination

morality: Babbitt on source of, 8–9; brutal imperialistic US tactics in Iraq and, 173; understanding different faculties of the soul and, 124–25

moral realism: Babbitt on contemporary leaders of the West and, 136, 153; Kissinger on Westphalian principles and, 167. *See also* amoral realism

More, Paul Elmer, 26, 28, 107, 108, 109, 122

Moscow. *See* Russia

Moynihan, Daniel Patrick, 168

Mozart, Wolfgang Amadeus, 104–5

muckraking journalism, 118, 150

Muhammad, 25. *See also* Islam; Islamic civilization

multiculturalism, cosmopolitanism compared with, 140

multipolar politics, Huntington on, 168–69

musical laws, Babbitt on, 104–5, 193*n*17

NAFTA (North American Free Trade Agreement), 172

Napoleon Bonaparte: Babbitt on repudiating spirit of, 114; Babbitt on Romantic assumptions about human nature and, 110–11; Chateaubriand and, 198*n*173; democratic outlook of, 133; on French Revolution and, 134; on imagination governing mankind, 126; as prodigy of energy yet spiritually indolent, 103; Prussian monarchy defeated by, 158; reign of, as culmination of French Revolution, 101–2

Napoleonic Wars, Kant's "Perpetual Peace" essay and, 112–13

Nation, 103, 109, 119, 145. *See also* "The Breakdown of Internationalism"; "The Political Influence of Rousseau"

National Humanities Institute, 13

National Interest, 157

nationalism: Babbitt on Rousseauistic propaganda and, 181; Babbitt's vs. Huntington's meaning for, 171–72; as challenge to liberalism, Fukuyama on, 160–61; German *Kultur* and Rousseau's influence on, 65–66; during Great War, Babbitt on French Revolution and, 111; literature of, Romanticism and, 144; Protestant religion and rise of, 128; rise of, threats to common culture and, 156; tempered by internationalism, Herder on, 103

nation-states, Westphalian principles and, 164

naturalism: Babbitt on forms of, 29–30; Babbitt on intellectual and moral errors underlying, 10–11; Babbitt on modern world's adoption of, 28; in ethics, Babbitt on, 106–7; not uniting human beings in peace, 129; obscuring dualism of humans, Renaissance roots of, 35–36. *See also* Rousseau, Jean-Jacques; scientific naturalism; sentimental naturalism

naturalistic political forms, in the West, 128–29

natural man, Rousseau's comparison of artificial man to, 61–62

natural rights, 66–67, 68, 94

nature, blissful state of, 90, 113–14, 119

Nazi Party, 183*n*1. *See also* fascism

neoclassical theater, French aristocratic culture and, 96

neoconservative foreign policy, 173

Neoplatonism, Babbitt on Christianity and, 25

Nevin, Thomas, 13, 14, 27–28, 31, 57–58

New Humanism, 12, 13, 28

The New Laokoon (Babbitt), 104–5, 121, 142, 193*n*22

Newman, Cardinal John Henry, 147

new world order, international rules and institutions and, 155

Nietzsche, Friedrich, 111, 187*n*67

nihilism, in modern democratic theory, 130

Nisard, Désiré, 144

nobles. *See* aristocratic leadership

noble savage, 41, 61–62, 92–93

oil, Babbitt on twentieth-century imperialism and, 135

oneness that is always changing, Babbitt on, 125

On the Social Contract (Napoleon), 101

open society, Huntington on international law and, 4
originality, 140–42. *See also* individuality
Orthodox civilization, 169, 171, 172
Ottoman Empire, Westphalian principles and, 164

Panichas, George, 13, 14
Pascal, Blaise, 35, 48, 79
passions: Burke on rights flowing from mastery of, 68; of democracy, Hamilton on leadership cooling, 70–71; loyalty oath at Champ de Mars rally and, 111, 194*n*48; Madison on safeguards against tyranny of, 182; natural, Robespierre's attempt to transform virtue into, 66; popular, Babbitt on class warfare and anarchic revolution and, 75
Patterns of Anti-Democratic Thought, 14
Paul, Saint, 25, 34, 60, 140, 147
peace: assumption that democracy is, 178; Babbitt on common ethical discipline and, 148; Babbitt on ethics and, 131; Babbitt on philosophy of naturalism thwarting, 129; Babbitt's world-city-soul principle and, 180–81; as disposition of character, 139; false cosmopolitanism as threat to, 144; international, Babbitt on intellectual and moral errors underlying, 4–5; *periagoge* (turning-around of the whole soul) and, 180; as spiritual agreement, Babbitt on, 18; US democratic imperialism and, 174; world, ethical work required for, 152; world, futility of humanitarian schemes for, 112–13, 134; world leaders capable of self-control and, 119, 175
Peace of Westphalia, 164
Peloponnesian War, 114
periagoge (turning-around of the whole soul), 180
"Perpetual Peace" (Kant essay), 112–13
Petition of Right (England, Scotland, and Ireland), 67
Phaedrus (Plato), 79
Phenomenology of the Mind (Hegel), 158
philanthropy, Babbitt on imperialistic personalities and, 149
picnicking on a battlefield, Babbitt on, 113–14
Plato: admiration for nature's beauty by, 79; Babbitt on Christianity and, 25; character types described by, 104; on city-soul principle, 180, 202*n*6; on individual character of leaders, 177; on justice, 148; on *periagoge* (turning-around of the whole soul), 180; on power of reason vs. power of will, 20
pleasure, cult of science and goal of, 39
plebiscitary democracy, Rousseauistic democracy as, 53–54
"The Political Influence of Rousseau" (Babbitt), 119
political leaders: Babbitt and Aristotle on education of, 55; Babbitt on Rousseau's hostility to aristocracy as, 87–88; Babbitt's democratic theory on development of, 75; personal introspection and ethical work by, 137. *See also* leaders
political philosophy: classical, Voegelin on, 8; Rousseau's, Mencken vs. Babbitt on, 54; social order built on Rousseauistic ethics and, 48
political violence, as essence of personal virtue, 81
The Political Writings of Jean-Jacques Rousseau (Vaughan), 55
popular majorities, Babbitt's opposition to use of, 73
popular opinion: capricious, leadership as bulwark against, 131–32; *The Federalist*'s cautions about, 77; legislative decision making and polls on, 78; politics of contemporary US culture and, 98. *See also* public opinion
popular sovereignty, Rousseau's: Babbitt comparing English checks and balances to, 64–65; chronic anarchy and, 134–35; on European war crisis of 1791 and 1792, 66; Louis XIV captivated by, 81–82; minority dictating political order of, 75; no limitations on will of the people and, 130; obscuring centrality of ethical leadership in a democracy, 70; as opposite to constitutionalism of *The Federalist*, 69
popular will: French Revolution leaders on acting for, 88, 150; Rousseau on aristocratic leadership vs., 132; Rousseau on humanity's natural goodness and, 51
populism: European nationalistic political parties and, 156; Rousseauistic, Babbitt on violent revolution and, 78. *See also* French Revolution

power, cult of science and goal of, 39
presidential veto, Babbitt's use of "veto power" compared to, 72
priests. *See* clergy
private property: Rousseau as inspiration for attacks on, 43; Rousseau on blissful state of nature and, 90
Profession, Voltaire's annotated copy of, 40
progressives, focus on institutional reform vs. ethical concentration of individuals by, 127
Project for an Everlasting Peace in Europe (Abbé de St. Pierre), 112
Promethean individualism, culture of, 114
"Prometheus Unbound" (Keats), 34
property: Rousseau's vs. Marx's view on, 90. *See also* private property
Prussia, Declaration of Pillnitz and, 192n1
public opinion: leader shaping by example of, 149–50. *See also* popular opinion
Pusey, Nathan, 13

Rabelais, François, 35–36
radical democracy, popular passion and, 75
radical nationalism, Rousseau's influence on, 65
rationalistic naturalism. *See* scientific naturalism
realism. *See* amoral realism; moral realism
reason: Babbitt on interplay between will, imagination and, 23; Eastern vs. Greek philosophers on power of, 20; Western thinkers on role of, 22
referenda, Babbitt's opposition to use of, 73
Reflections (Burke), 96
Reign of Terror. *See* Terror, Reign of
religion: Babbitt as ally of, 28; Babbitt on Asia as mother of, 24, 25; Babbitt on true cosmopolitanism drawing people together and, 145–46; Babbitt's world-city-soul principle and, 180–81; Burke on benefits of, 92–93; as challenge to liberalism, Fukuyama on, 161; as distinctly human experience, 97; as key to common values, Babbitt and Huntington on, 175; as obstacle to French Revolution goals, 88; Rousseau's bastardized form of, 89; sentimental Romantics on, 41; true cosmopolitanism of leadership based on, 151. *See also* Catholic Church; church; clergy
religious discipline, of Swiss peasants and New Englanders, 79–80
religious fundamentalism: as challenge to liberalism, Fukuyama on, 160; in Middle East, Westphalian principles and, 164–65; September 11 attacks and Middle East instability and, 162
religious political forms, 128
Renaissance: early, originality of art during, 141; naturalism obscuring dualism of humans emerging from, 35–36
Renan, Ernest, 25
Republic of 1848, 114
Review of Politics, 14
revolution: anarchic, Babbitt on unleashing popular passions and, 75; in Jacobin France and Rousseauistic democracy, 73–74; Jefferson's praise of, 78. *See also* French Revolution
revolutionaries, dividing society into "sublime" criminals and the "wicked," 81
revolutionary disorder in domestic politics, 11
Revolutionary Tribunal, Reign of Terror and, 102
Revolution of 1848, 106–7
Richelieu, Cardinal, 49
Robespierre, Maximilien: anticlericalism of, 50, 89; attempt to transform virtue into a natural passion by, 66; Babbitt on popular will or will of, 88; Babbitt quoting of, as most Rousseauist leader, 85; dividing society on basis of class not virtue or viciousness by, 86; on international democratic crusading, 100; judging by social groupings vs. personal merits, 86–87; on violence of the revolution, 84. *See also* Terror, Reign of
Rob Roy MacGregor, 57
Romantic democratist ideology, "end of history" and, 157–64
Romanticism: as appearance of cosmopolitanism, 140–41; Aristophanes as predecessor of, 114; Aristotle's definition of, 85; in art and literature, neoclassical critiques of, Babbitt on, 96; artificiality of neoclassical art and literature of, 142; Babbitt on natural rights theories and, 67; Babbitt on place for, Rousseau's fictitious world and, 86; Babbitt on political influence of, 105; Babbitt's critique of classical form of, 24; Babbitt's essay linking idealistic political movements to imagination of, 113; Babbitt's theory of imperialism and, 103–4; as intellectual, moral, and political disaster for the West, 181; literature of nationalism and, 144;

natural progression from science to, 40–41; rejecting religious and humanistic human nature, 145; rules of society discarded without ethical standards replaced by, 106; sentimental, roots of, 29; sentimental, Rousseau's direct democracy as, 70; sentimental naturalism as element of, 30; uncontrolled and undisciplined imagination and, 125–26; Western institutions transformed into restraints by, 47–48. *See also* Rousseau, Jean-Jacques

Romantics: ethical elevation of animals by, 44–45, 187*n*67; revolutionary, political violence against civilization by, 81

Le Romantisme Francais (Lasserre), 81

Rome, ancient: classics from, curriculum for a formative education and, 59–60; decadent imperialism of, 126–27; as democracy with imperial ambitions, 1, 3; epochs of decadence in, 115; late military ambitions of, American democracy compared with, 178–79; on man as creature of two laws, 19; popular governments of, Framers knowledge of, 78; weakening of religious traditions and constitutional republic in, 135

Rousseau, Jean-Jacques: on aristocratic leadership vs. popular will, 132; Babbitt on anti-intellectualism of, 97; Babbitt on influence of, 47; Babbitt's critique of, 12; Babbitt's views on theories of democracy of, 13–14; democratic theory of, 6; on Dijon Academy's essay contest and prize, 60–61; on education, 54–55; on genius as refusal to imitate, 140–41; German *Kultur* and nationalism and, 65–66; Harvard's Eliot influenced by, 58–59; idyllic quest to return human beings to blissful state of nature, 113–14; intellectual line to the Terror from democratic theory of, 84–86; inverted scale of values of, 44; as most influential Romantic and sentimental humanitarian, 41; as "musician" in Lausanne, 191*n*32; as musician in Lausanne, 86; Napoleon's idolizing of, 101; on nationalism and patriotic pride, 128–29; on nationalist love of country, 130; Rabelais as precursor to, 35–36; radical democracy theory of, 11; as rationalist about miracles, 40; rejecting Christianity as antinational, 145; role in inspiring revolt, Babbitt on, 79–80; Romanticism and, 29; Ryn's assessment of Babbitt's ideas about war and peace and, 15; sentimental naturalism and, 31; substitution of kingdom of man for Kingdom of God by, 33; Western ethical understandings and, 42–43. *See also* naturalism; sentimental humanitarianism

Rousseau and Romanticism (Babbitt): on devolution from humanistic into naturalistic philosophies, 35; on inverted scale of values, 45; linking Romanticism and imperialism, 108; Lovejoy's review of, 13; *Nation* 1915 article's themes similar to, 110, 194*n*44; *Nation* essays and publication of (1919), 121; on Seillière's view of Romanticism and imperialism, 120

Rousseauistic democracy: French Jacobins and, 66; Fukuyama's world order and, 163; as menaces abroad and domestic tyrannies at home, 102; on "natural" impulse in individuals and in the popular will, 73–74; as plebiscitary democracy, 53–54; as precursor to violent revolutions, Babbitt on, 87

rule of law, Western values and, Babbitt and Huntington on, 174

Russia: Babbitt on twentieth-century imperialism and, 136; Babbitt's prognostications on future of, 109; cultural changes in, 157; current tension with US and, 9; Fukuyama on return to nineteenth-century imperial or communism, 161; nineteenth-century authoritarian government and militarism by, 162; return to Orthodox and authoritarian roots, 156; US failure to recognize Orthodox civilization and, 173. *See also* Orthodox civilization; Soviet Union

Ryn, Claes G.: as Babbitt interpreter, 13; on Babbitt's characterization of idealism, 179; on Babbitt's idea of higher will, 26; Babbitt's influence on, 14–15; on Framers' understanding of decadent democracies' dangers, 78; on immunity of political idealism against condemnation despite links with brutality, 83; on international order in cosmopolitanism, 146–47; on interplay among will, imagination, and reason, 23–24; on peace and ethical character of cosmopolitan leaders, 151; on Rousseauistic democracy, 54; on *The Social Contract* revolutionary outlook in France, 84–85

Sainte-Beuve, Charles Augustin, 37, 106, 107
Schama, Simon: on atrocities of French Revolution, 77; on European war crisis of 1791 and 1792, 66–67; on French militarized nationalism, 101; on Jacobins on foreigners as enemy, 99–100; on revolution's justification for Terror, 87; on the Terror vs. noble goals of French Revolution, 83; on universal applicability of rights of man, 100
Scherer, M. Edmond, 32
scholastic philosophy, on role of reason, 22
science: Babbitt on deterrent effect of weaponry and, 137; Babbitt on military power and progress in, 136; Baconian worship of, American education and, 57; cult of, 39, 65–66
scientific enquiry: backlash against restoring outer authority of religion and, 36; as only true knowledge, 32
scientific humanitarianism: as agnostic to moral questions, 31–32; Babbitt on critiques of, 32–33; Bacon and modern version of, 33; as inspiration for sociology and government bureaucracies, 46; intellectual compatibility of sentimental naturalism with, 39–40; naturalism and, 30; as weakening obligation to improve individual character, 38–39
scientific naturalism (*libido sciendi*): Bacon and modern impetus for, 31; Bacon as intellectual father of, 33–34; distinguishing sentimental naturalism from, 41; sentimental naturalism of Romanticism and, 30, 40–41; spiritual emptiness in Taine's writings of, 37–38; utilitarian naturalism and, 29–30
Second Discourse (Rousseau): on abstract equality without reverence for leadership, 97; Geneva's Petit Conseil presented in, 80; revolutionary violence based on class warfare and, 89–91; unflinching individualism of, 63; Vaughn on influence of, 55; Vincennes vision and, 60–61. *See also Discourse on the Origins of Inequality*
Sedgwick, Ellery, 108
Seillière, Ernest, 119–20
self-mastery (self-control): American legislation micromanaging people refusing, 118; Babbitt on overemphasis of grace and, 27; Babbitt on political leaders and, 75; church's sale of dispensations and, 35; as cosmopolitanism prerequisite, 140; dualistic challenge

of, 34; humanitarianism and, 31; lack of, leading to conflict not peace, 44; law of contemporary US culture and, 98; Robespierre on virtue as overflowing feeling rather than, 85; Rousseau's repudiation of, 41, 43; scientific humanitarianism and, 39; Washington's struggle with, 73; of Western leaders, decadent imperialism and, 127–28
Senate, US, as bulwark against popular impulse, 71–72
sentimental humanitarianism: Babbitt on human law and, 6; Babbitt on radical democracy and, 11; Babbitt's analysis of, 45–47; cult of science leading to power and pleasure and, 39; as flattering to bottom of social hierarchy, 43–44; French Revolution and, 49–51; naturalism and, 30; Rousseau and modern version of, 33; Ryn on romanticizing human nature and, 151–52
sentimental internationalism, 174
sentimental naturalism (*libido sentiendi*): Babbitt on, 39–40; distinguishing scientific naturalism from, 41; intellectual compatibility of scientific humanitarianism with, 40; inverted scale of values of, 45; as passion for feeling at expense of self-discipline, 31; of Romanticism, scientific naturalism and, 30; Rousseau on, 33
September 11 attacks, 162, 177
service to humankind, as Harvard humanitarian goal, 57–58
Shaftesbury, third Earl of, 42
Shelley, Mary, 144
Siegfried, M., 6
Sinic civilization, 169, 171
Smilie, Kipton D., 13
Social Contract (Rousseau): on abstract equality without reverence for leadership, 96–97; hostility to Catholicism in, 88; individual disappears into collective will in, 63; on popular sovereignty, 134–35; revolutionary outlook in France after publication of, 84–85
social contract theory, Babbitt on, 93–94
social justice: Babbitt on minding everybody else's business and, 148; Babbitt on naturalism and struggle for, 30
social service, humanitarian concept of, 42
society: assisting individuals in mediating law

of measure, 19; progress for, humanitarianism and, 31; rights of, disorder by individuals and, 68

Socrates, 22, 24, 73, 107, 116

soft globalist foreign policy, 173, 179

Sophocles, 34

Sorbonne: "Democracy and Imperialism" (1923 lectures), 6–7, 8, 122; Reading Room murals of, 29

South Korea, 159

Soviet Union: Fukuyama on Gorbachev and reforms in, 160. *See also* Russia

spiritual efficiency, scientific humanitarianism improving mechanical efficiency vs., 38–39

spirituality: men coming together in common discipline and, 140. *See also* higher will

spiritual or moral indolence (*pamāda*), 22, 49

spiritual vigilance or strenuousness (*appamāda*), 22

Spitz, David, 14

Stanlis, Peter, 45

Statesman (Plato), 104

Stendhal, cult of Napoleon and, 111

Sterne, Laurence, 187n67

Stoics, Babbitt on Christianity and, 25

St. Pierre, Abbé de, 112

"sublime" criminals, as civilization destroyers, 81

subrational, Babbitt on difference between Rousseau and Burke and, 97

"Sultan Murad" (Hugo), 45

Supreme Court, US, as bulwark against popular impulse, 72

suprarational, Babbitt on difference between Rousseau and Burke and, 97

Swiss peasants, Rousseau's observations of, 79–80

Switzerland, French invasion of (1798), 113

sympathy, humanitarian peace-making schemes based on, 112

Tagore, Rabindranath, 136

Taine, Hippolyte, 37, 51

technology: clash of civilizations and, 174; information revolution and, 156; social media and, 162

temperament: brake on, Babbitt on Rousseau's ethical philosophy and, 91; democracies and, Rousseau vs. Burke on, 94; Teutonic, as expansive flattery of German soul, Babbitt on, 111; of world leaders, Kissinger on world order and, 166

Terror, Reign of: Babbitt on Romantic assumptions about human nature and, 110–11; cult of ruthless power and, 134; French Revolutionary Wars and, 102; in Jacobin France, 73; justification for, 87; as logical result of Rousseauism, 82–84

trade, international, as imperialistic, 135

traditionalism (traditional conventions): breakdown of, personal introspection and, 105–6; Burke and Babbitt on innovations in, 95; contempt in contemporary US culture for, 97–98; unimaginative defense of, Babbitt and Burke on, 96

true cosmopolitanism: Babbitt on positive path toward, 145–46; early Babbitt essay on, 144–45; of nations, Babbitt on, 149; peaceful disposition of leaders embodying, 150–51; Ryn on international order in, 146–47. *See also* cosmopolitanism

Trump phenomenon, 156

Turkey, after the Cold War, 155

twentieth century: hostile threats during, 156–57; radicalism, Babbitt on Rousseau's influence on, 79

Twitter, 162

Ukraine, 169, 173

"The Undesirability of Democracy" (Spitz), 14

United Nations Charter, 152

United States: Babbitt on Rousseauist characteristics of contemporary culture in, 97–98; civilizational blocs and diplomatic errors by, 172–73; cultural renewal prospects for, 181–82; current tension with Russia and, 9; decadent imperialism as potential for, 127; foreign policy, humanitarianism and, 4, 178; foreign policy, imperialistic, 1; foreign policy paradigms, Huntington on, 171–72; Huntington on moderation and restraint by, 173–74; imperialism and adoption of Fukuyama's outlook by, 163; international warfare by, 177–78; Kissinger on Westphalian order and democracy-crusading by, 167; Marx's classless society and egalitarianism in, 159; unionist tradition in, 74–75. *See also specific political leaders of*

universal standards, 125, 141
utilitarian and scientific naturalism, 29–30
utilitarian organization, as Harvard humanitarian goal, 57–58
utopianism, Babbitt's cosmopolitanism theory compared with, 152–53

Vaughan, C. E., 55, 187–88n4
veto power, 72–73
Viereck, Peter, 13
Villard, Oswald Garrison, 109
Vincennes vision, Rousseau's education goals and, 60–61
virtue: Babbitt on humanitarian activists exempting selves from laws of, 116; Babbitt on human nature and, 18–19; as commitment to social cause, 148–49; of Eastern and Western philosophies, commonalities in, 147; personal, contemporary US culture and, 98; Robespierre on, as overflowing feeling rather than self-control, 85; Rousseau on instinct and, 41–42; Rousseau's redefining of, 44, 47, 48, 132–33; Washington's struggle with self-mastery and, 73
vital impulse (*élan vital*), 22, 37, 105
Voegelin, Eric, 8
Voltaire, 40

war and peace: Babbitt on education and, 103; dearth of scholarship on Babbitt's views of, 14–15. *See also* peace
wars: endless, American democracy and, 178–79; Fukuyama on end of history and, 162; moral indolence or evil and, 10; overseas, US involvement in, 2, 177
Washington, George, 5, 69, 70, 73, 77, 171
Watson Institute, Brown University, 178
wealthy class: French revolutionaries' attacks on, 89–91, 99. *See also* class warfare
weaponry, as deterrence against war, Babbitt on, 137
Weekly Review, 131–32
West: altruism as elite virtue in, 39; Babbitt on commonalities of Western philosophical traditions with, 147; Babbitt on decadent imperialism in, 127; humanistic or religious traditions uniting people in, 145; moral crisis and Great War in, 108; role of reason for thinkers in, 22; Romanticism and institutional transformation into restraints, 47–48; Rousseau and ethical understandings in, 42–43. *See also* Europe; United States
Western civilization, 169, 171, 173, 174
Westphalian system, 164–67
Who Are We: The Challenges to America's Nationality (Babbitt), 170
Who will rule? Babbitt's applications of, 3
"wicked," as civilization protectors, Lasserre on, 81
will: Babbitt on Asian religions' emphasis on, 24–25; Babbitt on imagination shaped by, 22–23; Babbitt on restoring proper role of, 116; commonalities of Eastern and Western philosophies and, 148; controlled, mastery over imagination and, 125; *Democracy and Leadership* on shaping of, 123; of the people, as imperialistic, 149; of the people, popular sovereignty and limits on, 130; power of, Eastern vs. Greek philosophers on, 20–22; Ryn on ethical imagination and, 23–24. *See also* higher will
Will, Imagination, and Reason (Ryn), 13
Wilson, Woodrow, 150
Wordsworth, William, 57, 86
world-city-soul principle, as Babbitt Corollary to city-soul principle, 180–81
world order: Babbitt on peace and good relations and, 11; Huntington on theories of, 168; Kissinger on Westphalian principles and, 164–67; leaders uniting on a higher plane with respecting cultural diversity and, 175–76
World Order (Kissinger), 166
World War I. *See* Great War
World War II, Babbitt's prediction of, 135

Xi Jinping, 162

Yale Review, 109
yellow journalism, as accelerant ton inflame public opinion toward war, 150
YouTube, 162
Yugoslavia, former, as fault line between civilizations, Huntington on, 169